Protecting
Biological Diversity

Routledge Studies in Development and Society

Protecting Biological Diversity

The Effectiveness of Access and Benefit-sharing Regimes

Carmen Richerzhagen

Routledge
Taylor & Francis Group

LONDON AND NEW YORK

First published 2010 by Routledge
2 Park Square, Milton Park, Abingdon, Oxon OX14 4RN
52 Vanderbilt Avenue, New York, NY 10017

Routledge is an imprint of the Taylor & Francis Group, an informa business

First issued in paperback 2012

© 2010 Taylor & Francis

Typeset in Sabon by IBT Global.

Library of Congress Cataloging-in-Publication Data
Richerzhagen, Carmen.
    Protecting biological diversity : the effectiveness of access and benefit-sharing regimes / by Carmen Richerzhagen.
        p. cm. — (Routledge studies in development and society)
    Includes bibliographical references and index.
    1. Biodiversity conservation—Economic aspects.   2. Germplasm resources—Economic aspects.   3. Convention on Biological Diversity (1992)   I. Title.
    QH75.R487 2010
    333.95'16—dc22
    2009043111

ISBN13: 978-0-415-81062-3 (pbk)
ISBN13: 978-0-415-87224-9 (hbk)

Found

Once through the forest
Alone I went;
To seek for nothing
My thoughts were bent.
I saw i' the shadow
A flower stand there
As stars it glisten'd,
As eyes 'twas fair.
I sought to pluck it,
It gently said:
"Shall I be gather'd
Only to fade?"
With all its roots
I dug it with care,
And took it home
To my garden fair.
In silent corner
Soon it was set;
There grows it ever,
There blooms it yet.

Johann Wolfgang von Goethe
(translated by Edgar Alfred Bowring, 1815)

Contents

Figures

Tables

Acronyms

ABS	Access and benefit-sharing
ACP	African, Caribbean, and Pacific
ARA	Academic Research Agreements
ARCBC	ASEAN Regional Centre for Biodiversity Conservation
ARS	Agricultural Research Service
ASEAN	Association of Southeast Asian Nations
ASOEN	ASEAN Meeting Senior Officials on the Environment
AU	African Union
AWGNC	ASEAN Working Group on Nature Conservation
BCCM	Belgian Co-Ordinated Collections of Micro-Organisms
BMBF	German Federal Ministry for Education and Research
BMS	Bristol-Myers Squibb
BRCs	Biological resource centers
BTG	British Technology Group
BV	Bequest value
CBD	Convention on Biological Diversity
CBD-CHM	CBD's Clearing House Mechanism
CGIAR	Consultative Group on International Agricultural Research
CHM	Clearing House Mechanism
CIRAD	Agricultural Research for Developing Countries
CITES	Convention on International Trade in Endangered Species of Wild Fauna and Flora
CMS	Convention on the Conservation of Migratory Species of Wild Animals
CONAGEBIO	National Commission for the Management of Biodiversity
COP	Conference of the Parties
CRA	Commercial Research Agreements
DA	Department of Agriculture (Philippines)
DAO	Department Administrative Order
DENR	Department of Environment and Natural Resources (Philippines)

DFA	Department of Foreign Affairs (Philippines)
DNA	Deoxyribonucleic acid
DOST	Department of Science and Technology (Philippines)
DUV	Direct use values
EARO	Ethiopian Agricultural Research Organization
EC	European Community
EIAR	Ethiopian Institute for Agricultural Research
EMAS	EC Eco-Management and Audit Scheme
EO	Executive Order
EPA	Environmental Protection Authority (Ethiopia)
EU	European Union
EWCO	Ethiopian Wildlife Conservation Organization
FAO	Food and Agriculture Organization of the United Nations
GDP	Gross domestic product
GEF	Global Environment Facility
GNI	Gross national income
GNP	Gross national product
GPGs	Global public goods
GTZ	Gesellschaft für technische Zusammenarbeit
HDI	Human Development Index
IACBGR	Inter Agency Committee for Biological and Genetic Resources (Philippines)
IAMME	Informal ASEAN Ministerial Meeting on the Environment
IBC	Institute of Biodiversity Conservation (Ethiopia)
IBCR	Institute of Biodiversity Conservation and Research
ICBG	International Cooperative Biodiversity Groups
IFO	Institute for Fermentation
IMF	International Monetary Fund
INBio	National Biodiversity Institute (Costa Rica)
IPAF	Integrated Protected Areas Fund
IPC	Intellectual Property Code of the Philippines
IPEN	International Plant Exchange Network
IPPC	Intergovernmental Panel on Climate Change
IPRs	Intellectual property rights
ISD	Ethiopian Institute for Sustainable Development
ISO	International Organization for Standardization
ITPGRFA	International Treaty on Plant Genetic Resources for Food and Agriculture
IUCN	World Conservation Union
IUV	Indirect use values
LDCs	Least Developed Countries
LMMC	Like-Minded Megadiverse Countries

LPGs	Local public goods
MAT	Mutually agreed terms
MEA	Millennium Ecosystem Assessment
MINAE	Ministry of Natural Resources and Energy and Mines (Costa Rica)
MOSAICC	Micro-Organisms Sustainable Use and Access Regulation International Code of Conduct
MTA	Material Transfer Agreements
NCIP	National Commission on Indigenous Peoples
NGOs	Nongovernmental organizations
NIH	National Institutes of Health
NIPAS	National Integrated Protected Areas System
NPGs	National public goods
NRC	National Research Council
NUV	Non-use value
OAU	Organization of African Unity
OECD	Organisation of Economic Co-operation and Development
OPEC	Organization of the Petroleum Exporting Countries
OV	Option values
PCSD	Palawan Council for Sustainable Development
PCT	Patent Cooperation Treaty
PGRFA	Plant genetic resources for food and agriculture
PhP	Philippine peso
PIC	Prior informed consent
PLT	Patent Law Treaty
PVP	Philippine Plant Variety Protection
QOV	Quasi option values
RPGs	Regional public goods
SBSTTA	Subsidiary Body on Scientific, Technical, and Technological Advice
SCBD	Secretariat of the Convention on Biological Diversity
SINAC	System of Conserved Areas
SMTA	Standard Material Transfer Agreements
TEV	Total economic value
TK	Traditional knowledge
TPGs	Transnational public goods
TRIPs	Agreement on Trade-Related Aspects of Intellectual Property Rights
UK	United Kingdom
UN	United Nations
UNDP	United Nations Development Programme
UNEP	United Nations Environment Programme
UNFCCC	United Nations Framework Convention on Climate Change

UPOV	The International Union for the Protection of New Varieties of Plants
US	United States
UV	Use value
WCMC	World Conservation Monitoring Center
WCPA	World Commission on Protected Areas
WDCM	World Data Centre for Microorganisms
WHC	World Heritage Convention
WIPO	World Intellectual Property Right Organization
WSSD	World Summit on Sustainable Development
WTO	World Trade Organization
XV	Existence value

Acknowledgments

Without the help, support, guidance, and efforts of many people this book could not have been completed. Therefore, I wish to thank them.

This book is a revised version of the dissertation I wrote at the Institute for Food and Resource Economics, Department of Resource and Environmental Economics, at the University of Bonn. During this time I spent one research year at the Institute of Advanced Studies of the United Nations University (UNU-IAS) in Yokohama, Japan. I want to thank both institutes for providing me with an excellent working environment and great support that allowed me to conduct this research.

I would like to thank my supervisor Prof. Dr. Karin Holm-Müller. She patiently provided the guidance, encouragement, and advice necessary for me to complete my dissertation. I also would like to mention, with thanks, Prof. Dr. Thomas Heckelei, the second reviewer of this work.

Many thanks go to the Schaumann Foundation for the grant it awarded me to undertake my field research in the Philippines and Costa Rica. I owe a special word of gratitude to the Center for Development Research (ZEF) in Bonn and its staff for giving me the chance to participate in the coffee project. My special thanks go to Dr. Detlef Virchow. The research stay in Ethiopia helped me to advance my academic work.

I would like to take this opportunity to thank my former colleagues from the Institute for Food and Resource Economics for their support during all the good and the bad times. In particular I would like to thank: Marcel Adenäuer, Thomas Breuer, Ruth Delzeit, Hans Josef Greuel, Robert Hilden, Meike Henseleit, Gisela Julius, Sonja Macke, Bettina Rudloff, Sabine Täuber, and Christine Wieck.

I would also like to thank my former colleagues at UNU-IAS. I want especially to thank Brendan Tobin for giving me the chance to support his team in Yokohama and Nicolas Brahy for the invaluable and stimulating discussions and suggestions.

My research would not have been possible without the help of many people in the Philippines, Costa Rica, and Ethiopia. I would like to take this opportunity to thank them for their willingness to share their experience and knowledge with me.

I would also like to thank my colleagues from the German Development Institute/Deutsches Institut für Entwicklungspolitik (DIE) for their advice, support, and understanding.

My very special thanks to my invaluable network of supportive, forgiving, generous, and loving friends, without whom I could not have survived the long process.

I would like to thank my mother for her continuous support, for her faith in me, and her willingness to follow my ideas and spirit, even if that meant that I had to spend much time abroad.

Last but not least, I am grateful to Alexander for his love, support, encouragement, patience, and understanding in dealing with all the challenges I have faced.

1 Introduction

BACKGROUND

During the past twenty years the enormous global loss of biodiversity has received growing attention, not only from biologists, because biodiversity is one of the world's most important resources. Biodiversity serves many important purposes, e.g., in the form of life-support systems, ecosystem services, and cultural objects, but also as production inputs and goods.

Today genetic resources are highly regarded potential inputs of research and development. Due to recent, enormous technical progress, especially in the area of biotechnology, genetic resources have become more important for commercial sectors, including agribusiness and the pharmaceutical, cosmetics, and natural products industries. One well-known example is the rosy periwinkle (*Catharanthus roseus*), a tropical dry-forest plant from Madagascar. Two drugs derived from the rosy periwinkle, vinblastine and vincristine, are used successfully in the treatment of Hodgkin's disease and leukemia.

Genetic resources and the technology used for their exploitation are not equally distributed in the world. Biodiversity hot spots, centers of highly diverse but threatened genetic resources, occur mainly in tropical forests located in developing countries. Industries using genetic material for research and development are located in industrialized countries. Due to this unequal geographical distribution of resources and technology, the international trade in genetic resources has significantly increased in recent centuries. However, even in the past, trade in genetic resources played a very important role. Plant collections and informal and commercial trade in biodiversity and genetic resources have been, at all times, an integral part of socioeconomic and cultural evolution.

In the 1990s the increased demand for and the promising potential of the future use of genetic resources were thus recommended as a source of funds for habitat preservation. For the first time in 1991, the idea was applied when Costa Rica's National Biodiversity Institute (INBio) and the pharmaceutical company Merck & Co., Inc., announced an access-for-fee agreement. The concept was expanded into the Convention on Biological

Diversity (CBD), adopted in 1992, the aim of which is to promote both biodiversity conservation and sustainable development. In the past, genetic resources were treated as open-access resources in the sense of a common heritage of humankind. Consequently, the resources could be acquired free of charge and without any approval. The adoption of the CBD entailed enormous changes. The convention seeks to boost the use of and access to biodiversity, but also to conserve biodiversity by assigning the responsibility for biological resources to states and by calling for a fair and equitable sharing of the benefits arising out of the utilization of genetic resources. Since then, potential users have been required to seek the consent of providers of biological diversity or their representatives and to negotiate mutually agreed terms (MAT) on access and benefit-sharing (ABS) before they are allowed to bioprospect. Bioprospecting is understood as the specific search for and exploration of biological material or biological information of social and economic value. The underlying idea is to exchange genetic resources, on the basis of market-type contracts, for shares of the benefits generated, an approach expected to set incentives for resource conservation and promote economic development in the provider countries. The CBD is only a framework agreement and needs to be implemented in national or regional regulations. Today about forty countries have already adopted measures to regulate ABS with regard to their own biological resources, and many more are in the process of developing such measures (CBD 2007a).

Despite the protracted implementation of ABS regulations in provider countries and the improvements gained through experience and higher scientific interest, many parties to the CBD, mainly developing countries, have expressed their discontent with the existing situation. Plant genetic resources have been collected, used for research and development, and protected by intellectual property rights (IPRs), but the provider countries have neither approved their use nor received any share of the benefits. Natural products from neem and basmati rice are prominent examples of patents having been awarded for products that did not meet the conditions set for patents (e.g., novelty and invention). Besides these, many cases of misappropriation have been reported (McGown 2006). Such incidents have raised concern over the limitations of the present state of ABS regulation with regard to the effective protection of provider country interests.

In recent years, demands on user countries have been expressed more explicitly, urging them to work actively for implementation of the CBD regulations on ABS. The group of megadiverse countries has emphasized the fact that they do not consider themselves capable of enforcing ABS without the support of user countries. They are therefore calling for the creation of an international regime designed to induce user countries to take adequate measures to realize ABS in compliance with the CBD. The idea of developing such an international regime was accepted at the World Summit on Sustainable Development (WSSD), held in 2002 in Johannesburg, and subsequently included as an objective in the final report. CBD members are called on to negotiate an international regime to promote and safeguard the fair and equitable sharing of the benefits arising from the utilization of genetic resources (UN 2002, 44o). What this means in effect is that today's users of genetic resources have to be given more consideration and involved even more as important actors in the development of comprehensive international conservation concepts.

OBJECTIVES

The overall objective of this book is to analyze how the CBD's approach to ABS needs to be designed if it is to be an effective concept to ensure the conservation and sustainable use of biodiversity, to facilitate access to biodiversity, and to monitor the fair and equitable sharing of the benefits arising out of the commercialization of genetic resources. In short, what are the determinants of the convention's effectiveness?

The analysis is driven by three assumptions. First, the ABS concept, which is based on bilateral agreements, sets incentives to conserve biodiversity, but at the same time it has side effects (e.g., economic, social) that need to be taken into account. Second, there are certain critical factors that have a significant influence on the ABS concept and its goals. The effectiveness of the ABS concept depends on how these factors are shaped. Third, the ABS concept can be realized only through an international regime, i.e., provider- and user-side measures have to be in place.

The book's aim is to establish an analytical framework to measure the effectiveness of the ABS concept at the national and regional level. Effectiveness is defined here as the capability of the ABS regime: (i) to set incentives for the sustainable use and conservation of biodiversity,[1] (ii) to facilitate access to plant genetic material, and (iii) to enhance a fair and equitable benefit-sharing, which also implies prevention of the misappropriation and unapproved use of genetic resources. To measure the realization of these objectives, their determinants, so-called critical factors, need to be defined. They are derived from the application of economic theory to biodiversity loss and the ABS concept as well as from the empirical findings from four ABS case studies. The aim of these ABS case studies is to provide a comprehensive and comparative analysis of national and regional experiences in developing and implementing ABS policies, laws, institutions, and regulatory regimes. Three provider countries, Costa Rica, the Philippines, and Ethiopia, serve here as case studies. They are used to derive the critical factors and to test their feasibility by analyzing how these factors are shaped in a country-specific context, whether they are already addressed, and/or whether gaps still exist. On the user side, the European Union (EU) serves as an example of a group of user countries to identify and analyze potential user measures with regard to their feasibility, efficiency, and potential to address the critical factors. Because many EU measures are implemented at the national level, at some points a country perspective (Germany) is selected to illustrate a user country's actions and the possibilities open to it.

Furthermore, the book aims to explore the perspectives of ABS regimes. It analyzes the strengths and weaknesses of current ABS regimes in provider countries and user countries with a view to the critical factors. It seeks to identify options for developing measures that can be undertaken by countries in their capacity as providers and users of genetic resources to strengthen ABS governance and build an international regime.

The analysis of the effectiveness and perspectives of the ABS concept permits us to derive recommendations on improving and developing an international ABS regime. Measures that address the essential critical factors are identified and assessed. Furthermore, strategies are proposed on how best to implement such measures. The findings and results are not limited to the case studies presented. The analytic framework, consisting of the objectives and critical factors, can be applied to a range of countries faced with the need to implement the ABS concept. A comparative analysis of different case studies is only feasible with an analytic framework of the kind developed by the present book. The case studies provide experiences that may prove useful for other provider and user countries. Because the underlying questions of this book correspond with the issues with which international policy-makers are faced, the results may serve to support political discussions and negotiations and to propose options for further activities.

METHODOLOGICAL APPROACH

The effectiveness of the ABS concept can be measured on the basis of three objectives: conservation of biodiversity, facilitation of access, and enhancement of fair and equitable benefit-sharing. Analysis of the occurrence of the critical factors in a country-specific context is used to measure the realization of the objectives and assess the effectiveness of the ABS concept. Furthermore, the book presents and discusses the strengths and weaknesses of the approach.

The analysis integrates a multilevel approach by examining the implementation of the ABS concept at the national and international levels. The analytical framework is derived by applying some of the major theoretical aspects of the new institutional economics (i.e., property rights, bargaining solutions, transaction costs, and information asymmetries) to the ABS concept as well as on the basis of an analysis of qualitative empirical data collected on national and regional ABS regimes.

The book's main source of information is qualitative data collected in connection with the case studies, primary and secondary literature with a focus on environmental and new institutional economics and biodiversity and biodiversity-related topics, and information collected in connection with the author's observation of and participation in several political negotiations and international conferences related to ABS. The book's chronological order does not reflect the research process, and the empirical findings contribute to the development of the analytical framework presented in Chapter 5.

The empirical data from the four case studies (Costa Rica, the Philippines, Ethiopia, and the EU) constitute the core of the book. They provide practical insight into both the problem of biodiversity loss and the ABS concept and they serve as the empirical underpinning for the development of the critical factors. In view of the fact that the geographical location of the countries concerned (i.e., different continents) and their approaches to implementing ABS differ extremely, the case studies selected appear to be very useful. Both providers and users of genetic resources are an indispensable part of an international ABS regime. The present study, therefore, uses the case studies to capture both aspects. This EU case study is mainly a desktop study, but at the same time it is enriched with information gathered in workshops and at conferences. The provider case studies are based on field trips to the three developing countries. The reason why the author selected a qualitative approach involving collection of fieldwork data is that qualitative methods of data collection are regarded as methodologically adequate. These methods provide information useful for understanding the processes behind the observed results and peoples' perceptions (Creswell 1994; Denzin and Lincoln 2000).

Silverman (1997) characterizes qualitative research as a method used to collect and interpret "in-depth" material that is more meaningful than quantitative survey research data. In qualitative research, reality is subjective and seen differently by the interview partners. Such research therefore relies on reports from different voices and the interpretations of the informants. The researcher usually interacts with the persons she/he is studying, and she/he admits values and biases. The methodology allows for inductive approaches. Categories emerge from the informants rather than being identified *a priori* by the researcher. This emergence provides "context-bound" information and can lead to patterns or theories that explain certain phenomenon (Creswell 1994, 5–7). Qualitative research methods are therefore usually applied when the research subject is new and theories need to be developed.

As a research topic, ABS is not new. It has been analyzed from many different angles. However, what is missing is an adequate theoretical framework for an analysis of the concept's effectiveness. For this reason, it is necessary to develop a new analytical framework based on the insights of new institutional economic theory, but also on the findings of the case studies. The approach used in this book thus combines deductive and inductive reasoning processes to establish a new analytic framework. New institutional economic theory was chosen because it appears to be the most appropriate theory. It provides approaches suitable to analyzing the problems that occur during the implementation of ABS and offers adequate solutions for these problems.

The majority of relevant stakeholders or their representatives were identified and interviewed with a view to analyzing the country-specific context of ABS in the three countries concerned. The first field trip was undertaken in the Philippines between March and May 2002; twenty-seven stakeholders were interviewed. The second field trip took place in Costa Rica in November and December 2002, and twenty-three key informants agreed to provide information. The last field trip was conducted in Ethiopia in October 2003; fifteen persons were identified and interviewed.

The qualitative collection method varies depending on research subject. The main methods used are observation, textual analysis, interviews, and transcripts (Silverman 1997, 9). The data collection procedure used was the same in all three case studies. Semistructured interviews were used as a method to gather and analyze the qualitative data in the respective countries. The interviews were conducted with a fairly open framework that allowed for focused, conversational, two-way communication. According to Creswell (1994), interviews provide indirect information filtered through the views of the interviewee; they are useful when informants are able to provide certain kinds of background information and share their experiences. Stakeholder information and experiences are essential in order to analyze how ABS issues are perceived.

The semistructured interviews were prepared using an interview guide that lists a predetermined set of questions or issues that were to be explored during the interview. The questions and issues are based on a pre-analysis of economics literature regarding the loss of biodiversity and the ABS concept. The majority of questions were derived from the three general assumptions as well as from further country-specific assumptions. The guide for each country was therefore adapted to the specific country situation and widened to include country-specific questions. For example, in the Costa Rican case, explicit consideration was given to the outsourcing of the application process to a non-state actor.

The interviews were conducted with great flexibility, and the majority of questions asked materialized during the interview process. The guide covered the following problem areas: biodiversity conservation, property rights, win-win solutions, potential benefits, bureaucratic procedure, stakeholder interest, information distribution, political and legal situation, control and sanction mechanisms. Whereas the structure of the interviews gave a more systematic and comprehensive character to interviews with a number of different persons, it did not define the issues to be taken up in the interview.

The interview partners were identified as stakeholders, experts, or key informants. In the case of ABS, stakeholders are individuals or groups that are likely to be affected by ABS activities. Experts have specific knowledge on the issue and can provide detailed information. A key informant is an individual who has access to information valuable for the evaluator because of the former's knowledge, previous experience, or social status in a community. This information may include, e.g., insights about the functioning of society, its problems, and its needs. Key informants are a source of information that can help to understand the context of a program or project or to clarify particular issues or problems. The main stakeholders, people involved in ABS issues in their countries or at the international level, were identified as key informants. They can be assigned to different groups, such as, for example, government actors (i.e., civil servants), civil society groups, scientists, industry, local communities, farmers, and indigenous people.

The key informants were not selected at random. First, a set of people belonging to one of the identified groups was interviewed. These persons had been identified before the field research took place. Once the field research had started, the interviewed person recommended more interview partners. The author was aware that this principle might cause a bias. Interviewees were therefore carefully selected, with attention paid to including all important stakeholder groups.

All interviews were documented in the form of minutes. The qualitative data in this book is used and transformed in keeping with Wolcott's (1994) approach: "description," "analysis," and "interpretation." "Description" deals with a descriptive processing of information based on sorting and filtering. Once the empirical data had been collected, the information was assigned to different categories derived from economic theory. Useless information was sorted out. The "analysis" makes use of this information, identifying essential features and systematically describing interrelationships among them. The critical factors were defined and characterized in this phase. Apart from the factors identified on the basis of theory, new categories were identified by consolidating the theoretical and empirical findings. Furthermore, it proved possible to extend the existing categories. The interlinkages between the factors were also analyzed. The last step, "interpretation," is concerned with process-related questions of meaning and context. However, because the information collected was direct and significant, interpretation was rarely called for. The main approach used in this book to transform data is analysis based on prior description.

CONTRIBUTION AND OUTLOOK

The adoption of the CBD and the establishment of the ABS concept have given rise to controversial discussions over whether the approach is the most adequate one to protect biodiversity, ensure fair and equitable benefit-sharing, and support sustainable development. In the first years after the Rio conference, optimism was widespread and the hope was raised that the world's biodiversity could be protected by commercializing the "green gold" of the tropical forests. However, very soon it became evident that expectations were not being met and benefits were failing to materialize. It appeared that the concept was not working, and in the course of the political debate the international negotiations heated up.

At the same time, the volume of research on ABS issues had also increased, with international policy-makers coming to realize that they lacked knowledge on important governmental and nongovernmental actors, institutions, national regulatory and political frameworks, biodiversity-related economic values, the market for genetic resources (including users and providers), etc. Unlike the Climate Convention, which has established a scientific advisory committee, the Intergovernmental Panel on Climate Change (IPPC), the CBD has no such body. Research communities were therefore called on to provide scientific, technical, and especially socioeconomic information. The Millennium Ecosystem Assessment (MEA), initiated by UN Secretary-General Kofi Annan in June 2001 and completed in March 2005, is such a contribution. However, thus far this report has received only modest attention, although it has supplied some alarming findings on the future of ecosystems and biodiversity.

In the ABS context the scientific environment has increasingly focused on the analysis of national or regional ABS regimes in provider countries, mainly from the legal and policy perspective, concerning the development of national ABS laws in the past (see, for example, Reid et al. 1993; Columbia University 1999; Day-Rubenstein and Frisvold 2001). Whereas all these contributions have provided a useful catalogue of case studies and insights, they fail to develop an analysis framework that would make it possible to draw comparisons among different cases and reach conclusions on the effectiveness of the ABS approach promoted by the CBD. The analyses they present are more descriptive in nature and lack an assessment of the socioeconomic and ecological effects of ABS. Attempting to evaluate ABS regimes on a comparative basis, Dávalos and colleagues (2003) come up with some interesting results. However, despite their examination of case studies, their conclusions and recommendations often fail to encompass the whole of the ABS concept, remaining either very general or very specific and not dealing with the impacts of ABS on biodiversity conservation and economic development. The report released by the Organisation for Economic Co-operation and Development (OECD) mentions many very interesting aspects and attempts to come up with a general economic picture of ABS but, unfortunately, the report is not based on empirical findings and remains very sketchy (OECD 2003a). Barrett and Lybbert (2000) provide an interesting commentary on bioprospecting, but it covers only some of the essential aspects, e.g., the lack of distributional equity for benefits, and does not provide a general analytical framework. Some studies focus only on one aspect (reflected in the present book by the critical factors), analyzing it in isolation from the others. For example, Mulholland and Wilman (2003) look only into the information problem in ABS contracts.

Other published documents (Simpson, Sedjo, and Reid 1996; Rausser and Small 2000; ten Kate and A Laird 1999) estimate the private value of biodiversity as an input for research and development and discuss the commercial use of biodiversity from the point of view of the demand side. Whereas this may show the industry point of view, it does not attempt any evaluation from the point of view of society. Moreover, the existing work tends to focus on either the provider or the user side. No comprehensive approach has been developed thus far. For example, Artuso (2002) investigates the relationship between national ABS programs and the biotechnology capacity of provider countries, but the user side is totally excluded. Very little research has been done on user countries and user measures (Barber, Johnston, and Tobin 2003; Dross and Wolff 2005; Sarnoff and Correa 2006), and most of these studies focus on single user measures or are highly theoretical and not concerned with an existing user country. All in all, there is still a need for clarification of the effectiveness of the CBD's ABS approach as regards its objectives and its performance under an international regime.

The present book introduces a new focus into the discussion. The effectiveness of the ABS concept is measured in terms of its capability to reach three objectives: conservation, access, and benefit-sharing. It is operationalized by identifying the critical factors. The four case studies are analyzed in the light of these factors and on the basis of a comparative approach. The perspective of an international regime is used to integrate both sides, the providers and users of biodiversity, into the framework.

Nevertheless, this book cannot give answers to all the relevant questions and fill in all the gaps on ABS. It may, rather, be seen as a point of departure. Further research needs to be done in several areas, e.g., efforts to broaden the empirical base, examine a multilateral system, and assess the costs of user measures.

Three provider country case studies have been conducted and examined in the framework of the book. In order to test and improve the analysis framework developed here, it should be applied to more case studies. A number of other countries would be suitable for applying this approach. It would then stand on a broader empirical base.

The main focus of research in this book is the bilateral exchange system, as proposed by the CBD. Further research could step back and evaluate the concept of ABS in a multilateral exchange system, as suggested by the International Treaty on Plant Genetic Resources for Food and Agriculture (ITPGRFA). Furthermore, to determine the effectiveness of the ABS concept, it would be useful to evaluate the approach in comparison with other conservation concepts. The issue of payment for environmental services appears to lead to interesting results.

Whereas the analysis of user measures in this book remains quite theoretical, it is essential to look into user measures if the international community is to establish an international regime. Knowledge on the practicality, feasibility, and costs of user measures is very limited. Even when the EU is used as an example, we find that little information is available on the implementation of user measures. Pilot projects designed to implement a given measure in a specific sector (e.g., certificates of compliance in microbial collections) could provide needed information. Moreover, assessments of the economic impacts and implications would provide fruitful information for the ongoing debate.

OVERVIEW

Chapter 1 introduces the subject and the objectives of the book, outlining the methodological approach, including the analytical framework, the method used to gather information, the use made of the data collected, and the structure of the book. Chapter 2 presents the basic principles of genetic resources. It describes the present state of genetic resources and the places in which genetic resources originate, are distributed, and are used. It furthermore looks into different concepts of biodiversity conservation with a view to identifying the role of ABS within these concepts and describes the political and institutional framework in which ABS governance is set. Chapter 3 applies economic theory to the global problem of biodiversity loss and discusses the economic framework of the ABS concept, analyzing approaches to and problems of valuation, the relationship between biodiversity degradation and economic development, and market and policy failure as an explanation for the decline of biodiversity. The chapter also examines the ABS concept as a promising market-based approach to biodiversity conservation. Chapter 4 builds the analytic framework for the book based on economic theory and the empirical information gathered by means of the case studies with a view to measuring the effectiveness of the concept. In keeping with the objectives, it derives and defines the critical factors (property rights, time lags, good governance, information asymmetries, administrative complexity, and market structure) of an effective ABS regime. Furthermore, it identifies possible ways in which these factors can be addressed in countries that provide and use biodiversity. Chapter 5 consists of the four case studies: Costa Rica, the Philippines, Ethiopia, and the EU with a focus on Germany. The case studies analysis investigates how the critical factors occur in the respective countries. It applies the analytic framework derived, analyzing how the factors are addressed. Chapter 6 draws conclusions from the comparative analysis and formulates recommendations for ABS regimes at the national and international levels for use as instruments to protect biodiversity.

2 The Basic Principles of Genetic Resources as Regards ABS

The term *biodiversity* has become very prominent since it was coined in the 1980s.[1] At that time, the observed rapid extinction rates raised concerns and it became obvious that human activities constitute the main threat to the diversity of life. Biologists, ecologists, environmentalists, political leaders, and concerned citizens started to address the issue of biodiversity loss as a major worldwide environmental problem of the twentieth century.

The discussion on biodiversity has raised awareness in society about the environmental problem and its causes and has helped to understand in what ways biological organisms and processes are endangered. In the course of development and industrialization, humans have interfered with the natural environment in which important biological processes are embedded. Biodiversity is the foundation on which the ecosystem functions; indeed, it is the foundation of life itself. No environmental system is considered to be as complex, dynamic, and varied as the diversity of living organisms, and no system is thought to experience such dramatic changes caused by humans. Not only do these changes influence biodiversity, they also have tremendous impacts on human well-being (MEA 2005a, 18). The strategies developed to address this problem are conservation and sustainable use of biodiversity.

In order to fully understand the ABS concept and to assess its opportunities and its limits against the objectives stated, it is necessary to understand the basic principles behind the diversity of genetic resources. What follows provides an overview of the basic principles behind the diversity of genetic resources against the background of ABS. The chapter will identify and illustrate the major characteristics of genetic resources and their diversity and highlight the present state of the world's genetic resources. It will then go on to elucidate the distribution and origin of genetic resources and to characterize their provision and utilization. Based on this information, an attempt is made to assess the supply and demand situation—the potential market for genetic resources. The supply side is characterized by the increasing decline of biodiversity caused by various direct (e.g., habitat destruction, invasive species, climate change) and indirect (e.g., population growth, economic factors) factors. The demand side consists of a highly heterogeneous group of user sectors. The chapter looks into the composition of this group as well as its awareness and perceptions. Finally, the chapter introduces different conservation concepts, including ABS, and illustrates the institutional and political framework of international ABS governance.

THE PRESENT STATE OF THE WORLD'S GENETIC RESOURCES

Genetic resources are one component of biodiversity. Biodiversity is a collective term used to describe the totality and variety of life on Earth (Samper 2006). The CBD defines it as the "variability among living individual organisms from all sources including, inter alia, terrestrial, marine and other aquatic ecosystems and the ecological complexes of which they are part; this includes diversity within species, between species and of ecosystems" (CBD 1992, Article 2). It includes genetic resources, that is, organisms or parts of organisms, populations, or any other biotic component of ecosystems with actual or potential use or value for humanity. Consequently, genetic material is any material from plants or animals, microbial material, or other material from another origin containing functional units of heredity (CBD 1992, Article 2). Genetic resources are thus genetic material of actual or potential value for research and development.

Agrobiodiversity is a subcategory of biodiversity. It is, in other words, a subset of biodiversity that provides a basis for nutrition, livelihoods, and the maintenance of habitats and is of great importance to peoples' lives in the form of agricultural crops, productive livestock, raw materials, and medicinal plants (Wolff 2004, 338). However, agrobiodiversity consists not only of whole systematic units that contribute to people's livelihoods by providing food, medicine, feed for domestic animals, fiber, clothing, shelter, or energy (Shand 1997, 5). It is on account of their genetic properties that genetic crop resources, referred to as plant genetic resources for food and agriculture (PGRFA), are highly important in terms of the uses to which they are put. In particular, plant genetic resources, with their distinct characteristics, play a major role for food security. Their genetic material is used in the production of new cultivars and breeds or as a reservoir of genetic adaptability and serves as a buffer against potentially harmful environmental and economic changes (Food and Agriculture Organization of the United Nations [FAO] 1996, 19).

How many species actually live on the planet? Today's estimates of the number of species on the Earth range from three to one hundred million, a state of affairs that indicates the difficulties involved in assessing the total number of species. However, generally accepted estimates range between five and thirty million. The Secretariat of the CBD (SCBD) assumes that about thirteen million species exist today, 1.75 million of which have been described (SCBD 2000, 2). The estimates of the United Nations Environment Programme (UNEP), including fourteen million unknown species, are very close to this figure. Of the 1.75 million known species, 270,000 plant species have already been described (see Table 2.1).

Table 2.1 Number of Species Described

Species	Number
Bacteria	4,000
Protoctists (algae, protozoa)	80,000
Animals—invertebrates	1,272,000
Fungi	72,000
Plants	270,000
Total described species	1,750,000
Possible total, including unknown species	14,000,000

Source: UNEP (2002, 120).

The World Conservation Union (IUCN) regularly publishes statistics on globally threatened species as well as its Red List of Threatened Species. The IUCN comes to the conclusion that 1.9 of five to thirty million species have been described (Baillie, Hilton-Taylor, and Stuart 2004, 34). Most taxonomic work is concentrated far from the most species-rich taxa and regions, and, as a discipline, taxonomy is declining in general. This explains some of the uncertainty experienced when it comes to our knowledge on the existence of species (MEA 2005b, 88).

According to FAO (1997), it is assumed that between three hundred thousand and five hundred thousand species of higher plants (i.e., flowering and cone-bearing plants) exist, approximately 270,000 of which have been described. Of these, about thirty thousand are edible and some seven thousand have been cultivated or collected by humans for food and play a major role for food security. Despite the great number and vast diversity of PGRFA, only thirty crops provide 95 percent of all dietary energy. Three crops—wheat, rice, and maize—account for more than 50 percent of the world population's plant-derived energy intake. Sorghum, millet, potatoes, sweet potatoes, soybeans, and sugar account for an additional 25 percent (FAO 1997, 14). Today only 150 crops are commercialized on a significant global scale. The other species have fallen victim to agricultural simplification, a process that favors a handful of crops over others because of the comparative advantages they offer, including, for example, their ability to grow in a wider range of habitats, the ease with which they can be cultivated and processed, their storability, and their taste. These developments lead to enormous genetic erosion through a reduction of intra- and interspecific crop diversity. This is the reason why the level of vulnerability among users has increased, particularly in poorer societies dependent on diversity in crops. In addition, efforts to narrow the variety of nutrients have reduced the quality of food (Padulosi et al. 2002, 1).

Local communities in developing countries use a wider range of existing diversity. For example, in Mexico's Uxpanapa region, peasant farmers use 435 wild plants and animals and eat 229 of them, and people in a community in a Thai village eat 295 different local plants (Harrison and Pearce 2001, 159). Many minor species still exist, e.g., underutilized crops such as leafy vegetables in sub-Saharan Africa, and they play a vital role in local farming systems and in human well-being at subnational levels, although they tend to vanish in statistical aggregations at the national level (Williams and Haq 2002, 2). In recent years awareness of these neglected genetic treasures has risen, and researchers, policy-makers, and even industry have recognized the need to keep up and improve the uses made of these underutilized or neglected crops, which are left aside by research, technology, marketing systems, and by conservation efforts (Padulosi et al. 2002, 1). Underutilized crops have promising economic potential as food security products in local and regional markets and as niche products in international markets.

THE SUPPLY SIDE

On the supply side, the countries that hold biodiversity are referred to as "provider countries." Countries in which given genetic resources originate are "countries of origin." Both provider and user countries can be identified by analyzing the origin and the distribution of material. Generally speaking, most of the diversity and the regions of origin of genetic resources are found in the southern hemisphere, in developing countries, whereas most of these resources are used and processed in the northern hemisphere, in industrialized countries. Even though this may be a simplification that applies in many cases, it is necessary to take a closer look at actual distribution because natural distribution is not always in harmony with the CBD's understanding of ABS. Even though the distribution of genetic resources is not bound to territorial borders, the CBD defines states as the responsible actors.

The supply of biodiversity is compromised by its continuing loss. The greatest threat to biodiversity is the human-induced destruction of habitats for the purpose of converting forest into agricultural land. This indicates that the decline of biodiversity is above all a question of opportunity costs. Other land uses are economically more attractive than biodiversity conservation. This shows that a market-based approach like ABS may be a concept adequate to counteract the ongoing loss of biodiversity in that it provides economic incentives for conservation.

Origin and Distribution

Species have migrated on Earth for ages. Migration is one important aspect of evolution and the development of biodiversity. Crops in particular have been spread around the world by human interventions and activities. Wild plant genetic resources have also migrated in the course of time. Questions regarding the origin of species and today's distribution of genetic resources must therefore be seen as legitimate.

The CBD relies on the concept of origin. The parties to the CBD agreed that the "country of origin of genetic resources" would be understood to mean countries that possess these genetic resources in situ conditions (CBD 1992, Article 2); whereas "country providing genetic resources" refers to the countries that supply genetic resources collected from in situ sources. These include populations of both wild and domesticated species, or populations taken from ex situ sources that may or may not have originated in that country (CBD 1992, Article 2). When it comes to benefit-sharing, a country of origin of a given resource or a country that has acquired the genetic resource in accordance with the CBD should be the recipient of shared benefits (CBD 1992, Article 15).

The first noteworthy comprehensive attempt to identify the origin of major crops was undertaken in the 1900s. Having undertaken numerous collection missions, the Russian scientist Vavilov identified centers of plant origins. In 1926 he published his work "Studies on the Origin of Cultivated Plants," which documented his theories on the origin of crops. The main finding of his research was that each crop has a characteristic primary center of diversity, which is also its center of origin. He argued that degree of diversity was indicative of how long the crop had been grown in that area. Therefore, species show the greatest genetically variation at or near their center of origin. According to his theory, all major crops were first domesticated in these centers. Vavilov identified eight areas: China, India (with a related center in Indo-Malaya), Central Asia, the Near East, the Mediterranean, Abyssinia (Ethiopia), southern Mexico and Central America, and South America (Peru, Ecuador, and Bolivia), with two lesser centers—the island of Chiloe off the coast of southern Chile and an eastern secondary center in Brazil and Paraguay (Hawkes 1997). Vavilov's centers show similarities, with all of them located between 20 and 45 degrees latitude in mountainous regions with temperate climate (Fowler and Mooney 1990).

Vavilov's theory has since been enlarged and modified. Today scientists agree that there are one or more centers of origin where a crop is domesticated and that these centers are usually the primary centers of in situ diversity for that crop (see Figure 2.1). The continued gene flow between crops and their wild relatives in these areas can contribute to new variability. Center of origin is not a synonym for center of diversity, and these centers are not necessarily the starting point of domestication. Certain varieties of crops have originated outside of centers of both origin and diversity (FAO 1997, 20).

In many cases it is difficult to determine the origin of plant genetic resources and assign them to countries, or even regions. However, technical advances in the field of molecular biology have made it increasingly possible to identify origin (Hardon, Vosman, and van Hintum 1994, 13).

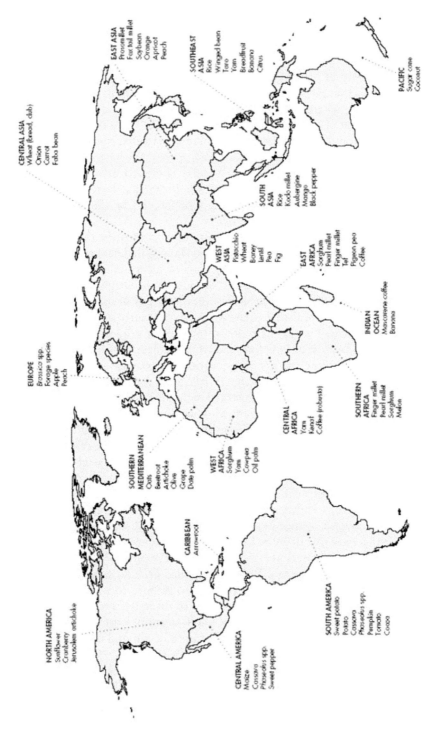

Figure 2.1   Regions of diversity for major cultivated plants. Source: FAO (1997, 21).

Plants are not bound to territorial borders. In many cases plants exist in three or even more neighboring countries, and many plants have migrated and been distributed by people and animals. For example, the place of origin of guava (*Psidium guajava L.*) is assumed to be an area extending from southern Mexico into or through Central America. Traditionally guava is used to treat diarrhea, gastroenteritis, and other digestive complaints. *Tamarindus indica*, used as a refrigerant for fever and as a laxative, is native to tropical Africa, a region that consists of more than forty countries (Morton 1987, 115ff., 356ff.).

The evolution that Vavilov had already described for crops applies equally for biodiversity in general. Biodiversity is not evenly distributed in the world. In the context of biodiversity conservation, tropical forests are areas known specifically for their rich diversity, whereas drier ecosystems are far more important for crop resources (FAO 1997, 20). As already mentioned, the greatest species density is generally found in the southern hemisphere. According to UNEP, 70 percent of the world's species is found in just twelve countries: Australia, Brazil, China, Colombia, Costa Rica, Ecuador, India, Indonesia, Madagascar, Mexico, Peru, and the Democratic Republic of Congo (UNEP 2002).

More than twenty-five thousand plant species—some 10 percent of the world's flora—can be found in the Hindu Kush-Himalayan belt (UNEP 2002, 131). Tropical forest ecosystems are the most species-rich environments. Although they cover less than 10 percent of the world's surface, they contain 90 percent of its species. Coral reefs and Mediterranean heathland are also highly species-rich. In some countries endemism is high. Ninety-eight percent of Madagascar's land mammals, 92 percent of its reptiles, 68 percent of its plants, and 41 percent of its breeding bird species are endemic (Harrison and Pearce 2001, 167). The Amazonian flora contains the greatest tree diversity on earth: in 1,000 km^2 of terra firme forest near Manaus (Brazil) thirteen hundred tree species have been identified. A world record was discovered in the Peruvian lowland forest near Iquitos, with three hundred tree species identified on one hectare (Parolin 2002).

Different concepts have been developed to assess the existence and distribution of biodiversity. Mutke and Barthlott (2005) have developed a world map of the species numbers of vascular plants as an indicator of plant biodiversity (see Figure 2.2).

The concept of "biodiversity hotspots" is another approach to identifying biodiversity-rich areas. Originally it was developed by Norman Myers (2000) to identify priority areas for biodiversity conservation. When the study was published, these biodiversity hotspots were characterized by both exceptional levels of plant endemism and serious levels of habitat loss. The concept was later revised and the definition redefined. Today a hotspot is defined by the presence there of at least fifteen hundred endemic species of vascular plants (> 0.5 percent of the world's total) as well as the loss of at least 70 percent of its original habitat. Twenty-five hotspots have been identified (Myers et al. 2000).

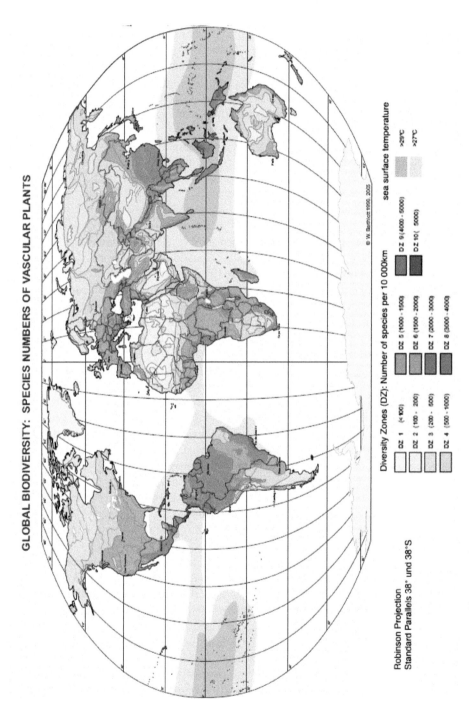

Figure 2.2   World map of the species numbers of vascular plants. Source: Mutke and Barthlott (2005, 525).

The concept of hotspot identification is evolutionary in character, reflecting changes in nature and advances in science. In 2005 Conservation International published a set of new figures. The number of biodiversity hotspots was extended to thirty-four, reflecting the ongoing loss of biodiversity. The key findings are:

- Over 50 percent of the world's plant species are endemic to the thirty-four biodiversity hotspots; these thirty-four hotspots once covered 15.7 percent of the Earth's land surface.
- 86 percent of the hotspots' habitat has already been destroyed; intact remnants of hotspots now cover only 2.3 percent of the Earth's land surface.
- Hotspots hold at least 150,000 plant species as endemics, 50 percent of the world's total.
- The overall number of species occurring in hotspots is much greater— approaching four-fifths of the world's total (Mittermeier et al. 2005).

Both concepts depend on the conventional measure used to count species, and the results tend to be predictable. Most of the world's biodiversity is concentrated in a very small area within the tropics. There are different reasons that lead to species concentration. Higher solar energy and greater variety of habitats and microclimate in the tropics are good examples. Isolation, as in the case of islands (e.g., Galapagos, Madagascar), promotes endemism. However, endemism also weakens species and makes them vulnerable to outside interference due to their limited distribution and weak resistance to diseases (Harrison and Pearce 2001, 167).

Some questions have been raised as to whether the hotspot concept serves to set the right priorities for biodiversity conservation because species-rich hotspots do not necessarily overlap with hotspots of endemic species richness or with a high number of threatened species. Furthermore, the concept totally excludes social and economic factors, e.g., the cost of conservation action (Possingham and Wilson 2005, 920). The issue is too complex to permit assessments of biodiversity to rely on one indicator only.

Decline of Biodiversity

In the past, certain species became extinct and biodiversity declined due to natural incidents such as climate change or tectonic movements leading to continental interchange. Today most of the world's supply of genetic resources is affected primarily by human activities. IUCN estimates that 99 percent of threatened species are at risk due to human activities (The World Conservation Union 2006b).

What have we lost so far and at what pace have we lost it? If we are to look into ABS as an instrument, it is necessary to identify the problem of loss because it has a decisive impact on the supply of genetic resources. The decline we find in biodiversity is enormous. The current rate of species extinction is approximately one thousand times higher than the natural rate (also called background rate) that has prevailed over the Earth's history. Even if, globally, the net rate of conversion of some ecosystems has begun to slow (one reason being that there is increasingly little habitat left for further conversion), it can be observed that across a range of taxonomic groups, the population size or range of the majority of species is declining (MEA 2005a, 3).

Information on extinction rates and the existence of species is provided by the IUCN Red Lists of Threatened Species. It lists the species that are threatened with extinction. The 2006 Red List of Threatened Species indicates that about 16,119 species, 8,394 of which are plants and lichens, are threatened with extinction.[2] In the major species groups, the percentage of threatened species ranges between 12 percent (birds) and 52 percent (cycads). The species mainly affected are found in the tropics, especially on mountains and islands (The World Conservation Union 2006b). These species are very relevant for ABS. All wild plants, and especially those found in the tropics, are of high interest for research and development due to their specific characteristics.

In addition to species diversity, genetic diversity has declined globally, especially among domesticated species. This decline lowers the resilience and adaptability of domesticated species. Genetic erosion is a consequence of the replacement of local varieties with improved or exotic varieties and species. If old diverse varieties are substituted by newer homogenous varieties, and if the total number of cultivated varieties is reduced by the introduction of commercial varieties in traditional farming systems, genetic erosion will occur. For example, in Ethiopia traditional barley and durum wheat varieties are suffering serious genetic erosion due to displacement by introduced varieties (FAO 1997, 33–35). The "Green Revolution" has significantly boosted the intensification of agricultural systems and led to a fundamental decrease of intraspecies diversity in farmers' fields. Furthermore, specialization by plant breeders and the harmonizing effects of globalization have also led to a substantial reduction in the genetic diversity of domesticated plants in agricultural systems (MEA 2005a, 5).

It is not only the amount of the total loss of biodiversity that is alarming. The distribution of species has also become more homogenous, and this means that species found at very different locations resemble one another. The reasons for this are that unique species tend to experience higher extinction rates and die out earlier, and that invasions of alien species tend to disperse at accelerating rates, choking out other species (MEA 2005a, 4). Looked at in terms of the use of genetic resources as inputs for research and development, this homogenization is very dramatic because the amount and the quality of diversity increase the probability that new active substances or breeding material may be found.

What are the drivers of biodiversity loss? Drivers are considered to be natural or human-induced factors that directly or indirectly cause a change in an ecosystem. Direct drivers unequivocally influence ecosystem processes. Indirect drivers operate more diffusely, by altering one or more direct drivers (MEA 2005c, 175). Identification of drivers is crucial for the selection, and success, of adequate countermeasures. Instruments that serve to increase the economic value of a given resource may be seen as effective measures to respond to the decline of biodiversity, assuming that the drivers of biodiversity loss are caused by the economic inferiority of the resource conservation towards other activities, e.g., land use change due to agricultural production.

According to the MEA (2005b), the most important direct negative impacts on biodiversity are habitat destruction, the introduction of alien species, overexploitation, disease, nutrient pollution, and climate change. Whereas habitat change, loss, and degradation are seen as the most effective drivers of biodiversity loss, it is assumed that disease, nutrient pollution, and climate change will play a more important role in the future. Climate change and invasive species are considered threats that initiate irreversible processes (MEA 2005b, 96). These direct drivers heavily influence the state of biodiversity, and will do so even more in the future. The relative importance of these drivers differs from one ecosystem to another. Land conversion tends to be most intensive in tropical forests and less intensive in temperate, boreal, and Arctic regions. The highest rates of atmospheric nitrogen deposition are reported for northern temperate areas close to cities. The introduction of exotic species is related to human activity. Areas remote from human intervention are generally observed to have fewer introduced species (UNEP 2002, 121).

Habitat change due to clearing or degradation has been the major threat to terrestrial ecosystems and their biodiversity. The problem is most apparent in areas where humans and species compete for space. We can observe two developments. First, agricultural land is expanding. In the coming thirty years, developing countries will need an extra 120 million hectare for crops, an overall increase of 12.5 percent. The rate varies from region to region, but Latin America, sub-Saharan Africa, and South and Southeast Asia are the regions most affected. However, less new agricultural land will be developed in the future than in the past (FAO 2002, 3). Second, the world's forests are diminishing. The FAO reports regularly on the state of forests (FAO 2003), and it estimates that every year in the 1990s 0.38 percent of the world's forests were converted to other land uses (i.e., deforested). At the same time, large areas were reverting to forest, and this indicates a net annual loss of 0.22 percent, and an even greater loss of biodiversity. Fragmentation is one visible consequence of habitat change. In the case of agricultural crops, intensification of agriculture based on the use of agricultural chemicals, the building of large-scale irrigation systems, clearance of hedgerows, etc., causes habitat destruction (FAO 1997, 36). The fact that human-induced habitat destruction and the intensification of agriculture have been shown to be the major causes of biodiversity decline indicates that the economic incentives set for conservation are too low. Market-based instruments for biodiversity conservation may thus be said to be an adequate response.

The introduction of alien species and diseases in recent years has increased enormously. Globalization of markets and population growth, made visible by increased international trade and travel, work in favor of the introduction of invasive species and pathogens. Alien species are nonnative species that are introduced, deliberately or not, outside their natural habitats, in places where they become established, proliferate, and spread. Existing native populations may be negatively affected. The same goes for the introduction of pathogens. Once a disease has attacked a population, the result is a decline that can lead to depopulation and even extinction. Invasive species and pathogens are recognized as one of the greatest biological threats to biodiversity—second only to habitat loss (MEA 2005a, 8; Reinhardt et al. 2003). Pimentel and colleagues (2001) estimated the annual economic and environmental costs caused by introduced pests in crops, pastures, and forests. The economic costs are estimated to be nearly US$230 billion and the environmental costs amount to US$100 billion in the United States (US), the United Kingdom (UK), Australia, South Africa, India, and Brazil. ABS is not related to this problem.

Overexploitation of resources or unsustainable harvesting of, for example, wild plants used for food, medicine, the ornamental flower trade, and timber is another important cause of genetic erosion. Many of these wildlife products and derivates can be found in international markets, where they are in great demand. Pressure on resources has increased along with population growth. Even though the trade in wild plants and animals and their derivatives is poorly documented, the costs are estimated to exceed US$160 billion (Traffic 2002). ABS can be relevant for this problem because users of genetic resources in some cases, e.g., in the botanical medicine sector, depend on a large and continuous supply of genetic resources. In this case, ABS may intensify the problem.

Climate change is likely to have considerable impacts on most or all ecosystems. The natural distribution limits for species may be affected by changes of temperature, rise of sea levels, changes in precipitation patterns, and increased frequencies of extreme weather events. As a consequence, species may migrate in response to changing conditions, although in many cases natural or human-induced barriers will hinder the movement of species and consequently lead to their extinction. For example, most national parks and protected areas are surrounded by urban and agricultural landscapes that prevent the migration of species beyond their boundaries. Scientists believe that the reason why the golden toad is extinct is climate change (Pounds, Fogden, and Campbell 1999, 611–615). Climate change does not affect all species in the same way. Some species are more vulnerable than others because they have different attributes (e.g., reduced mobility, isolated or small populations) and face different barriers (e.g., restricted habitat requirements). It is assumed that the present trend in climate change will continue, giving rise to greater impacts on biodiversity. Some scenarios indicate that as much as 30 percent of species will be lost as a consequence of such change (Thomas et al. 2004). ABS is not related to this problem. However, the problem of climate change indicates that there is urgent need for action.

The main indirect factors that influence the state of biodiversity are demographic, economic, and sociopolitical (MEA 2005c, 175). All of these factors are related to ABS.

Population growth is not evenly distributed in the world. Fifty years after World War II, the world's population has grown immensely and multiplied more rapidly than ever before. High growth rates can be observed for the most part in less developed countries, but population growth is also projected to continue in the US. Today more than 6.5 billion people live on Earth; twenty years ago the figure was only 4.2 billion. According to estimates, by 2050 more than nine billion people will live on the planet (Population Reference Bureau 2005). More people need more living space and more resources to meet their needs, and this will increase the pressure on the environment and resources. Increased land use changes are the consequence. More people will make the issue of ABS more complex because resource holders play an important role for the concept.

Economic aspects play a key role in the loss of biodiversity. The world economy and per capita incomes have grown along with population. Between 1950 and 2000, world gross domestic product (GDP) grew on average by 3.85 percent per year, resulting in an average per capita income growth rate of 2.09 percent (MEA 2005c, 175). Economic growth is not equally distributed across the world, and inequities in the distribution of wealth and resources persist. Rising income implies increased consumption and changes in consumption patterns. Economic growth depends on resources such as, e.g., land and fossil fuels. Another consequence is increased generation of waste and pollutants. International trade is set to increase, and economies will be more closely interlinked, further aggravating the problem. One other problem driving biodiversity loss is the lack of economic incentives designed to guarantee the provision of biodiversity, or the existence of adverse incentives that lead to depletion (see Myers 1995, 111ff.; Chapter 3, this volume). Economic distortions caused by taxes and subsidies (e.g., to clear forests) may have negative impacts on the environment. All of these developments have a decisive impact on resources and the environment. ABS and the market for genetic resources are closely linked to other markets and compromised by distortions. ABS needs to provide for compensations designed to offset the need to abandon other destructive activities.

Sociopolitical factors have developed positively in many countries in the last decades (United Nations Development Programme [UNDP] 2005, 19ff.). The importance a given country attaches to biodiversity also depends on how political leaders view environmental issues. Elected democracies have displaced authoritarian governments, local communities and indigenous people have gained rights and recognition, nongovernmental organizations (NGOs) play an increasingly large role in the decision-making process, and many environmental issues are discussed in multilateral forums, including, for example, the CBD (MEA 2005b, 74–75). These developments put biodiversity on the political agenda of many governments, but they have also made societies more familiar with the issue, even though awareness is still at a very low level. International conflicts often entail destruction of the natural environment in the area of conflict. In some countries war and civil strife have contributed significantly to genetic erosion. In Angola and Cambodia they contributed to the loss of many traditional varieties as people moved from one area to another in search of safety. Farmers were unable to preserve their local varieties (FAO 1997, 38). Sociopolitical factors also play an important role for the ABS system and its critical factors. Only where the sociopolitical factors support it can a system of this kind work.

THE DEMAND SIDE: UTILIZATION OF GENETIC RESOURCES

This section will characterize the demand for genetic resources in terms of the importance of genetic resources for the demand side and the actors (users) operating in the market. Apart from providers, users are the most relevant actors in ABS. The scope and size of their demand will be shown in exemplary form for the pharmaceutical sector, with natural inputs serving to illustrate what role genetic resources play for research and development. The market is also shaped by the heterogeneity of users. The main commercial user sectors of biodiversity will be described in the following. They include the health care sector, with pharmacy, botanical medicine, cosmetics, and personal care; the agricultural sector, with plant breeding and pest control; and the horticulture and the biotechnology sectors. These sectors point to different areas and possibilities of commercial utilization. The sectors differ in terms of many aspects, including, for example, market value, market structure, material acquisition, and benefit-sharing practices.

Importance of Genetic Resources for Industry

Biodiversity is a treasured good. At a conference held by the International Society of Chemical Ecology in Sweden in 1990, it was noted that "Natural products constitute a treasury of immense value to humankind. The current alarming rate of species extinction is rapidly depleting this treasury, with potentially disastrous consequences" (MEA 2005a, 273–274). However, not all potential users of genetic resources acknowledge their importance. Especially today, users from private sectors stress that their need for genetic resources as inputs for research and development has significantly decreased.

The user industries of genetic resources can be generally described as research- and development-intensive industries that invest over 10 percent of their gross revenues in the development of new approaches (Swanson and Goeschl 2000, 78). The pharmaceutical sector is the biggest and most promising user industry of genetic resources, in terms of their potential in monetary terms. A short overview of one selected market, the market for drugs based on natural inputs, is presented to show in exemplary form the role that genetic resources play for the development of commercial products.

In the past ten years companies have de-emphasized natural product drug discovery, arguing that the share of drugs that rely on natural inputs is relatively small and decreasing. The interest of industries in natural products drug discovery has diminished because other technologies, including combinatorial chemistry, promise to be successful future solutions (Sittenfeld, Cabrera, and Mora 2003). According to Newman, Cragg, and Snader (2003), the trend began in the early 1990s and was driven primarily by practical motives. Advances in the drug-discovery process (e.g., automation, robotics, fast personal computers, and high-throughput screening) have meant a need for huge numbers of compounds for screening. Natural products drug discovery has not satisfied this demand because the approach is slow and labor intensive. Besides, combinatorial chemistry libraries are more successful than natural product drug discovery in further developing or optimizing the process from hits of screens to leads and to approved drugs. However, this is not the case for pure discovery and the development of *de novo* combinatorial compounds leading to an approved drug. Here, natural products drug discovery is still the main method used. Moreover, this method has become less difficult to use thanks to technological advances (e.g., separation technologies, speed and sensitivity of structure elucidation; Newman, Cragg, and Snader 2003).

The statistics bear out both these developments and the importance of natural products and genetic resources as inputs for and sources of new drugs and lead compounds useful for further drug development. Butler (2004) determined that natural products or related substances accounted for 40 percent of the top thirty-five worldwide prescription drug sales in 2000, a figure that ranged between 24 percent in 2001 and 26 percent in 2002. A further indicator of the importance of certain groups of drugs is the number and economic value of prescriptions. According to Grifo and colleagues (1997), 84 of a representative sample of 150 prescription drugs in the US fell into the category of natural products and related drugs.

Users of Genetic Resources

The use of genetic resources for research and development depends on a wide variety of species, but it also involves a wide variety of users and users groups. The term *user*, or *user country*, is widely used in reference to the utilization of biodiversity, and especially ABS. At the country level, and in relation to the term *provider country*, it is used to describe the amount of biodiversity in a country and the occurrence and development there of biotechnological, pharmaceutical, and agricultural industries. Due to the unequal distribution of resources and research and development capacities in the world, biodiversity-rich developing countries are classified as provider countries, whereas most of the industrialized countries that have distinct biotechnology capacities are referred to as user countries. However, neither the distinction nor the generalization hold in all cases. For example, Australia and Brazil are at the same time important providers and users of genetic resources (Barber, Johnston, and Tobin 2003, 18). In this book, the term *user countries* refers to countries that have high demand for genetic resources and the capacity to use them in research, development, and commercialization, regardless of whether or not they also provide biodiversity. At the individual level, the term characterizes the agents on the demand side of genetic resources. Users are those agents who obtain genetic resources for commercial or scientific purposes. The term *user countries* refers to the competent legal and political authorities under whose jurisdiction the users of genetic resources act and operate (Barber, Johnston, and Tobin 2003, 18). Even though it is widely used, the term *user* seems too broad because intermediaries or other agents also demand genetic resources. Whereas the latter are recipients of the material, they are not necessarily its final users. However, in the international debate recipients are classified as users. To speak in the same language, the term *user* is used synonymously with the term *recipient* throughout this book.

The User Sectors

The health care sector, including pharmacy, botanical medicine, cosmetics, and personal care; agriculture with plant breeding and pest control; and horticulture and biotechnology, are the most relevant user sectors of plant genetic resources (see Figure 2.3). Research institutions (e.g., universities and research institutes) and ex situ collections often act as intermediaries, forwarding genetic resources, derivatives, or intermediary products to these sectors. They are more research than development oriented and can be assigned to the sectors identified. However, because more and more patents are based on innovations made at universities, these users will in the future have to be considered as an important user group. The number of US academic patents quadrupled from approximately eight hundred in 1988 to more than thirty-two hundred in 2003. The increase in patents was highly

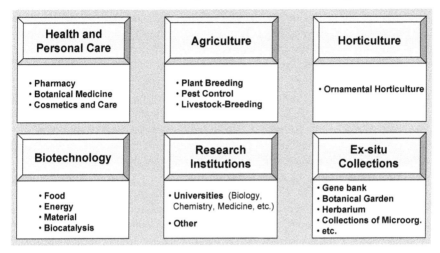

Figure 2.3 User sectors.
Source: Holm-Mueller, Richerzhagen, and Taeuber (2005, 18).

concentrated in life sciences applications (National Science Board 2006, 5–51). In 2005, the University of California received more than 390 patents for innovations, followed by the Massachusetts Institute of Technology (MIT) with 136 patents (United States Patent and Trademark Office 2007).

Pharmacy

Pharmaceutical companies invest a higher share of their profits in research and development than other innovative sectors. In general, these expenditures have risen significantly, but the companies are always looking for ways to cut their costs. Most pharmacy-related research and development is conducted in the US, followed by the UK and Switzerland. Estimates are that the development of a new medicine costs about US$500 million, and it takes an average of fifteen years for a product to reach the market (ten Kate and A Laird 1999, 47).

The main technologies used for drug development are screening of libraries for synthetic compounds and natural products and rational drug design based on genomics. Both technologies are very elaborate and the probability of success is quite low. When screening is used, only one of five thousand to ten thousand synthetic compounds is likely to be approved as a drug. The ratio for natural products is only one to thirty thousand or forty thousand (Onaga 2001, 264). However, the potential profits are remarkable. In 1997, seventy-one drugs earned more than US$500 million each and twenty-seven blockbuster drugs earned more than US$1 billion each per year. Estimates for the pharmaceutical sector indicate an increasingly significant role for genetic resources in the development of pharmaceuticals.

Today more than half of the drugs in the market are natural products or derived from natural products. It has been estimated that the pharmaceutical industry earns about US$32 billion a year in profits from products derived from traditional remedies (Harrison and Pearce 2001, 162).

According to a survey by Newman, Cragg, and Snader (2003), 61 percent of the 877 small-molecule new chemical entities introduced as drugs worldwide during 1981–2002 can be traced back to natural products. This figure breaks down as follows: natural products account for 6 percent, natural product derivatives for 27 percent, synthetic compounds with natural product–derived pharmacophores for 5 percent, and synthetic compounds designed on the basis of knowledge gained from a natural product (natural product mimic) for 23 percent. In therapeutic categories the share is even much higher. Seventy-eight percent of antibacterials and 74 percent of anticancer compounds are natural products or have been derived from or inspired by a natural product. Other important categories are antiulcer, cholesterol-lowering, hypertension, antidepressant, hematologic, and antihistamine drugs.

The most popular example of a natural-based drug is Taxol (paclitaxel), which was introduced by Bristol-Myers Squibb (BMS) in 1993 to treat ovarian cancer. The company earns about US$1.6 billion a year from Taxol. Its development is based on the bark of the Pacific yew tree (Firn 2003, 212). Other examples are vinblastine and vincristine from *Catharanthiis roseus*, the rosy periwinkle, from Madagascar. In the 1950s, Eli Lilly and Company discovered that a leaf extract from *C. roseus* could affect the progress of leukemia. As a result, the pharmaceutical company introduced anticancer drugs known as vinca alkaloids in the 1960s. Vinblastine is used to treat Hodgkin's disease, a cancer of the lymphatic system, and vincristine is used to treat pediatric leukemia, a cancer of the bone marrow and other blood-cell-producing organs. Annual revenues were in excess of US$200 million (Wilson 1992, 283).

In 2004 the pharmaceutical market topped US$500 billion (Wynberg and A Laird 2005, 7). This is a 7 percent increase over 2003 and a 28 percent increase compared to 2001. The industry is concentrated in the US and Europe, followed by Japan. The already large and profitable pharmaceutical industry has been rapidly consolidating over the past few years. The top ten companies (by sales) account for 45 percent of the market (see Table 2.2).

The greatest rates of growth can be observed for generic and biotechnology companies. However, consolidation of the market also had some negative impacts on research and development, and in 2003 many companies had lower market shares than the sum of their components in 1998 (Wynberg and A Laird 2005, 8).

In the pharmaceutical sector most genetic material is acquired via intermediaries. A few companies, most of them larger, collect raw materials (i.e., wild plants or microorganisms) themselves in the countries of origin. Collections may be random and blind in a determined geographical area, ecology driven and led by observations, chemotaxonomic and based on

Table 2.2 The Top Ten Pharmaceutical Companies, Ranked by Sales, 2004

Company	Revenues US$ billion	Market share (percent)	R&D spending US$ billion
Pfizer	50.9	9.25	7.5
GlaxoSmithKline	32.7	5.96	5.2
Sanofi-Aventis	27.1	4.93	3.9
Johnson & Johnson	24.6	4.47	5.2
Merck	23.9	4.35	4.0
Novartis	22.7	4.13	3.5
AstraZeneca	21.6	3.93	3.8
Hoffmann-La Roche	17.7	3.22	5.1
Bristol-Myers Squibb	15.5	2.82	2.5
Wyeth	14.2	2.58	2.5

Source: adopted from Diller and Satlas (2005).

knowledge of taxa, or ethnobotanical, using local people's knowledge about plant properties. Many companies own libraries of compounds, extracts, and dried plant material. The amount of material obtained depends on the company's size and its research and development strategy. It is assumed that the users of this sector are relatively familiar with the CBD and adopt progressive ABS procedures (ten Kate and A Laird 1999, 57–77).

Botanical Medicine

The botanical medicine industry is growing worldwide, and especially in Germany. In 1997 the German population accounted for approximately 30 percent of the consumption of nonprescription pharmaceuticals containing botanical medicine. Besides Germany, the largest markets are found in China, Japan, the US, France, Italy, the UK, and Spain (ten Kate and A Laird 1999, 79).

For the most part, whole plant material is used for botanical medicines. Prominent examples include *Ginko, enchinacae,* and Saint John's wort. The botanical medicine industry usually imports the whole body of the plant. The botanical market in the US is estimated at approximately US$1.6 billion per year. It is estimated that Europe annually imports about four hundred thousand tons of medicinal plants, with an average market value of US$1 billion, from Africa and Asia. After Hong Kong, Japan, and the US, Germany ranks fourth on the list of international importers. However, most of the material used is native to the region where it is sold. According to estimates, the global trade in medicinal plants amounts to US$800 million per year (Horaeau and Da Silva 1999).

The plant material is either collected from the wild or cultivated. Because the market is growing by more than 10 percent per year, wild collections can have a negative impact on the environment and biodiversity. Products are sold in the form of dried and fresh raw material, tinctures, extracts, and phytomedicines. Currently, China is the largest exporter of plant material, followed by India. The material is acquired through supply companies (i.e., cultivators, wholesalers, processing companies). On its way to the consumer it passes through many hands, including manufacturing companies and consumer sales organizations. Traditional knowledge (TK) is widely used to identify promising material, whereas intensive research in the field is limited due to the multicompound characteristics of botanical medicine. Applications for patents appear unrealistic in these cases. Two-thirds of the fifty thousand medicinal plants used worldwide come from the wild (wildcrafting), and these plants account for the majority of plant material used in this sector. At present, though, there is a trend toward cultivated material because continuity and quality are important supply criteria (Schippman, Leaman, and Cunningham 2002, 4–5). ABS is not very common in this sector. Monetary benefit-sharing is mainly practiced in the form of payment per weight unit of raw material, and only in a small number of cases are advance payments and royalties used (ten Kate and A Laird 1999, 78–116).

Devil's claw is an excellent example. In 1972 it was discovered that an extract derived from its roots has anti-inflammatory properties. From then on, the product boomed. In 1999, in Germany, sales amounted to €8 million, rising by 113 percent the following year and by 59 percent, to €27 million, by 2001. All sales are based on collections from the wild, but it has become clear that these collections will not be sufficient to sustain the supply in the long term. The global market currently demands between 600 and 700 metric tons of raw materials every year, and the plant needs to grow for four years or more before it is ready for harvesting. Company-based cultivation projects were initiated to substitute for wild collection and to teach collectors how to harvest the rhizome in a sustainable manner in order to preserve the populations. One collateral effect discovered was that the cultivated material is of better quality than the wild plant in terms of purity, identity, and active constituent content (Nutraingredients 2004). The volume of trade indicates that revenues are quite large in this sector. According to estimates, in Germany annual revenues from phytopharmaceuticals amount to about €900 million (Bundesverband der pharmazeutischen Industrie 2005, 37).

Cosmetics and Personal Care

With an 8 to 25 percent growth rate per year, the natural cosmetics and personal care industry is growing at a disproportionately high rate within the overall cosmetics and personal care sector (3 to 10 percent). The natural segment anticipates gaining a share of up to 10 percent of the overall sector. The industry uses wild or cultivated plant genetic material in a wide range of products, including, for example, baby and skin care, cosmetics, and hair products. The European and US markets for personal care were estimated to be worth US$86 billion in 2004 (Datamonitor 2006).

As in the botanical medicine sector, the agents here can be broken down into supply companies, manufacturers, and marketers. Companies only seldom engage in collecting activities of their own. Similarities between these two sectors are due to the identical raw material input, that is, dried plants and oils from a wide variety of species. The demand of users in this sector for new genetic resources is relatively low. One reason for this is the large variety of plants already in use, another the highly cost-intensive and time-consuming process involved in introducing new ingredients. Yet the research and development strategies of some companies in this sector also include the use of new genetic material. If ABS agreements are concluded, providers are usually compensated on the basis of payments per kilogram or sample (ten Kate and A Laird 1999, 276–292; Holm-Mueller, Richerzhagen, and Taeuber 2005, 20).

Agriculture: Seed Industry

The seed industry has gone through a period of structural change in the past thirty years. Mergers and acquisitions have created a new structure dominated by large companies. Already in the mid-1970s, when the seed market was growing, many multinational companies that earlier focused on pharmaceuticals and chemicals entered the seed market. With the development of genetic engineering in the 1980s, many companies evolved into "life science groups," seeking to harness the strong potential for complementarity between crop protection and seeds. One prominent example of this complementarity is Monsanto's product Roundup Ready[3] (United Nations Conference on Trade and Environment [UNCTAD] 2006, 7).

The global commercial seed market is estimated to range between US$21 and US$25.2 billion. As in the pharmaceutical industry, what we see here is domination of the market by a handful of companies with concentration strategies (see Table 2.3). Whereas ten companies control 49 percent of the

Table 2.3 The Top Four Seed Companies, Ranked by Sales and Market Share, 2004

Company	Seed sales (million US$)	Market share (in percent)
DuPont/Pioneer	2,624	10
Monsanto	2,277	9
Syngenta	1,239	5
Limagrain	1,239	5
Others	17,821	71
World	25,200	100

Source: adopted from UNCTAD (2006, 9).

market, four companies account for a total of about 30 percent (UNCTAD 2006, 8; Action Group on Erosion, Technology, and Concentration 2005, 2).

It is difficult to separate the seed and pest control sectors because the same companies dominate both markets. However, in addition to the large companies, many small seed companies (about fifteen hundred) are also active in the market, six hundred of which are based in the US and four hundred in Europe. In many countries the provision and distribution of seeds is still under government control. The public sector accounts for about 20 percent of the global seed market (James 1996, 18). In addition, there are international research organizations like the Consultative Group on International Agricultural Research (CGIAR) that support agricultural research for food security.

The main actors in this sector are breeders of agricultural crops. Although most material used for breeding was originally taken from the wild, today most material is obtained from seed banks held by corporations, universities, botanical gardens, and regional, national, or international gene banks. Intermediaries are, therefore, important actors in this sector. However, wild species are also essential for the sector. The existence of a wide gene pool is important if breeding is to adapt to future challenges posed by a changing environment. If certain wild plants had been extinct in the past, it would not have been possible to domesticate rice and wheat (Devlin and Grafton 1999, 95). The development of a wheat variety can involve thousands of plant breeding crosses and many different individual lines from many countries and over many centuries (MEA 2005a, 281). Other actors in the market operate in seed production, seed conditioning, and seed marketing and distribution.

Development of new varieties takes about eight to fifteen years and costs something in the range of US$1.0 to US$2.5 million for a traditionally bred variety and US$35 to US$75 million for a transgene variety.

Wynberg and A Laird (2005) assume that the CBD and ABS play an important role in this sector. Benefit-sharing by private companies is generally based on arrangements involving payment of license fees for the use of germplasm. Monetary benefit-sharing is not common among public institutions. They generally arrange for access to genetic resources on a mutual basis and promote capacity-building by transferring knowledge and technology to the countries of origin (ten Kate and A Laird 1999, 131–157).

Benefit-sharing arrangements have been covered by the ITPGRFA since this multilateral agreement came into force. Bilateral contracts play a role only when the crops used for plant breeding are not covered by the treaty (see Chapter 4, this volume).

Agriculture: Crop Protection

Following a period of stagnation, the market for agrochemicals (i.e., herbicides, insecticides, fungicides, and other agrochemicals) has grown since 2002. Market value has recently been estimated at US$32 million (UNCTAD 2006, 3). The concentration in this market is obvious. In 2004 six companies accounted for about 77 percent of the market, with three of them accounting for some 50 percent.

Major concentrations of the agrochemical industry are found in North America, Europe, and Japan. Whereas production is in the hands of a small group of companies, other small companies, government agencies, universities, and research institutions are involved in the research. In 1997 herbicides accounted for 48 percent of the market, insecticides for 27 percent, and fungicides for 20 percent (ten Kate and A Laird 1999, 189).

The costs involved in discovering a new commercial chemical pesticide may range between US$40 and US$100 million, and it takes up to fourteen years to develop the product. Of one hundred thousand chemicals tested, only about two result in a product. It is estimated that crop protection products derived from genetic resources account for about 10 percent of annual global sales (ten Kate and A Laird 1999, 194–195).

Demand for access to genetic resources in the sector of agrochemicals is very likely to grow in the future. All companies and institutions that work in this sector depend on access to new genetic resources. The users obtain material through their own collecting activities in the countries of origin and via intermediaries, but also from ex situ collections. Many companies maintain libraries of genetic material. A genetic resource is usually needed for a single screening, and thus extraction takes place only once. However, some methods of pest control require a regular, large supply of the genetic material that constitutes a direct component of the product. Public institutions, universities, and research institutions guarantee the traditional mutual exchange of genetic material, engaging in research in cooperation

Table 2.4　The Top Six Agrochemical Companies, Ranked by Sales and Market Share, 2004

Company	Agrochem sales (million US$)	Market share (percent)
Bayer	6,155	19
Syngenta	6,030	18
BASF	4,165	13
Dow	3,368	10
Monsanto	3,180	10
DuPont	2,249	7
Others	7,519	23
World	32,665	100

Source: adopted from UNCTAD (2006, 3).

with the countries of origin. Most private companies practice monetary benefit-sharing in the form of single-access fees or up-front payments (ten Kate and A Laird 1999, 210–227).

As agrochemicals, biological control systems aim at crop protection but rely much more on biodiversity. Biological control is seen as an alternative to chemicals because it uses predators, parasites, or pathogens or their products to protect crops. No data is available to estimate the share of biological control in the crop protection sector. Pimentel (1992) suggests using the cost of pesticide use for food production (e.g., health costs, veterinary costs, surface and groundwater contamination, and pollinator losses) in the US as a reference. These factors were estimated to amount to US$8 billion per year, costs that could be avoided by substituting biological control agents for agrochemicals (MEA 2005d, 279).

Crop protection is also used in the horticulture sector, and it could therefore be assigned to this sector. Because crop protection in the field of agriculture involves significantly greater dimensions, and in order to simplify matters, crop protection is here assigned to the agricultural sector.

Horticulture

Horticulture is a very broad field and includes intensive, large-scale, and commercial production of vegetables but also gardening as a hobby. This book considers only the part of horticulture that uses genetic resources to develop new horticultural products. It is, however, difficult to define its scope in relation to agriculture, and there is some question as to the accuracy of the data available. The horticultural market for vegetables is larger than the market for ornamental horticultural products. Annual sales of horticultural seeds, including flower and vegetable seeds, amount to US$1.80 billion (A Laird and ten Kate 2002, 256). The issues surrounding access to genetic resources for vegetables are very similar to those discussed for agricultural seeds. Things are slightly different for the case of ornamental horticultural (i.e., potted plants, bedding plants, cut flowers), and we will therefore take a brief look at the matter here.

The major producing countries are the Netherlands, Japan, and the US. Market concentration is also an important feature of this sector. Ten multinational seed companies (e.g., Novartis/Switzerland, PanAmerican/US, Sakata/Japan, Goldsmith Seeds/US) account for 90 percent of global sales of seed for ornamental varieties. Whereas the costs involved in developing a new ornamental variety from scratch may range from almost nothing to US$5 million (on average US$2 to US$4 million), the time needed may vary from one or two years to up to ten years (ten Kate and A Laird 1999, 165).

As far as the use of genetic resources is concerned, the horticulture sector breaks down into two groups. One group mainly uses breeding material that is already in commercial use. The use of wild plants as a source of new genetic material is of relatively minor interest for these breeders. The second group consists of those breeders who depend on access to new genetic resources. Their sources include botanical gardens, national collections, and commercial providers. It is difficult to assess the size of each of the groups.

At present one feature characteristic of this sector is widespread ignorance of the CBD (Wynberg and A Laird 2005, 26). Benefit-sharing is relatively uncommon. Traditionally, plant material was exchanged free of charge between breeders. Guaranteed mutual access to plant material still constitutes an essential form of nonmonetary benefit-sharing. There are, though, some cases where so-called royalty fees are paid to share benefits (ten Kate and A Laird 1999, 172–187).

Biotechnology

Biotechnology is understood as the application of science and technology to living organisms, as well as parts, products, and models of such organisms, to alter living or nonliving materials for the production of knowledge, goods, and services (OECD 2005, 9). The biotechnology sector includes, e.g., activities in the fields of health and agriculture, but also in energy, materials, biocatalysts, functional food (novel food), and diagnostics. Its most important genetic resource inputs are microorganisms. In 2004 the revenues of the biotechnology industry amounted to US$54.6 billion. The US dominates the sector, with 78 percent of global public company revenues. Biotechnology products have experienced a 17 percent increase in market share. Consolidation is evident here as well. Eighty percent of the biotechnology market is held by ten companies (Wynberg and A Laird 2005, 8–13). Because biotechnology products are quite diversified, it is not possible to assess the development time and cost of a new product. In the case of a novel enzyme product, it may take from two to five years and cost between US$2 and US$20 million before the product is sold in the market (ten Kate and A Laird 1999, 239).

The biotechnology sector also comprises both users who collect their genetic material themselves in the respective countries of origin and companies and research institutions that obtain their genetic resources mainly from intermediaries, including, for example, collections (Wynberg and A Laird 2005, 16).

In the biotechnology sector various monetary and nonmonetary benefits are provided in exchange for rights to use genetic resources. These measures can be described as benefit-sharing, even though the users consider them more as expenditures for important input factors (ten Kate and A Laird 1999, 242–261).

Other Minor Sectors

The term *biomimetics* refers to biologically inspired technologies developed by industry. Prominent examples are shells of various mollusks, which have inspired the ceramic industry, or the lotus leaf, which repels water droplets and particles of dirt. Biomonitoring is an industry that is needed to track down sources of pollution. Whereas this would otherwise require a vast amount of instrumentation, the status of the environment can also be monitored by using organisms that sample the environment. Freshwater can be monitored, e.g., by fish and mussels, soil by earthworms, and air by bees (MEA 2005d, 279–281). These two sectors are examples of sectors of minor relevance compared to the others, and it is difficult to assess annual sales and market potential. However, these emerging markets are growing and may play a more important role in the future.

Experiences, Awareness, and Participation of Users

In 1999 ten Kate and A Laird analyzed basic trends and differences within European user sectors. One important finding of their book is that the majority of users in all sectors are insufficiently informed about the CBD and its associated legal framework regarding the use of genetic resources. Positive attitudes towards the CBD are most common among those companies that are already participating in the political process. Among other things, the users express the following expectations for the CBD: improvement of legal security for issues concerning access to and use of genetic resources and more clarity on questions of property rights to genetic resources. According to some user points of view, the CBD can assist in developing guidelines for best practice in the use of genetic resources, helping to address image problems in the user sector (ten Kate and A Laird 1999, 296). The experiences of users with the impact of the CBD have led to a more critical attitude towards the CBD. The problems and disadvantages mentioned by users include insufficient levels of information, inconsistent implementation of access regulations by the different countries of origin, excessive bureaucratic expenses, unrealistic expectations on the part of the countries of origin regarding benefit-sharing, negative incentives for research and development, and in general the negative impact of high transaction costs due to complicated regulations (ten Kate and A Laird 1999, 296–300).

As far as the CBD regulations on benefit-sharing are concerned, users tend to hold the opinion that the actual value of a genetic resource arises only from user capital expenditures in the context of research and development. Users are therefore inclined to offer transfers of knowledge and technology in exchange for access rights, rather than to show themselves capable of and willing to practice monetary benefit-sharing. In addition, the industry always argues that it has alternative approaches to product discovery other than genetic resources and that demand for access will decline in the future (ten Kate and A Laird 1999, 6–7).

Until recently, the comprehensive book on the EU published by ten Kate and A Laird was the only study that attempted to identify the structure of the user sector, user awareness, and user perceptions. This information is essential for undertaking user-orientated measures and formulating policies with regard to genetic resources. Now, some governments of user countries (e.g., Germany in 2004, the UK in 2004, and Belgium in 2006)[4] have initiated studies conceived to assess, in their countries, the user structure as well as user attitudes and levels of user awareness and participation. The survey on users of genetic resources in Germany was the first published in this series, and its major findings are outlined here. Its results confirm many of the findings presented by ten Kate and A Laird in 1999, but it also provides a set of new insights on users of genetic resources.

In Germany the majority of users receive their material from trading partners, rather than collecting or reproducing it themselves. The same applies to the UK (Latorre 2005, 6). Providers from the countries of origin and from other countries constitute the most important supply sources for all sectors. Above all, users at universities and other research institutions as well as ex situ collections and users from the field of biotechnology engage in collecting activities "of their own."

Most users directly approach providers in the countries of origin, establish cooperation in the countries of origin, and/or contact ex situ collections. Only a small number of users obtain prior informed consent (PIC) from authorities in the country of origin before they make use of genetic resources or conclude material transfer agreements (MTA) with the countries of origin.

The main reasons for German researchers and companies not to work with genetic resources are the difficulty in finding an appropriate responsible contact person to arrange access modalities in the country of origin and the image problem arising from the use of genetic material.[5] The problem of excessive costs resulting from benefit-sharing is not identified as a major problem. This seems rather unexpected because commercial users in particular often complain about disproportionate expectations in terms of monetary benefit-sharing.

The most relevant finding of the study is that many German users are generally not familiar with the CBD and the obligations arising from the agreement. They see themselves as insufficiently informed on the international regulations on ABS. Users are apparently aware of the lack of information. The study cannot confirm the assumption that larger companies and institutions tend to be better informed, as noted by ten Kate and A Laird. Groups of users of similar size and structure do not automatically have the same level of information. The majority of users in all sectors are not informed about the CBD. Ex situ collections were found to be most familiar with the CBD, followed by universities and other research institutions. The awareness of survey participants from the private sector turns out to be considerably lower than that of users from the public sector. As regards the question of whether users see their interests properly represented in the international CBD negotiations, statements tend to differ, and they do not yield a clear picture. The most important sources of information about the CBD include, in descending order, the Internet, trade associations, and scientific journals. Firsthand information from German authorities (e.g., national focal point, delegation members) is consulted by no more than a few users.

In the UK the picture is slightly different. The level of awareness there of the CBD and ABS provisions is higher, even though the majority of users appear to lack detailed understanding. Large organizations seemed generally more knowledgeable and experienced concerning ABS. However, they too rely mainly on intermediaries to obtain material (Latorre 2005, 6).

More than 50 percent of the users interviewed believe that it has become more difficult for German users to gain access to genetic resources since the CBD entered into force. The same experience is reported for the UK (Latorre 2005, 5). However, the majority of users report an approximately constant use of genetic resources. In the future, the importance of genetic resources is expected to grow for users. This finding is surprising because many private-sector users stress the decreasing importance of "wild" plant genetic material for research and development.

CONSERVATION CONCEPTS

How can we bridge the gap between the immense decline in biodiversity and the increasing demand for and importance of biodiversity? And what role does ABS play in relation to other conservation concepts?

At the World Summit in Johannesburg in 2002, the international community acknowledged that the ongoing loss of biodiversity had not been halted, and it put biodiversity protection and the 2010 target on the list of priorities. The 2010 target, formulated in 2002 by the CBD Conference of the Parties, is now an essential component of the Convention's implementation, and this implies that the parties' aim is to achieve a significant reduction of the current rate of biodiversity loss at global, regional, and national levels by 2010 (CBD 1998, Decision VI/26). A series of global and outcome-oriented targets were adopted to facilitate monitoring of progress toward 2010. These targets cover the following focal areas: understanding and documenting plant diversity, conserving plant diversity, using plant diversity sustainably, promoting education and awareness concerning plant diversity, and building capacity for the conservation of plant diversity. The targets are very ambitious. They include, for example, conservation of 10 percent of each of the world's ecological regions, conservation of 50 percent of the areas most important for plant diversity, conservation in situ of 60 percent of the world's threatened species, and conservation of 70 percent of the genetic diversity of crops and other major socioeconomically valuable plant species and associated indigenous and local knowledge. Under the targets, 30 percent of plant-based products should be derived from sources that are sustainably managed, no species of wild flora should be endangered by international trade, and the importance of plant diversity and the need for its conservation should be incorporated into communication, education, and public-awareness programs (CBD 2004, Decision VII/30).

There are a number of different conservation concepts that are used in an attempt to stem the ongoing loss. ABS is only one of them. The main conservation concepts can be broken down into two groups: in situ and ex situ conservation. In situ conservation is "the conservation of ecosystems and natural habitats and the maintenance and recovery of viable populations of species in their natural surroundings and, in the case of domesticated or cultivated species, in the surroundings where they have developed their distinctive properties," whereas ex situ conservation refers to "the conservation of components of biological diversity outside their natural habitats" (CBD 1992, Article 2). Ex situ approaches are regarded as complementary to in situ approaches rather than as rivals because it is recognized that both methods address different aspects of genetic resources. On their own, neither is sufficient and adequate to conserve the total range of genetic resources that exist. In situ conservation is essential for several reasons. Not all elements of crops, e.g., wild and weedy relatives of crops as well as perennials and species with recalcitrant seeds, can be held in ex situ facilities. Ex situ institutions can store certain genetic materials of a plant and maintain the material in the state in which it was collected—but not the surrounding ecosystem, which influences the plant's generation. In situ conservation can serve to support the maintenance of a changing system; this also allows for the loss of certain species (Brush 2000, 7–8).

With a view to better understanding the role that ABS plays among other conservation concepts, the following sections categorize the different approaches and possibilities available. The characteristics of in situ compared to ex situ conservation are of major importance for a later analysis of ABS because ex situ collections may appear to represent competition for provider countries.

In Situ Conservation

Protected areas are the strongest instruments used for the in situ protection of biodiversity. These areas are like a genetic reserve in which the genetic diversity of natural wild populations is conserved within defined zones. Since the late nineteenth century establishment of protected areas has been the leading response to such challenges. Both increased technical capacities to design protected areas and the realization that protected areas have the potential to contribute effectively to the protection of forests have led to a consolidation and expansion of the network of protected areas (Adams et al. 2004, 1146). The 2003 United Nations List of Protected Areas lists[6] 102,102 protected areas that cover 18.8 million km². This figure is equivalent to 12.65 percent of the Earth's land surface. In 1962 protected areas only amounted to 9,214 sites and 2.4 million km². In 1992 there were 48,388 sites and 12.3 million km under protection; 4,116 of these protected areas contain marine and coastal elements, covering 4.3 million km². The largest protected marine area is the Great Barrier Reef Marine Park in Australia (345,400 km²) (Chape et al. 2003, 21, 26, 27).

The CBD sees the establishment and effective management of a global series of protected areas as a key instrument to protect biodiversity. The CBD defines a protected area as: "a geographically defined area which is designated or regulated and managed to achieve specific conservation objectives." IUCN has formulated a broader definition conceived to include cultural aspects. It views protected areas as "areas of land and/or sea especially dedicated to the protection and maintenance of biological diversity, and of natural and associated cultural resources, and managed through legal or other effective means" (The World Conservation Union 1994, 7).

Protected areas play a key role in reaching the CBD's objectives. The seventh Conference of the Parties (COP) of the CBD ended with a major advance on protected areas when it adopted a program of work on protected areas. The overall purpose of the work program is to support the establishment—by 2010 for terrestrial areas and by 2012 for marine areas—of an effective global network of protected areas. The program of work on protected areas recognizes that the Least Developed Countries (LDCs) and those with economies in transition need help to strengthen the skills necessary to implement the objectives and measures adopted (CBD 2004, Decision VII/28).

Protected areas serve the purpose of supporting in situ conservation, but also of providing sources for bioprospecting and ABS (A Laird and Lisinge 2002, 127). In some countries, including, for example, Costa Rica, bioprospecting material is collected only in protected areas, and as implementation of the ABS concept progresses, demand for samples from protected areas will grow. In the past, protected areas have yielded valuable inputs for research and development. In 1969, US scientists reported a new species of bacterium, which they named *Thermus aquaticus*. This thermophilic organism was isolated from hot springs in Yellowstone National Park, and it has contributed to significant developments in biotechnology. The bacterium is the source of the enzyme Taq DNA (deoxyribonucleic acid) polymerase, one of the most important enzymes in molecular biology and one widely used for industrial and scientific research. Yellowstone's thermophilic bacteria attract many researchers and many research projects are carried out in the national park. In 2001, forty-nine microbiology research projects were conducted in Yellowstone (Yellowstone Center for Resources 2002). Another example is cyclosporine, which is derived from a soil sample taken from Hardangervidda National Park in Norway in 1969. An immunosuppressive agent, it is used to reduce the body's natural immunity in patients who receive organ transplants. It was the thirty-third top-selling drug worldwide in 2000, with sales of US$1.2 billion (Mulongoy and Chape 2004, 45).

In situ conservation can be financed and promoted either directly or indirectly. Since it became clear that developing countries, which hold the most diverse biological resources, do not have sufficient resources to maintain them, industrialized countries have assumed some responsibility and contributed to conservation activities in these countries aimed at altering behaviors. Whereas in industrialized countries conservation initiatives tend more to emphasize direct investments (e.g., performance payments, tax relief, land purchases, and easements), conservation in developing countries has tended more to emphasize indirect approaches such as integrated conservation, development projects, and community-based natural resource management. The aim of these projects is to encourage rural communities to maintain biodiversity by using it sustainably. They appear to contribute to achieving both conservation and development objectives. Although many such conservation projects have been carried out, biodiversity continues to decline (Ferraro and Kiss 2002, 1718–1719). One criticism leveled at the indirect approach is that in most developing countries the political, social, and economic conditions needed to set indirect incentives are not given. It has therefore been suggested that a switch should be made from indirect to more direct investment forms and direct payments to people for conserving biodiversity, the reason being that these approaches entail fewer institutional demands, stimulate local markets, and are more cost-efficient (Ferraro and Simpson 2001, 17–18).

ABS is characterized as a more indirect investment, like ecotourism, sport hunting, and wild coffee production, because the approach supports the establishment of markets to commercialize biodiversity goods, and it is hoped that commercialization will set incentives for conservation. Biodiversity conservation is only a by-product, but its value for research and development is widely recognized (see Chapter 3, this volume).

Payments for environmental services, such as carbon sequestration, biodiversity conservation, watershed protection, and landscape values, are another indirect approach. Here private land users are compensated for the environmental services they contribute. Sales of the services provided, e.g., carbon sequestration by forests, serve to generate funds and to increase the private benefits of forest conservation to individual land users and to change their incentives or to generate resources that can be used by government or the public (Landell-Mills and Porras 2002, 193; Pagiola, Bishop, and Landell-Mills 2002, 4). For biodiversity in particular, the concept is a promising one. Much of the world's biodiversity is found not in protected areas but in surrounding and neighboring areas. It is for this reason necessary to find solutions for biodiversity outside of the protection zones. Costa Rica is a prominent example not only for pioneering efforts regarding ABS, but also for payments for environmental services.

Debt-for-nature swaps are a financial instrument that may be used to fund either direct or indirect approaches (Ferraro and Simpson 2001, 20). The instrument serves to channel financial support from industrialized countries or NGOs to developing, poor, but biodiversity-rich countries. These initiatives reduce debt obligations and generate funds for the environment. They typically involve restructuring, reducing, or buying a portion of a developing country's outstanding debt, with a percentage of the proceeds being used to support conservation programs in the debtor country (Sheikh 2004, 1). Recent examples are debt-for-nature swaps designed for the protection of forest areas. They have been pursued by the US with El Salvador (US$14 million), Belize (US$9 million), and Thailand (US$9.5 million) (Grafton et al. 2004, 445).

On-farm conservation—understood as the sustainable management of the genetic diversity of locally developed traditional crop varieties along with associated wild and weedy species or forms within traditional agricultural, horticultural, or agri-silvicultural cultivation systems—is a direct approach (Dhillon et al. 2004, 558). On-farm conservation can be realized automatically when farmers, through their day-to-day farming practices, maintain genetic resources in the form of local, diverse crop varieties (landraces) in their natural environment. If farmers choose to cultivate modern, broadly adapted, or higher-yielding varieties instead, on-farm conservation is reliant on the financial support provided by specific projects and programs. National governments, international programs, and private organizations directly finance these programs and projects. These measures are an attempt to encourage farmers to continue to select and manage local crop populations (Brush 2000, 4). However, indirect approaches have also been established, including, e.g., development of markets for niche products. One example of a successful green marketing program designed to promote in situ conservation is an effort undertaken in the US, by Cherokee farmers in North Carolina, to maintain and utilize ancestral maize. Another market approach would be sale of genetic landrace resources under ABS agreements.

Whereas, from the conservationist's point of view, direct payments for conservation may be the most effective instrument in the short term, other factors are also relevant for the long term. Here direct payments will depend on ongoing financial commitments. They may, for instance, merely serve to shift the pressure from one site to another that was not previously exploited. Another aspect is property rights. In developing countries land tenure is often ambiguous. Such conditions are quite unattractive for funding agencies, which need to know how their investments are being used (Nicholls 2004).

Ex Situ Conservation

Biological resource centers (BRCs) are the heart of ex situ conservation; they are also the heart of the use of genetic resources for research and development. They hold collections of culturable organisms (e.g., microorganisms, plant, animal, and human cells), replicable parts of these (e.g., genomes, plasmids, viruses, cDNAs), viable but not yet culturable organisms, cells, and tissues, as well as databases containing molecular, physiological, and structural information relevant to these collections and related bioinformatics. BRCs may be microbial culture collections, viral repositories, herbaria, botanical gardens, zoos, or ex situ plant and animal genetic resource collections (OECD 2001b, 11, 14). However, with a view to the analysis of the ABS concept, ex situ plant collections, botanical gardens, and microbial collections are of the highest importance, as will be illustrated in the following.

In the past, ex situ conservation of plant genetic resources was the main instrument used for conservation. The material was for the most part stored in botanical gardens and seed banks. In the early 1960s the FAO strongly promoted ex situ conservation of crop genetic resources, and in the 1970s and 1980s germplasm was collected intensively. It is estimated that today the existing global ex situ collections contain approximately six million accessions of plant genetic resources for food and agriculture. About six hundred thousand of these accessions are maintained within the CGIAR system, whereas the remainder is stored in regional or national gene banks (SCBD 2001, 205). CGIAR is a group of countries, international and regional organizations, and private foundations that supports fifteen international agricultural centers (e.g., the International Plant Genetic Resources Institute and the International Rice Research Institute).

Ex situ collections are not evenly distributed in the world. Twelve countries hold more than 45 percent of the germplasm accessions held in national collections. Most gene banks are found in Europe and Asia. Ex situ collections may be seed gene banks, in vitro collections, and field gene banks. Seed storage is the most common and most cost-effective plant conservation method for orthodox seeds. Seed storage accounts for about 90 percent of total accessions held ex situ (Dhillon et al. 2004, 557). Over 40 percent of all accessions in gene banks are cereals, whereas minor crops, e.g., yams, are poorly represented (FAO 1997, 90–91).

Ex situ collections differ in terms of the type of material they preserve. Botanical gardens serve to conserve living plant material, seed banks to preserve seeds, and microbial collections to store microorganisms. There are, in a total of 153 countries, more than two thousand botanical gardens with over six million accessions (Botanic Gardens Conservation International 2001, 5, 28). Many institutions also maintain germplasm collections for the conservation of ornamental species, indigenous crop relatives, and medicinal and forest species, and some of them conserve germplasm of cultivated species, including landraces and wild food plants and other noncultivated species for local use. Other ex situ germplasm collections often lack such species, and botanical gardens therefore play an important complementary role in ex situ collection systems (SCBD 2001, 206). Due to their task of conserving both a broad-spectrum species and as many individual species as possible, botanical gardens conserve considerable amounts of interspecies diversity but little intraspecies genetic diversity (FAO 1997, 84).

The majority of botanical gardens are found in developed countries in Europe and North America. According to estimates, 90 percent of all living plant collections in botanical gardens was collected and stored prior to the CBD. The ABS rules therefore do not apply to these collections (Botanic Gardens Conservation International 2001, 5–6).

Most developed countries and a small number of developing countries maintain national collections of microorganisms as an essential resource for science and industry. There are 483 culture collections in sixty-five countries registered in the World Data Centre for Microorganisms (WDCM). Together these collections maintain over 1.1 million microbial cultures, including around eleven thousand species or subspecies of bacteria (445,000 cultures), twenty thousand species or subspecies of fungi (375,000 cultures), ten thousand virus collections, ten thousand cell lines, and 277,000 other microbes. Microbial collections handle thousands of transactions per year. For example, the Agricultural Research Service (ARS) Culture Collection in Illinois distributes four thousand subcultures per year and adds one thousand to two thousand new accessions per year to its collection of around eighty-five thousand cultures. The Institute for Fermentation (IFO) in Japan maintains around eighteen thousand strains and distributes around eight thousand samples per year (Cunningham et al. 2006).

BRCs may be owned either publicly or privately. Public collections usually depend on public funding. It has been reported that many BRCs, especially in developing countries, have problems in obtaining adequate funding to maintain and develop their collections (Day-Rubenstein et al. 2005, 21). Public collections are publicly accessible, whereas private industry collections are withheld from public access to protect financial investments and industrial secrets. In many cases, private industrial biological resources are made accessible to the wider scientific community only if they are protected by patents or if they are no longer deemed to be of specific economic value (OECD 2001a, 37).

INSTITUTIONAL AND POLITICAL FRAMEWORK OF INTERNATIONAL ABS GOVERNANCE

The CBD is the most important biodiversity agreement. It is a pure biodiversity convention, and its aim is to conserve biodiversity not only through protection but also through sustainable use and sharing of the benefits arising from the resource's utilization. Other conventions that have protection objectives but deal with more specific issues include the Ramsar Convention on Wetlands, the World Heritage Convention (WHC), the Convention on International Trade in Endangered Species of Wild Fauna and Flora (CITES), and the Convention on the Conservation of Migratory Species of Wild Animals (CMS).

Between the 1970s and 1980s, it became evident that neither the public nor the private sector in biodiversity-rich countries—for the most part developing countries—were able to provide sufficient funds for nature in general and biodiversity conservation in particular. The concern and general willingness found among the international community to conserve biodiversity was not sufficient to counterbalance these deficiencies. In 1987 a discussion was launched, in the framework of the UNEP, on the elaboration of an international agreement on the conservation of biodiversity (Henne 1998, 114). Following protracted negotiations, the CBD was finally adopted during the Earth Summit in Rio de Janeiro in 1992. The essential objectives of the CBD are conservation of biological diversity, sustainable use of its components, and fair and equitable sharing of the benefits arising out of the utilization of genetic resources (CBD 1992, Article 3). This includes facilitated access to genetic resources and appropriate transfer of relevant technologies. ABS was included under pressure from the developing countries. Because the issue of harmonization and strengthening of international patent law was under discussion in parallel to the negotiations on the CBD, the developing countries came out in favor of creating a counterbalance within the CBD. The negotiations ended when, in 1995, the World Trade Organization (WTO) was established following the adoption of the Agreement on Trade-Related Aspects of Intellectual Property Rights (TRIPs). Under the WTO, TRIPs sets minimum standards and harmonizes national regulations and responsibilities for IPR protection. The TRIPS agreement has a powerful enforcement mechanism backed by trade sanctions, and it is a stronger framework agreement than the CBD in that it is directly linked with trade interests.

Today (March 2009) the CBD has 191 parties (CBD 2009). Due to the fact that the majority of countries are members, protection of biodiversity has come to be considered one of the world's biggest environmental priorities. However, whereas the US has signed the CBD, it has yet to ratify it. The decision is bound up with the inclusion of ABS in the convention. When the CBD was adopted, the instrument of ABS assumed binding force for all parties to the convention. The US feared negative impacts from ABS for its user industries.

The CBD covers all fields of biodiversity: ecosystems, species, and genetic resources. It extends to in situ biodiversity and biological material that has been stored in ex situ collections since the adoption of the CBD (CBD 1992, Article 2). It links traditional conservation efforts to the economic goal of sustainable utilization of biological resources. The CBD recognizes that biological resources can at the same time be conserved and used, without jeopardizing their protection (SCBD 2000, 8). In keeping with its objectives, the agreement sets out principles for the fair and equitable sharing of benefits arising from the use of genetic resources. To ensure that this goal is reached, the CBD is based on a bilateral system geared to the exchange of genetic resources and compensation. This concept is illustrated and analyzed in Chapter 3, this volume. The agreement also covers the rapidly expanding field of biotechnology, and it addresses the issues of technology development and transfer as well as benefit-sharing and biosafety.

The CBD's Governing Body is the COP, which consists of all governments and regional economic integration organizations that have ratified the convention. The COP is entitled to make amendments to the convention, create expert advisory bodies, review progress reports by member nations, and collaborate with other international organizations and agreements. Nonparties can also be admitted to attend COP meetings as observers. Not a static entity, the CBD is a flexible agreement that is constantly advanced through regular general meetings (COPs) and expert meetings (e.g., the Subsidiary Body on Scientific, Technical and Technological Advice [SBSTTA] and Working Groups).

The SBSTTA is a committee composed of experts from member governments and a subsidiary body of the COP. It provides scientific advice and information to the COP on scientific and technical issues related to the CBD, including, for instance, scientific and technical assessments of the status of biological diversity or innovative, efficient, and state-of-the-art technologies.

The SCBD, based in Montreal, organizes meetings, drafts documents, assists member governments in the implementation of the program of work, coordinates with other international organizations, and collects and disseminates information. Whereas confirming that the Secretariat's work is well organized and managed, a paper also notes that it has no more than modest impacts on external stakeholders and other actors, such as national governments, industry, and NGOs (Siebenhuener 2007, 271).

The COP also sets up working groups, including, for instance, the Working Group on Article 8(j)[7] and the Working Group on ABS, created to address the CBD's TK and ABS articles. This shows that TK and ABS, the central issues of the CBD, are too complex to be handled by the COP on its own.

COP 4 set up a regionally balanced panel of experts appointed by governments and composed of representatives from the private and public sectors, as well as representatives of indigenous and local communities, to:

> "draw upon all relevant sources, including legislative, policy and administrative measures, best practices and case-studies on access to genetic resources and benefit-sharing arising from the use of those genetic resources, including the whole range of biotechnology, in the development of a common understanding of basic concepts and to explore all options for access and benefit-sharing on mutually agreed terms including principles, guidelines, and codes of conduct of best practices for access and benefit-sharing arrangements." (CBD 1998, Decision IV/8, 3)

The Ad Hoc Open-Ended Working Group on ABS was set up by COP 5 to develop guidelines and other approaches for submission to the COP and to assist parties and stakeholders in addressing, for instance, the need to clarify and define terms. The major result of the first meeting was the development of the Bonn Guidelines on access to genetic resources and the fair and equitable sharing of the benefits arising from their utilization; the guidelines were adopted by COP 6. They furnish guidance for providers and users in their efforts to implement the CBD's ABS specifications.

Besides the working groups and the SBSTTA, the work of the COP is also supported by the CBD's Clearing House Mechanism (CBD-CHM), an Internet-based network. The aim of the CBD-CHM is to ensure universal access to the convention's official records as well as to additional information such as case studies, national reports, etc. Another of its aims is to increase public awareness of convention programs and issues. The CBD-CHM furthermore supports the efforts of providers and users to establish contacts needed to start cooperation and to facilitate the dissemination of information (SCBD 2005, 222ff.).

The CBD is based on a number of major principles that will be elucidated here. The convention recognizes every state's sovereignty over its own biological resources and assigns responsibility for the conservation and sustainable use of biodiversity to the provider countries (CBD 1992, Article 3). The CBD states that governments are responsible for establishing national regulations on dealing with their biological resources and regulating ABS and that users are obliged to recognize the sovereign rights of states over their natural resources (CBD 1992, Article 15.1). At present, though, the definition of and the consequences of the principle of state sovereignty are particularly clear. Whereas it is the responsibility of governments to establish and design national ABS regulations as well as to define and to assign property rights to biological resources, the conditions set are required to ensure facilitated access to genetic resources (CBD 1992, Article 15.2). The difficulties arising from this principle will be addressed in Chapter 4 of this volume. Arrangements for access to valuable biological resources must be reached on "mutually agreed terms" (MAT) and be subject to the "prior informed consent" (PIC) of the country providing the genetic resources (CBD 1992, Article 15.1/4/5). These important criteria are not laid down in more detail in the CBD. It is the responsibility of national governments to establish rules and regulations concerning PIC. Furthermore, the CBD stresses that scientific research should be conducted, to the greatest extent possible, in the country of origin of the genetic resource and with the participation of the contracting party. The benefits resulting from any use of genetic resources should be shared with the country providing the material under MAT and in a fair and equitable way (CBD 1992, Article 15).

The PIC and benefit-sharing provisions of the CBD are established with respect to the "country providing genetic resources" and not the "country of origin." Access to genetic resources shall be subject to prior informed consent of the Contracting Party providing such resources, unless otherwise determined by that Party (CBD 1992, Article 15.5).

> "Each Contracting Party shall take legislative, administrative or policy measures, as appropriate, [. . .] with the aim of sharing in a fair and equitable way the results of research and development and the benefits arising from the commercial and other utilization of genetic resources with the Contracting Party providing such resources. Such sharing shall be upon mutually agreed terms." (CBD 1992, Article 15.7)

This clarification is important for the implementation of any ABS regulations in provider and user countries. The CBD calls for benefit-sharing with the provider countries of in situ material thus and necessarily with the countries of origin.

Since the CBD was adopted, its implementation has focused more on the establishment of ABS regulations in biodiversity-rich provider countries that address the behavior of agents in provider countries. That has led to an imbalance regarding the efforts of provider and user countries to realize the convention's objectives. However, in stipulating that access to valuable biological resources must be based on MAT and is subject to the PIC of the providing country, the CBD addresses the behavior of users in provider countries. The agreement also places responsibility on user countries to contribute to its implementation. Realization of the third objective, fair and equitable benefit-sharing in the form of transfer of monetary or non-monetary benefits, including, for example, technology, requires measures to be taken in user countries. In particular, users are obliged to promote and carry out transfers of technology and biotechnology to the providers of relevant resources (CBD 1992, Article 15.7, 16, 19).

Although the CBD has been in place for more than fifteen years now, biodiversity continues to decline, and there is thus some reason to question the convention's effectiveness. During COP 6 the parties decided to adopt the Strategic Plan for the Convention on Biological Diversity to guide the convention's further implementation at the national, regional, and global levels. The main objective is to effectively stop the loss of biodiversity so as to secure the continuity of its beneficial uses based on the conservation and sustainable use of its components and the fair and equitable sharing of benefits arising from the use of genetic resources (CBD 2002, Decision VI/26). The parties are committed to achieving, by 2010, a significant reduction of the current rate of biodiversity loss at the global, regional, and national levels as a contribution to poverty alleviation and to the benefit of the whole of society.

The funding system of the CBD is based on a multilateral system that provides support for capacity-building and investment in projects and programs in biodiversity-rich developing countries. The Global Environment Facility (GEF), established in 1991, finances projects in developing countries that are designed to forge international cooperation and fund actions to address four critical threats to the global environment: biodiversity loss, climate change, depletion of the ozone layer, and degradation of international waters. The projects are managed by the implementing agencies, viz. by the UNEP, the UNDP, and the World Bank. By 2006 (fiscal year), the GEF had financed, in a total of 155 countries, 752 projects worth US$2.2 billion. A total of US$5.17 billion has been leveraged in cofinancing. All together, the total contribution of the GEF's initiatives in biodiversity conservation amounts to about US$7.3 billion (GEF 2006b, 4).

The CBD places emphasis on recognition of and consistency with IPRs, especially patents in the field of biotechnology (CBD 1992, Article 16). The convention affirms the need to extend IPRs as a precondition for bioprospecting and ABS as sustainable form of exploitation. IPRs play a major role in the biotechnology industry and have a great impact on developments in these knowledge-intensive sectors. In 2002 biotechnology patents already accounted for about 7 percent of all US patents (OECD 2006b, 45). The possible use of IPRs as a means to protect inventions that involve high research and development costs is seen as offering a guarantee for ongoing development work (Lele, Lesser, and Horstkotte-Wesseler 2000, 7). However, the CBD recognizes at the same time that patents and other IPRs may have negative impacts, and it states that IPRs should not run counter to the convention's objectives (CBD 1992, Article 16).

At the international level there has been heated debate as to whether the international regimes and agreements on biodiversity may conflict with or be seen as in line with IPRs. It is important for biodiversity policy to consider both the positive and the negative effects of the establishment of IPR systems and to seek to overcome potential conflicts between them by finding an adequate degree of protection for these rights.

At first sight, IPRs appear to be positive for the ABS regime. They provide exclusive rights for inventions and products derived from the use of genetic resources. As a rule, these rights are combined with an obligation to disclose knowledge on relevant inventions. From the user point of view, exclusivity is at once a prerequisite and an incentive to conclude bilateral ABS agreements. Exclusive rights serve to mitigate the investment risk faced by the potential user of genetic resources. Growth in research and development activities in the fields of plant breeding and biotechnology creates new options for the use and commercialization of genetic resources. Successful commercialization raises the value of the biological material concerned and sets incentives for both the conservation and sustainable use of biodiversity, provided that fair and equitable sharing of the benefits arising from the utilization of genetic resources is applicable.

However, the CBD and IPR protection systems like the Agreement on Trade-related Aspects of Intellectual Property Rights (TRIPs) have divergent policy objectives. IPRs regimes aim to protect new knowledge through exclusive rights, whereas biodiversity regimes aim to protect genetic resources through market-based mechanisms. IPRs may have negative effects on the provider side. IPR protection can result in restricted access to genetic resources, e.g., if the resources concerned are covered by a patent that threatens food security. IPR protection may also distort benefit-sharing if the resource holder is unable to participate in these rights (Rosendal 2006, 438). Furthermore, a protected product may have intellectual similarity with traditional products, and IPRs may limit or prevent traditional consumers from continuing to use certain biological resources. A new commercial product, being less expensive, may also serve as a substitute for a traditional product, driving traditional producers out of the market. If IPR protection entails a greater marginal loss for a local provider, she/he will have fewer incentives to conserve the resource (Bhat 1999, 392, 402).

Furthermore, there are concerns that IPR protection may encourage biopiracy (Anuradha 2001, 27). Many cases have occurred in which nations have been forced to challenge natural product patents based on TK, motivated by principles of justice rather than by the economic forces usually behind patent disputes. For example, a 1995 patent, "Use of Turmeric in Wound Healing," was canceled in 1998 after an investigation established that use of turmeric to promote wound healing had been known for generations in India (Gollin 2001).

IPRs have been widely criticized because of ethical concerns. Throughout history biological resources and related technologies and knowledge have been exchanged freely. Millions of people continue to depend on these inputs in their day-to-day lives. The patenting of life forms is therefore regarded as unethical, and sometimes even criticized as "intellectual colonialism" (Bhat 1996, 207).

Both the IPRs regime and its reciprocal influences need to be taken into account in the formulation of ABS policies. This makes it possible to harness synergies, indeed even for the ABS concept embodied in the CBD to benefit from and make use of the IPRs regime.

Recent discussions in the COPs and working groups have led to a call for more responsibility on the user side. The group of megadiverse countries has called for an international regime, arguing that provider countries are not capable of enforcing ABS without the support of user countries. This line of argument was adopted by the WSSD in Johannesburg in 2002. The Johannesburg Plan of Implementation calls upon the parties to the CBD to negotiate an international regime to promote and safeguard the fair and equitable sharing of the benefits arising from the utilization of genetic resources (UN 2002, 44o). The Bonn Guidelines, which were adopted in 2002, also address the roles and responsibilities of providers and users as defined with a view to ABS. The guidelines set out a number of measures that user and provider countries should consider when implementing the CBD's ABS specifications. At COP 7 the parties decided to mandate the Ad Hoc Open-Ended Working Group on ABS to elaborate and negotiate an international regime on ABS with the aim of adopting instruments to effectively implement the provisions of Article 15 and Article 8(j) of the convention as well as of its three objectives. At COP 8 a decision was taken to continue on with efforts to elaborate and negotiate an international regime, and the ABS Working Group was instructed to complete its work at the earliest possible time before the COP 10 in 2010.

These developments indicate user countries have been urged to stand up for the implementation of the CBD regulations on ABS. What this means in effect is that today, more than ever before, users of genetic resources need to be given due consideration and involved as important actors in the development of comprehensive international conservation concepts.

3 The Economic Framework of the ABS Concept

ABS has been discussed mainly from a legal or political perspective. The aim of the present book is to contribute to the international debate by seeking to shed light on the approach by adopting an economic point of view. The ABS concept has been developed as an instrument to stop, *inter alia*, the decline of biodiversity. To analyze ABS from an economic point of view and assess its effectiveness, it is necessary to step back and place biodiversity loss in an economic framework. This chapter starts out by exploring the economic issues bound up with biodiversity loss. The relevant economic issues are valuation, economic development and poverty, market and policy/institutional failure. The first section describes the problems faced by and the results of attempts to come up with economic valuations of biodiversity. A number of different studies have been undertaken to assess the pharmaceutical value of biodiversity; only a small number seek to assess the agricultural values of genetic resources. However, these studies come to the conclusion that there are in fact certain economic values for genetic resources. The section furthermore explores the links between biodiversity conservation, ABS, and poverty. ABS is an instrument that has the potential to contribute to poverty alleviation. Finally, the section identifies market and policy/institutional failure as a factor responsible for the loss of biodiversity. Investigating the promise of ABS to contribute to biodiversity conservation and economic development, the second section outlines the economic framework of the ABS concept. It evaluates the ABS approach to biodiversity conservation by means of commercialization and deals with how IPRs play in ABS.

ECONOMIC ISSUES OF BIODIVERSITY LOSS

The Difficulties Involved Valuing Biodiversity

"The value of biodiversity is the value of everything there is. It is the summed value of all the GNPs of all countries from now until the end of the world. We know that, because our very lives and our economies are dependent upon biodiversity. If biodiversity is reduced sufficiently, and we do not know the disaster point, there will no longer be any conscious beings. With them will go all value—economic and otherwise." (Norton 1988, 205)

Today it is not possible to estimate the future relevance of biological diversity for the global economy as well as for social welfare. Biodiversity has many benefits that have yet to be discovered, and conservation of this resource can thus be justified with reference to the precautionary principle. But even today many of the values of biodiversity can be identified. Biodiversity has values in itself, spiritual and intrinsic as well as existence and bequest values, but it also contains values generated by its use as inputs. The resource plays an important role within the planet's life-support system and at the same time provides many ecosystem services: mitigation of greenhouse gases, watershed protection, protection of scenic beauty (Sedjo 2000, 110). Beyond that, biodiversity, and especially wild plant genetic resources, are used as production inputs by research institutions and in "life science" companies, many of which consists of pharmaceutical, food, seed, and chemical divisions. The following sectors are building important markets for genetic resources: pharmaceuticals, crop protection, agricultural seeds, horticulture, botanical medicine, cosmetics and personal care (A Laird and ten Kate 2002, 246). Enormous technical advances have made biotechnology ubiquitous in industry, and its widespread use raises expectations that the potential of biodiversity will be tapped more efficiently in the near future. Biodiversity's economic value has increased.

But what is the point of seeking to identify the economic values of biodiversity? It may be said that biodiversity protection generates costs, or that the non-use of the resource implies forgoing benefits (e.g., logging prohibitions). Biodiversity conservation activities often compete with other human-induced activities that harm the environment. The values of competing activities need to be identified in order to determine whether some values and benefits of resource use are more important than others. Economic valuation of biodiversity can, for example, support decisions on land use options for conservation or other uses, promote efforts to raise awareness and set priorities for biodiversity conservation, and prove useful in assessing biodiversity losses and choosing instruments to conserve biodiversity (OECD 2002, 23–24). It was only after the commercial value of biodiversity had been identified that the idea of developing the ABS concept emerged. Assessment of this commercial value is essential both to the ABS concept and negotiations between users and providers regarding fair and equitable benefit-sharing. It is only valuation that can put negotiation on a solid basis.

However, the commercial research and development value of biodiversity and genetic resources determines only a small share of the total economic value (TEV) of biodiversity, which encompasses all the values of biodiversity, including plants and plant genetic resources. The ABS concept aims to internalize this value. As Figure 3.1 shows, TEV consists of use value (UV) and non-use value (NUV). The UV arises from the actual use of the resource. According to Pearce and Moran (1994), UVs can be divided into direct use values (DUV), which refer to actual uses of biodiversity for food, clothing, etc.; indirect use values (IUV), which refer to the benefits deriving from ecosystem functions; option values (OV); and quasi option values (QOV), which are something like an insurance value and approximate an individual's willingness to pay to safeguard the option of using the resource in the future.

DUV refer to values that reflect those elements of biodiversity that can be directly consumed, traded, or used as an input for commercial activities. DUV can generally be estimated by identifying the market prices of a specific product or close substitutes. In the case of biological resources, this may, for instance, be the use of a forest for timber or recreation, or the use of plant genetic resources for biotechnological research and development. UVs are usually realized at the individual level if property and use rights are clearly assigned and tradable (OECD 1999, 29). The benefit of the commercial use of genetic resources is also realized at the individual level by users as economic agents.

IUV are delivered to humans at the local, regional, or global level by ecosystem services, including, for instance, flood control, purification of water supplies, or carbon sequestration. They are not realized at an individual level. Their provision, therefore, requires action at a broader level. It is more difficult to measure IUV than UVs, because it is difficult to measure quantities of services like carbon sequestration and to distinguish between several ecosystem inputs of produced goods. Indirect values can be estimated by calculating the amount of money that would be needed to invest in technologies to substitute for them (Brown et al. 1993, 13; OECD 1999, 29).

The terms OV and QOV describe the value implied by having the ability to make choices in an uncertain future. OV address possible options if preferences change in the future, whereas QOV refer to the need to maintain

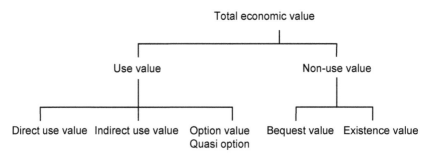

Figure 3.1 Total economic value.
Source: adopted from OECD (2002, 83).

the ability to respond to future information, regardless of preferences. Both OV and QOV reflect all direct and IUV of biodiversity. Benefit-sharing contracts for genetic resources try to capture the OV of these resources (OECD 1999, 31).

There are more problems associated with efforts to define and estimate NUV. NUVs are broken down into bequest value (BV) and existence value (XV) (Pearce and Moran 1994, 12). BV concerns the possibility to maintain a given resource for future generations, and XV refers to the value a resource has by virtue of its existence (OECD 1999, 31). Environmental policy addresses the XV of biodiversity in the form of bilateral and multilateral transfers from industrialized, biodiversity-poor countries to developing, biodiversity-rich countries through international organizations and funds like the GEF.

The individual values add up to the TEV of an environmental resource such as biodiversity: TEV = UV + NUV = (DUV + IUV + OV + QOV) + (XV + BV).

It has been recognized that the use of TEV is problematic, because the individual categories cannot be separated in any case and in part overlap. This can lead to double counting. Besides, caution is also called for here in that some values cannot be added together because they are mutually exclusive (Baumgaertner 2002, 11). Some argue that XV is not relevant for economic valuation because it may represent counterpreferential values based on moral concern, obligation, duty, etc. (Brown et al. 1993, 13). However, the concept has been widely accepted as illustrating the different benefits that an environmental good offers and that need to be considered for its valuation.

In order to give an idea of the TEV of ecosystems, reference is made to two prominent studies that attempt to estimate it. Costanza and colleagues (1997) published an article in *Nature* estimating the value of the world's ecosystem services and natural capital. The estimate was based on a small number of original calculations as well as on the analysis and synthesis of material from more than one hundred studies carried out to estimate the monetary value of ecosystem goods and services. The studies estimate the current economic value of seventeen ecosystem services for sixteen biomes. The conclusion they reached was that the value of the entire biosphere is in the range of US$16–54 trillion per year, with an average of US$33 trillion per year, whereas total global gross national product (GNP) amounts to around US$18 trillion per year.

Another approach, published by Balmford and colleagues (2002) in *Science*, compares, on the basis of five case studies, the economic gains and losses of sustainable and converted ecosystems. The authors come to the conclusion that the TEV of sustainably used ecosystems is higher than the TEV of converted ecosystems, because the loss of ecosystem services like flood protection, carbon sinks, and tourism outweighed the marketed private benefits that came with conversion. At first, conversions may have some benefit to local society, but at the global level the costs of conversion exceed the benefits. According to the estimates, the TEV of intact ecosystems ranged from 14 percent to nearly 75 percent above the TEV of converted ecosystems.

The debate over the value of plant genetic material for research and development is very lively, and it is characterized mainly by two distinct views. The first, assuming a social point of view of the kind mainly advanced by conservationists, suggests that the economic value of plant genetic resources with pharmaceutical potential is huge; the second, assuming a private point of view, is that this value turns out to be very marginal when converted to economic values per hectare. This argument is often supported by industry (International Chamber of Commerce 2004; Finston Kling 2004).

Pearce and Moran (1994) have performed a rough calculation of the economic value of tropical forests. Their results suggest that at the local level a tropical forest area may yield anything from US$300–9,000 per hectare in present value terms (see Table 3.1). Minor forest products (e.g., honey, nuts, rattan, rubber) and medical plants play the main role when it comes to economic value. However, the results are quite imprecise, and the authors regard the upper range of their results as unrepresentative.

In their study, Costanza and colleagues (1997, 256) estimated that the economic value of genetic resources used as inputs for medicine, products for material science, genes for resistance to plant pathogens and crop pests amounts to US$79 per hectare per year.

Three separate studies have estimated the value of plant species as a source of leads in new product research by asking what companies would be willing to pay to preserve threatened genetic resources. An article by Simpson, Sedjo, and Reid (1996) argues that the commercial value of the "marginal species" is likely to be extremely small, thus providing little

Table 3.1   Economic Values of Biodiversity—Tropical Forest (Values US$/ha 1992)

Benefit	Local	Global	Local and Global
Use Value: Direct			
Medical Plants	250–750	12–250	262–1,000
Tourism	20–1,250	20–1,250	
Minor products	> 0–7,000	> 0–7,000	
Use Value: Indirect			
Carbon fixing	0	500–1,500	500–1,500
Flood control	23	23	
Non-use value	+	5	+ 5
Total	> 293–9,023	1,017–4,255	1,310–13,278

Source: Pearce and Moran (1994, 90).

incentive for companies to invest in habitat conservation. Their result is based on a static model that assumes that the probability that any given species contains commercially valuable information is independent and identical across species. The model they used calculates the value of a species by deriving its incremental contribution to the probability that a particular product of commercial value will be discovered. One restriction is that it is assumed that the different products derived from different species are either perfect substitutes or absolutely unrelated.

Simpson and Craft (1996) seek to avoid this weakness by using an approach that assumes that different products derived from different species may be imperfect substitutes for one another. Furthermore, the authors not only attempt to capture the value of genetic resources for pharmaceutical companies, they also try to estimate social welfare, i.e., both the consumer surplus and the profit of bioprospecting. They come to the conclusion that the social values of biodiversity prospecting may provide a motivation for habitat conservation in some areas. These values are likely to be small relative to land value in other uses, even in some of the more biologically rich regions of the world.

Rausser and Small (2000) challenge these findings, noting that firms focus their research efforts on the most promising species, and that auspicious leads command an information rent because of their role in lowering search costs. For the most promising ecosystems, they find that the value of preservation may be much more promising than what is suggested in the previous study by Simpson, Sedjo, and Reid (1996); indeed, that it may be large enough to support market-based conservation of biodiversity. As Table 3.2 shows, the studies under consideration suggest that plant genetic material with pharmaceutical potential may increase the value of certain land areas up to several hundred or even thousands of US dollars per hectare.

Among practitioners, these results have sparked an intense debate on values. For example, Barrett and Lybbert (2000, 295) state that to analyze whether the rents calculated are sufficient to provide an incentive for conservation, it is essential to bear in mind that the estimates are very context-specific and can only be proved by empirical research. Firn (2003) argues that current biotechnological developments will further erode the value of bioprospecting by easing the present dependence on biological resources.

Costello and Ward (2006) assert that the studies of Simpson and colleagues and Rausser and Small differ only in terms of their use of different parameters, not because they assumed the use of different search methods. The authors recalculate the marginal values of land for bioprospecting from thirty-four hotspots based on a new and updated set of parameters. They conclude that marginal land values are too small to provide conservation incentives. Assuming homogenous leads (all species are homogenous), they estimate that the values amount to a figure between US$3.18/ha (mean estimate) and US$5.70/ha (upper 5 percent quantile). Assuming ordered search

Table 3.2   Pharmaceutical Value of Marginal Land (US$/ha)

"Hotspot"	Simpson, Sedjo, and Reid (1996)	Simpson and Craft (1996)	Rausser and Small (2000)
Western Ecuador	20.6	2,888	9,177
Southwestern Sri Lanka	16.8	2,357	7,463
New Caledonia	12.4	1,739	5,473
Madagascar	6.9	961	2,961
Western Ghats of India	4.8	668	2,026
Philippines	4.7	652	1,973
Atlantic Coast Brazil	4.4	619	1,867
Uplands of western Amazonia	2.6	363	1,043
Tanzania	2.1	290	811
Cape Floristic Province of South Africa	1.7	233	632
Peninsular Malaysia	1.5	206	539
Southwestern Australia	1.2	171	435
Ivory Coast	1.1	160	394
Northern Borneo	1.0	138	332
Eastern Himalayas	1.0	137	332
Colombian Choco	0.8	106	231
Central Chile	0.7	104	231
California Floristic Province	0.2	29	0

Source: based on Simpson, Sedjo, and Reid (1996); Simpson and Craft (1996); Rausser and Small (2000).

of heterogeneous leads (i.e., some species are known to be more likely than others to yield success), their estimates rise to US$14/ha (mean estimate) and US$65/ha (upper 5 percent quantile). However, they expect that in the future, with the extinction rate rising, values will increase accordingly.

But plant genetic material has played an important role not only for the pharmaceutical sector. Swanson (1997) indicates that as a source of germplasm, wild and unknown species account for 6 percent of the plant-breeding sector and definitely contribute to the genetic enhancement of crops. A study by Hein and Gatzweiler (2006) estimates that in terms of disease resistance, low caffeine content, and increased yield, the value of Ethiopian genetic coffee resources for breeding programs amounts to US$1,459 million at a 5 percent discount rate and US$420 million at a 10 percent discount rate. Successful examples of the use of wild relatives in crop improvement would include the introduction of resistance to potato late blight, the increased soluble solid content in tomatoes (a trait worth US$240 million per year), and the development of a rice variety resistant to a virus that represented a major threat to the Asian rice crop in the 1970s (International Plant Genetic Resource Institute 2005, 28; Heal 2000, 11).

The value of wild species for plant breeding is estimated to be much higher than this percentage indicates, because wild species have a maintenance function for the overall breeding system. Wild relatives and early landrace varieties have been recognized as an essential pool of genetic variation that will be critical for future plant improvement (McCouch 2004, 1508).

Biodiversity Conservation, ABS, and Poverty

Does ABS have the potential to alleviate poverty? When the CBD and the ABS concept were adopted, poverty alleviation was not the primary concern of policy-makers. However, both direct biodiversity conservation and ABS have positive effects on poverty. It is therefore necessary to analyze the relationship between ABS and poverty in a broader framework, including biodiversity loss and conservation.

ABS represents a new income opportunity for poor countries. If local resource providers are included in ABS activities as partners, the concept can alleviate poverty. Monetarization of biological resources offers new income opportunities for developing countries, and the transfer of benefits, in the form of technologies, money, or capacity, from resource users to providers should place them in a better position to escape from poverty (Barrett and Lybbert 2000, 293; Henne et al. 2003, 58). If bioprospectors establish research institutions, train local staff, and produce drugs or new breeds in provider countries, ABS has the potential to promote economic development. However, development may threaten biodiversity, as examples from the past show. Biodiversity has been undermined and destroyed by attempts of developing countries to reach their development objectives through intensification of, e.g., land use, urbanization, infrastructure development, or food production. Habitat destruction has been identified as the major threat to biodiversity (see Chapter 2).

As far as biodiversity decline and conservation are concerned, there is a clear-cut relation to poverty. Biodiversity loss exacerbates poverty, and because poverty is a major threat to biodiversity, what we have is a vicious circle. Biodiversity provides the basis for the lives of many people, especially poor people. According to the *Human Development Report 2005*, one in five people in the world, that is, more than one billion people, still survive on less than US$1 a day. This is a level of poverty that threatens survival. Another 1.5 billion people live on US$1 to US$2 a day. This means that more than 40 percent of the world's population is faced with poverty. Income poverty is closely linked with hunger. More than 850 million people, including one in three preschool children, are still trapped in a vicious circle of malnutrition and its effects (UNDP 2005, 24).

Biodiversity plays an important role for poor people in terms of food security and health, income generation and livelihoods, and reduced vulnerability to shocks, as well as cultural and spiritual values. The lives of poor people depend directly on the availability of a wide range of natural resources and ecosystem services, and these people are thus hardest hit by their degradation. Conservation of biodiversity, but also access to the resources, is a condition for the survival of many people. In low-income countries, environment-based wealth accounts for 25 percent of total wealth, compared to less than 4 percent in OECD countries (OECD 2006a, 9). In many developing countries biological resources continue to be the basis of consumption and production and a major source of economic income. Twenty-two percent of the world's population works in the agricultural sector, relying heavily on biodiversity and ecosystem services. An estimated 1.6 billion poor people are heavily dependent on forests for their livelihoods, including food security (i.e., fruits and vegetables), health (i.e., medicinal plants), shelter (i.e., building materials), and energy (i.e., fuelwood and charcoal). Harvesting and trading in fishery products, fuelwood, wild fruits, nuts, bush meat, and other natural resources provide informal and formal employment, trading opportunities, and jobs. As mentioned earlier, other sectors, including, e.g., tourism, medicinal plants, and herbs, generate billions of dollars per year. Bioprospecting accounts for a substantial share of these activities. For many indigenous and traditional people, nature and biodiversity are directly linked with identity, culture, and spirituality (The World Conservation Union 2006a, 33).

In addition, biodiversity protection supports and secures ecosystem resilience. It alleviates vulnerability to factors like climate changes or pests. Mangroves and coral reefs can slow down coastal storms and cyclones and reduce the vulnerability of local people to extreme weather events (IUCN 2006a, 33). For example, in Bangladesh hoar swamp forests have been cleared to make way for agricultural land and human settlements. This has led to the disappearance and depletion of biodiversity and natural barriers. Forests protected the population against the unavoidable wave action during the monsoon season. As a consequence, people have been compelled to increase spending every year to protect their tiny homesteads (Steele, Oviedo, and McCauley 2006, 224).

It is poor people who are hardest hit by biodiversity loss. They lack the resources, the ability, and the option to substitute for or offset local losses of biodiversity and its services by shifting their production and harvesting activities to other regions or switching to other income possibilities. Another important fact is that whereas developing countries are the most vulnerable to environmental degradation, they are also the richest in biodiversity, i.e., what we find in such countries is a geographical overlap between biodiversity and poverty. Mapping global development and biodiversity shows that some of the world's LDCs are located in hotspot areas of great importance for biodiversity (UNEP/GRID-Arendal 2004).

Even though the benefits of biodiversity conservation are high for the local population, Brockington and Schmidt-Soltau (2004) note that the impacts of conservations measures (e.g., protected areas) on the poor are often negative due to the loss of income opportunities and living space they entail. Creation of protected areas denies farmers future land use options and leads to potentially significant economic opportunity costs. Conservationists are aware of the problem. In 2003, at the World Parks Congress, it was stressed "that many of the costs of protected areas are borne locally—particularly by the poor communities—while the benefits accrue globally" (World Parks Congress 2003). However, there is still a strong body of opinion behind the idea that it is possible to combine poverty elimination and conservation under the concept of "pro-poor conservation," although in practice it is quite difficult to realize such win-win solutions (Adams et al. 2004, 1147).

Adams and colleagues (2004) identify four models on how poverty alleviation and conservation can be implemented jointly. ABS reflects the third model. First, poverty and conservation can be regarded as separate policy fields. Focused solely on the preservation of biodiversity, this conception leads to conservation strategies aiming at the establishment of protected areas or of approaches such as direct payments for conservation carried out by the state or by private owners. Second, poverty can be viewed as a critical constraint on conservation. In this case, poverty reduction is undertaken only to achieve more conservation. Conservation measures may include park outreach strategies (e.g., employment of local people) and income-generating projects (e.g., sharing of the revenue from tourism in protected areas) designed to address the poverty of critical protected-area neighbors. Third, it can be argued that conservation should not compromise poverty reduction. Compensation for the opportunity costs arising from conservation measures and social impact assessments of protected areas are measures in line with this concept. Another possibility is income generation through nonextractive uses (e.g., ecotourism, sustainable harvesting, and bioprospecting). Fourth, poverty is at the center of attention when it is assumed that livelihood depends on resource conservation. In this case conservation is a tool used to achieve poverty reduction, one that could lead to rejection of protected areas and priority for sustainable use concepts designed to optimize economic returns for poor people. The aim here would not be the preservation of species but their sustainable harvest. Projects would, for example, promote the local management of common-pool resources.

Biodiversity Loss Through Market Failure

That biodiversity decline has reached its present extent is a consequence of market failure. Market failure is a situation in which existing markets do not efficiently allocate resources because their full costs and/or benefits are not reflected in market prices. The costs of biodiversity conservation are borne by the entity in charge of resource management. This entity may be a landowner, a local community, or a government agency, depending on the distribution of property and use rights for biological resources. The benefits of biodiversity and its conservation accrue at the same level, but also beyond it. At the global level, the world population benefits from biodiversity through NUVs and UVs, including, for example, esthetic considerations and ecosystem stability. Market failure is caused by:

- externalities
- the characteristics of public goods

These two causes and their impacts are explained in the following sections.

Externalities

The reason for the failure of the market for biological diversity is the existence of externalities. Externalities occur when a decision gives rise to costs or benefits for individuals or groups other than the person making the decision. In this case the decision-maker neither bears all of the costs nor reaps all of the benefits from his actions. In other words, externalities arise from the disparity between the private and social costs and benefits of biodiversity use and conservation (Dixon and Sherman 1990). Biodiversity conservation has positive externalities in the form of benefits, and biodiversity decline has negative externalities in the form of costs that are only separated by a baseline. At the private level, the direct user or provider of biodiversity perceives the private benefits of conservation or the costs of loss, whereas at the social level it is the whole of society that perceives the social benefits or costs.

The individual decision of a private landowner or government agency may be rational and optimal from her/his/its point of view but suboptimal from the point of view of society. The private costs of exploiting species and converting habitats do not include the opportunity costs of foregone global biodiversity benefits. In the case of biodiversity, externalities are spillover effects arising from the "production" and conservation of biodiversity. Whereas biodiversity is maintained locally, it leads to positive global externalities (Barbier 2000, 80). These externalities are achieved especially through the indirect UVs and NUVs of biodiversity. If biodiversity is conserved in a tropical forest, the beneficiaries include not only the local population but also the populations of other countries. This is due to either the XVs of biodiversity or the fact that biodiversity contributes to important ecosystem services.

Because in a competitive market the individual's benefits and the private value of producing the good will be lower than the benefits gained by society (i.e., social value), an insufficient amount of biodiversity will be provided from society's point of view. The outcome is not socially optimal. The private value of biodiversity and its components varies from individual to individual. This private value is critical for biodiversity conservation because it determines decisions and economic behavior bearing on biodiversity (Simpson 1999). People will convert biodiversity-rich forests into cultivated land if this enables them to increase their income. Biodiversity can only be maintained if the private benefits of conserving biodiversity exceed the private benefits of cultivating land, or of any other biodiversity-damaging activity (e.g., commercial logging).

$$[B_c - C_c] > [B_a - C_a]$$
B_c: benefits of conservation C_c: costs of conservation
B_a: benefits of activity C_a: costs of activity

The $B_a - C_a$ differential reflects the opportunity costs of conservation. The provider of biodiversity needs to receive compensation for conserving biodiversity that is at least equal to these opportunity costs, otherwise she/he will convert the areas concerned for alternative land uses and not conserve the species found there.

Pearce and Moran (1994) distinguish between local market failure and global market failure. Local market failure refers to the inability of markets to capture local, regional, and national benefits of biodiversity conservation, or, in other words, local market failure refers to the failure of markets to take into account the external costs of biodiversity loss due to, e.g., land conversion. For the authors, global market failure results from the fact that biodiversity conservation yields external benefits that accrue at the global level to actors other than the decision-makers themselves.

Figure 3.2 illustrates this kind of market failure. The horizontal axis shows the amount of land converted into, e.g., agricultural land. The vertical axis indicates price. MPB_i is the marginal private benefits of land conversion, the extra revenue a farmer receives by converting forested land into agricultural land. MC_i is the marginal costs accruing to the farmer for converting the land. The "rational" farmer will equate MC_i and MPB_i in order to maximize profits, and the amount of land conversion that actually takes place is Lp. If the farmer is subsidized to convert the land, the private costs will be lower and the marginal cost curve will shift from MC_i to $MC_i - SUB$, where SUB refers to the subsidy. The quantity of land converted will expand to Lp+s. The Lp – Lp+s differential is a measure of government failure (GF). The issue of government failure is discussed later in this chapter.

However, Lp and Lp+s are not optimal decisions on land use because they are based on the private costs and benefits of the farmer. If the social costs of land conversion, including the externalities that accrue locally, are known, it is possible to achieve a better result for land use. A higher level of conservation Ln is realized by internalizing the externalities and holding the farmer accountable for them by levying taxes and fees on him because

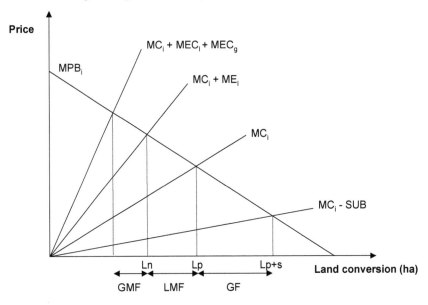

Figure 3.2 Measuring economic failure.
Source: adopted from Pearce and Moran (1994).

the land concerned is zoned for conservation, the reason being that in this case the cost curve shifts from MC_i to $MC_i + MEC_i$. The Ln – Lp differential is a measure of local market failure (LMF). Less land will be converted. If even the social costs of society as a whole are internalized, the cost curve will shift even further, to $MC_i + MEC_i + MEC_g$, making it possible to prevent global market failure (GMF). Internalizing the externalities of land use involves less land conversion and hence more biodiversity conservation.

In reality, the externalities of land conversion are internalized only in very rare cases, and biodiversity declines as a consequence of incomplete and missing markets, i.e., for lack of markets that fully reflect the overall costs and benefits of biodiversity.

Publicness of Biodiversity

In the economic literature biodiversity is often characterized as a public good. But is this true? With a view to answering this question, the following section will identify the characteristics of biodiversity and compare them with the classification of goods.

Public goods are characterized by a particular kind of externality. The benefits of public goods are available for everyone. A pure public good can be characterized by its nonexcludability and nonrivalry, meaning that no one can be excluded from the good's consumption and that the good can be consumed by one person without affecting its simultaneous consumption by another. Public goods can yield benefits on all levels. They are broken down into local public goods (LPGs), national public goods (NPGs), regional public goods (RPGs), transnational public goods (TPGs), and global public goods (GPGs). In contrast to NPGs, TPGs provide nonrival and nonexcludable benefits to people in two or more countries. If they entail global spillovers, they are called GPGs. If the benefits are confined to a well-defined location in two or more countries, the good is called an RPG. For example, cleaning up a local ecosystem is such an RPG (Sandler 2006).

Private goods are excludable and rival in consumption, meaning a person who does not pay for a good or does not meet certain access criteria can be excluded from its consumption, and that a good consumed by one person cannot be consumed by another person. Impure public goods represent in-between cases. They possess benefits that are either partially non-rival and partially excludable or partially rival and nonexcludable (Sandler 2001, 10). Club goods are one category of impure public goods. If a good is excludable but nonrival, it is a club good. Difficulties arise in setting the right price for access, in defining the group of users who can share the good, and in striking a balance between the gain implied by additional users and the potential loss implied by increased use.

Common property resources constitute another group. These are goods that are subject to rivalry. Common property is usually shared in an uncontrolled manner among its owners, although others can be excluded from its use; or it may take the form of an open-access regime under which it is difficult to place any restrictions at all on use (OECD 2003b, 14). In his article "Tragedy of the Commons," published in *Science*, Hardin (1968) described the implications of an open-access resource. In his opinion, only two institutional arrangements—centralized government and private property—are able to sustain common-pool resources, including, e.g., air, water, and forests, in the long run. To illustrate his point, he uses an example drawn from the use of public lands by herdsmen. The pasture is open to all. This arrangement works for a while, even for centuries, until each herdsman realizes he can make a profit by adding more and more cattle to his herd. Hardin concludes that in a world in which resources are scarce and individuals pursue their own best interest, the freedom of commons brings ruin to all.

Hardin's theory can also be applied to the problem of biodiversity loss. If biodiversity occurs in the form of a common-pool resource, e.g., in the form of a common-access forest, it will be exploited and biodiversity will decline. In 1999 Ostrom and colleagues (1999) revisited the commons and challenged Hardin's theory. The authors are convinced that Hardin is mistaken in his assumption that users can be pictured as trapped in a situation that they cannot change and that calls for external authorities needed to address the problem. The authors argue that many social groups have been successful in managing common-pool resources and that they have often devised long-term, sustainable institutions for governing these resources. The authors, furthermore, indicate that private and state-managed resources have been subject to failures, and they define the conditions needed to create durable and successful institutions to manage common-pool resources.

Biodiversity may assume the features of one of four categories: pure public good, common good, club good, and private good (see Figure 3.3). As far as ABS is concerned, the most relevant problems are those bound up with common goods as well as with club goods. Biodiversity and its components have characteristics of both public and private goods. Whereas many of the benefits of biological diversity accrue to the public as a whole, some benefits have a private character and can only be captured privately (OECD 2003b, 23ff.). The existence of ecosystems and the provision of local ecosystem services are often pure public goods, i.e., they are nonrival in consumption and nonexcludable, whereas individual components of ecosystems are often private goods, e.g., edible plants. However, these goods generate only a small return when sold on the market (Heal 2000, 110).

Biological resources in the form of wild plants are rivals in consumption. If such resources are harvested in greater quantities, as is the case, for

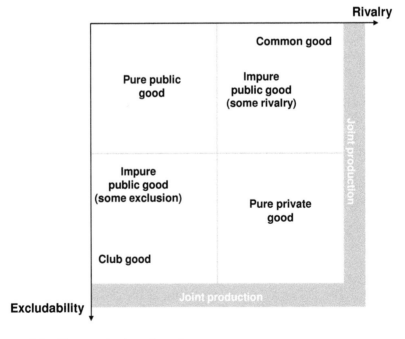

Figure 3.3 Characterization of goods.
Source: own presentation.

example, for wild coffee or wild medicinal plants, they will grow scarce, and if they are not subject to property rights, no one can be excluded from their use. In this case they must be seen as common goods, or even as open-access resources.

Nonrivals are genetic resources whose information is used merely as a blueprint. If the structure of an active chemical compound is known, it can be used in various forms, and each additional use will have no impact on the previous user (OECD 2003a, 11). In the case of biodiversity, we can distinguish between two levels of excludability. The first level refers to physical access to biodiversity. Those who hold property rights to the resource can exclude others from its use. If a state controls access to its biological resources or protects biodiversity in its national parks, charging entrance fees for admission, biodiversity is exclusive and available only to a certain group of individuals. Domesticated and cultivated plants that are already widely distributed cannot be made exclusive. The second level refers to the genetic information contained in the biological resource. Information is excludable if the technology needed to extract this information is not widely available (e.g., protected by IPRs). In this case, biodiversity can be characterized as a club good.

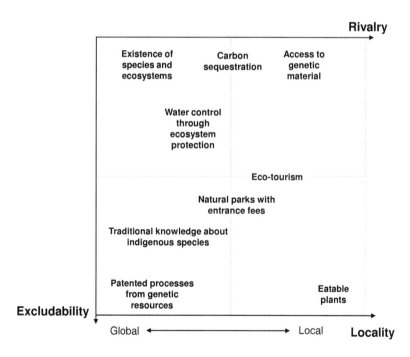

Figure 3.4 Characteristics of biodiversity goods and services.
Source: adopted from OECD (2003b, 30).

Because biodiversity cannot be assigned definitively to one of the four categories (private good, public good, common good, club good), the resource must be seen as an impure public good. Some of its benefits may be captured privately, others may accrue to everyone (Perrings and Gadgil 2003, 535). According to Cornes and Sandler (1984), public goods that provide private and public benefits are the result of joint production; the authors refer to them as joint products. They yield two or more outputs that vary in their degree of publicness. Jointly produced outputs may be purely public, impurely public, or private. Tropical forests are considered to be such a joint product. Actions undertaken to preserve the forest yield not only LPGs (e.g., watershed, ecotourism, and local climate stability) but also GPGs (e.g., existence of biodiversity and carbon sequestration). The provision of joint products depends on the ratio of excludable benefits (i.e., contributor-specific and club-good benefits to total benefits). If the share of excludable benefits is high, markets and clubs will evolve to efficiently allocate the resource. If the share is low and all jointly produced benefits are nonexcludable, underprovision or overutilization will result and an intervention will be needed. However, joint products offer an opportunity to reduce the problem of underprovision of public goods in a decentralized economy. Efforts designed to augment private and excludable benefits may serve to set incentives for potential supporters (Sandler 2006). ABS is a concept that relies on biodiversity as a joint product.

Like other goods with public good characteristics, biodiversity and its conservation are vulnerable to free riding. Countries and individuals have an incentive to free-ride on the efforts of others because this behavior enables them to enjoy additional benefits without having to pay for them. As long as no other rules are in place, conservation efforts of countries and individuals are determined by the private value they can capture through the use or existence of biodiversity. Without internationally coordinated action, neither individuals nor countries will undertake conservation measures that go beyond their own interests. Free riding appears at both the local and the global level (Perman et al. 2003, 131–132).

The related discussions show that the property rights regime and the institutional form under which resources are governed can have a decisive impact on the conservation and sustainable use of resources. Property rights, be they private, communal, or state, are essential for addressing the problem of nonexcludability as well as for efforts to maintain a given resource (Coase 1960; Barzel 1997, 7). The underlying conception is that holders of property rights have a long-term view of their asset and will therefore use it in a sustainable manner. No property rights (i.e., open access) will lead to the depletion of the resource, whereas private, communal, and state property rights may be an adequate basis for negotiation and have the potential to set incentives for conservation measures. Property rights arrangements have distinctive characteristics. *Open access* refers to a situation where there are no controls on how much of a resource individuals consume and there are restrictions on the number of individuals that use the resource, i.e., there are no property rights to the resource. The term *state rights* refers to property rights that are vested in a central governing authority. These rights may coexist with other property rights regimes, including, for example, open access, if the state chooses not to exercise its rights. Community rights are one of the earliest forms of property rights over natural resources. These rights often exclude persons outside of a community from using a resource and establish rules governing how resources are to be used and exploited. The term *private rights* describes the rights individuals have to own, control, and enjoy the things they possess as well as their right to sell, rent, or exchange these things or parts of them (Devlin and Grafton 1999, 73ff.). IPRs are a special category of private property rights. The role they play in relation to biodiversity will be analyzed later in this chapter.

These different property rights arrangements have different allocation and distribution effects. Whereas private, state, and communal property are promising property rights regimes, they also may have some negative aspects and problems, as shown in Table 3.3.

Table 3.3　Allocation and Distribution Effects of Different Property Rights Regimes

Property rights arrangement	Allocation	Distribution effects	Problems	Solutions
Open access	Unlimited extraction	Depends on "who comes first"	"Tragedy of the unmanaged commons"	Assignment of property rights
Private property	Investment in appropriate values	Intergenerational unfairness	Doubtful preservation of nonappropriable values	Restrictions
National patrimony	Depends on political decisions	Possibly problematic in regard to local people	Weak governments lead to open-access problems	International, political, and financial support
Communal property	Depends on communal decisions	Those who control the asset will benefit	Can lead to open-access problems without regulation	Set of regulations
Patents	Include incentives to invest in biological resources	Can effect "North-to-South flows"	Ethical concerning "patent on life"	Patent law must be embedded in environmental regulations

Source: adopted from Lerch (1998, 292).

Biodiversity Loss Through Institutional and Policy Failure

Besides market failure, biodiversity degradation may also be a consequence of missing policies and institutions. The market failure and undervaluation of various resources described earlier, which lead to decline of biodiversity, can be addressed through government action. Government is often in a position to intervene and correct market failure. Such interventions can be the outcome of policies and instruments designed to conserve biodiversity and develop institutions that assume responsibility for implementing such policies and managing the resource. Examples would include the creation or improvement of property rights and recognition of social benefits (Grafton et al. 2004, 447).

In reality, it can be observed that government interventions do not stop environmental degradation. Often appropriate policies are either absent or compete with other policies that have adverse effects on biodiversity. Most such policies seek to promote economic development, and they tend to ignore environmental impacts. For example, agricultural subsidies and land grants may promote agricultural production and land conversion, in this way increasing biodiversity loss. Such land conversion is a consequence of the overvaluation of the assets converted, and it generates the same outcome as the undervaluation of biodiversity (Swanson 1995, 6).

Part of the difficulties that governments have in establishing effective biodiversity policies is rooted in the lack of a global and a national consensus on biodiversity preservation priorities and the influence of changing societal preferences on the policy-making process.

The CBD suggests four different types of policy measures intended to offer orientation for national policy-makers. The first type consists of positive incentives for conservation, including, e.g., monetary inducements paid to landowners to reimburse them for providing biodiversity. The second category includes disincentives designed to adjust economic decisions. Disincentives may, for example, be based on the polluter pays principle and the imposition of costs (e.g., user or pollution fees) on actors who harm biodiversity, in order to discourage these activities. A double dividend can be achieved if these new financial resources are channeled to other actors, e.g., farmers and landowners, to incentivize biodiversity conservation. The third type of policy measures is indirect incentives. These incentives are based on a mechanism that creates or improves market signals that encourage conservation and make it possible to derive benefits from biodiversity values. ABS is such an indirect incentive, as are afforestation programs geared to obtaining benefits from carbon sequestration. The last category refers to the removal of perverse incentives with a view to accelerating biodiversity conservation. This would include reform of agricultural policies and reduction of production subsidies (Grafton et al. 2004, 448).

The nature of policy failure may differ and vary from country to country. Public participation in the policy-making processes is often not very high.

An environmental regime may not be in place, or if a developing country is able to formulate a comprehensive set of environmental regulations, it may well lack the institutions, resources, and—sometimes—the political will needed to implement them. Effective policies and policy instruments require efficient and strong implementing institutions. According to North (1990), institutions reduce uncertainty by providing a structure for political, social, and economic interactions. They affect the performance of the economy by affecting the costs of exchange and production, including transaction costs, and they determine the profitability and feasibility of engaging in an economic activity. In other words, institutions provide the incentive structure of an economy. Property rights are considered to be such an institution. Effective biodiversity policy needs effective institutional structures that provide stakeholders with the incentive structures they need.

Policy failure is also observed in developed countries. Whereas the latter's institutions tend to be stronger, in these countries biodiversity is turned over to other pressures. Consumption and standards of living tend to be far higher—and to aggravate the pressure on natural resources (Bhattarai and Hamming 1998, 12).

THE PROMISE: BIODIVERSITY CONSERVATION BY MEANS OF BIODIVERSITY COMMERCIALIZATION

The promise held out by the ABS concept is biodiversity conservation by means of biodiversity commercialization. The concept furthermore implies that commercialization will lead to economic development. ABS is regarded as an instrument that can even foster sustainable development. Because ABS internalizes the commercial benefits of users of genetic resources, it can also be described as a market-based approach. The central elements of the concept are (i) the principle of state sovereignty, which is characterized by the allocation to states of a quasi property right to their biological resources, and (ii) bilateral contracts between providers and users of genetic resources covering both the exchange of these resources and compensation. Even though theory suggests that bilateral contracts are a Pareto-optimal solution, practical experiences indicate that that there are many factors that obstruct the optimal outcome. IPRs are a special category of property rights, one eminently important for the ABS concept. The debate on the pros and cons of IPRs will be outlined at the end of this section.

ABS: A Market-Based Approach to Sustainable Development

ABS and sustainable development are closely interlinked, but what is sustainable development? Very few concepts have found their way as rapidly and pervasively into policy discourses as the concept of sustainable development. The concept was introduced with the Brundtland report in 1987,

which defined it as "development that meets the needs of present generations without compromising the ability of future generations to meet their
own needs" (World Commission on Environment and Development 1987,
54). During the Rio Summit in 1992 sustainable development was the main
concept around which the debates crystallized. The main Rio documents,
the Rio Declaration and Agenda 21, further defined the concept, giving it
a more policy-oriented content. The emphasis of the concept was on the
need to balance economic, social, and environmental issues. The overarch-
ing policy goal of the international community should, it is argued, be the
creation and maintenance of a stable economy that produces sufficient welfare for the whole of society and distributes the benefits in an equitable
way. Since the Rio conference in 1992, the concept has been embedded
in many policy agendas. The main principles of sustainable development
include policy integration, equity regarding the costs and the benefits of
production and consumption, intergenerational solidarity, internalization
of social costs and benefits, and participatory policy-making (Bruyninckx
2004, 266ff.).

The CBD, one of the Rio agreements, reflects the concept of sustainable
development. First, the CBD is a global multilateral agreement that accords
due consideration to the conservation of biodiversity. Due to its global externalities, it calls for globally coordinated action. Second, the CBD's main
mechanism for conserving biodiversity is a bilateral, market-based instrument designed to combine conservation and development efforts by conserving biodiversity through the commercialization of plant genetic resources.

Biodiversity-rich countries alone are not able to preserve their resources.
In 1995 Norton-Griffiths and Southey estimated the opportunity costs
of biodiversity conservation in Kenya on the basis of the potential net
returns of agriculture and livestock production, comparing them with the
net returns from tourism, forestry, and other conservation activities. They
found that at the national level, agricultural and livestock production in
Kenya's parks, reserves, and forests could generate gross annual revenues of
US$565 million and net returns of US$203 million, the opportunity costs
of biodiversity conservation in Kenya. In 1995 the combined net revenues
from wildlife tourism and forestry were US$42 million, a figure inadequate
to cover the opportunity costs for land. The authors come to the conclusion
that Kenya alone—standing in for many developing countries—is unable to
solve this problem and that there is a strong need for international cooperation. Developed countries benefit from the conservation efforts of developing countries, and they need to contribute to covering these costs if they
want to see these efforts continue (Norton-Griffiths and Southey 1995).

However, even before any such calculations had been done, international policy-makers realized that the biodiversity-rich countries, mostly
developing countries, would not be able to provide sufficient funds for the
conservation of nature in general and biodiversity in particular. It was clear
that innovative financial instruments were needed to tackle the problem.

Already between the 1970s and 1980s, scientists, stakeholders from different developing and industrialized countries, and representatives of environmental NGOs began to develop strategies to stop the ongoing loss of resources. Market-based approaches were the focus of attention because they offered policy-makers new, cost-efficient ways to reach conservation objectives; such approaches use market forces to achieve their objectives. Command and control approaches became less popular. The underlying idea of market mechanisms is to capture the global, external benefits of biodiversity (Heal 2000, 21ff.). These approaches were driven in particular by changes in exploitation and a change in the property rights status of biodiversity and particular genetic resources.

The market-based approach has become manifest not only in the adoption of the CBD but also through other conventions and institutions geared to the conservation and sustainable use of resources. Examples would include the United Nations Framework Convention on Climate Change (UNFCCC) and the GEF, which channels financial resources from industrialized to developing countries as a means of supporting conservation activities. Perception of the need to involve industrialized countries in conservation strategies in developing countries is one important factor that has advanced the concept: biodiversity conservation by means of biodiversity commercialization.

The Principle of Sovereignty

The CBD's market approach is based on recognition of the principle of state sovereignty. The assumption is that assigning property rights to and responsibility for biodiversity serves to boost the exclusivity of biodiversity as a resource. In the case of crop diversity, the principle of state or national sovereignty, or the assignment of private property rights, had of course existed before it was laid down in the CBD. During the colonial era, ownership of potentially valuable plant species was an established principle. With advances in breeding in the mid-1950s, economic values of biological material shifted from the species to the variety level. This entailed a shift from colonial claims to national sovereignty to the declaration of a "common heritage." Biological materials were seen as belonging to humans in general. However, ownership could accrue only to the creator of a new, distinct, uniform, and stable variety (Petit et al. 2001, 4).

Wild genetic resources that may be found by chance in forests, on grassland, etc., long continued to be regarded as a "common heritage of mankind." The "common heritage" status of the wild genetic resources remained in place until it was dethroned by a new acknowledgment of the principle of national sovereignty. The principle is regarded both as a legal regime and as a precondition for the introduction of bilateral market-like contracts between holders and users of biodiversity (Boisvert and Caron 2002, 152).

From the point of view of institutional economics, the adoption of the CBD, affirming the principal of state sovereignty over genetic resources, is the result of improvements in the technologies needed to use genetic resources. Demsetz (1967) recognized that property rights emerge as a means to internalize externalities caused by open access, assuming that it makes economic sense to internalize such externalities. Only if the benefits of internalization exceed the costs of internalization will property rights emerge. Demsetz describes two effects that can alter the cost–benefit ratio. First, an increased value of a given asset increases the benefits or gains from ownership, leading to the creation of property rights. For example, new property rights can evolve through value enhancement driven by technical progress. Second, a decline in the costs involved in implementing property rights likewise entails positive effects on the cost–benefit relation involved in establishing property rights. Demsetz's theory is based on empirical observation of the development of land ownership by American Indians in the Quebec region in the eighteenth century. A growing trade in and value of pelts resulted in the definition of property rights to beaver populations as well as a form of privatization.

Lerch (1998, 285) applies Demsetz's theory to the case of genetic resources. Both demand for genetic resources and their utilization have increased as a result of technical advances in the field of biotechnology. Consequently, the benefits arising out of the use of genetic resources have increased, regardless of what parts of genetic resources are used (i.e., tangible versus intangible). This is the reasoning behind the creation of property rights for genetic resources and the adoption of the principle of sovereignty by the CBD or by private IPRs. Aside from the increase in their value, another aspect that has had an influence on the emergence of property rights is the cost factor. This applies not at the level of the biological material but at the level at which genetic information is processed and advanced. The transaction costs involved in assigning and enforcing such rights have been lowered by the establishment of property rights institutions, including, for instance, IPRs protection regimes. The existence of such created institutions or regimes serves to facilitate the emergence of IPRs in the field of genetic resource utilization (Sedjo 1992, 207–208)

Internalization of Commercial Externalities

The innovative framework of biodiversity management under the CBD takes up a number of different developments that have occurred over the past twenty years: the increasing loss of species and new insights about biodiversity conservation, but also technical progress in the field of biotechnology and increasing demand for biological material. This includes access to genetic resources and appropriate transfer of relevant technologies.

To recall the findings presented in the previous section: biodiversity and its components have characteristics of public and private goods. Whereas many of the benefits of biological diversity accrue to the public as a whole in the form of cultural, social, and economic benefits, a number of its components have private values (OECD 2003b, 23ff.). It assumed that the public value of biodiversity is very large (see the section "The difficulties involved valuing biodiversity" in this chapter). Starting from there, every effort would be made to conserve the planet's life-support system or certain ecosystem services. However, the private value of any specific status of biodiversity varies and depends on the concrete institutional setting. But it is this private value that determines decisions and economic behavior when it comes to biodiversity (Simpson 1999). People convert biodiversity-rich forests into cultivated land if this serves to increase their incomes. Conservation of biodiversity through market-based incentives is a realistic option only if the private benefits of conserving biodiversity exceed the private benefits of cultivating land, or of any other biodiversity-damaging activity (e.g., commercial logging).

Utilization of biodiversity as an input in research and development embodies a private value. In the form of evolution and the process of selection, nature provides a number of successful strategies that can be used against the dynamic occurrence of existential threats, for instance, pests and predators of the primary food system or incurable diseases. This is the reason why various wild plant genetic resources are of high interest (Swanson 1996, 3). The main user sectors are the pharmaceutical industry, the crop protection sector, the agricultural seed business, horticulture, botanical medicine, cosmetics and personal care, and so-called life science companies, which often consist of pharmaceutical, food, seed, and chemical divisions. All these sectors have a high interest in obtaining genetic resources for research and development. This was pointed out in Chapter 2 of this volume. The demand function for genetic resources is not well known. Reid and colleagues (1993) already stressed that demand for biochemical resources for the pharmaceutical industry is likely to respond elastically to price changes, that is, if the price for access to natural products rises, pharmaceutical firms can respond by stepping up their investment in synthetic chemistry and reducing their investment in natural products research.

The contribution of natural products to the sales of the world's top pharmaceutical companies ranges from 10 to more than 50 percent. Natural products accounted for 42 percent of the twenty-five best-selling drugs worldwide in 1997, with a total value of US$17.5 billion (ten Kate and A Laird 1999, 34). The potential for the commercial use of genetic resources is thus evident. Even though some companies have recently scaled down or closed their natural product development departments, all leading companies still run natural product programs either themselves or through subsidiaries (A Laird and ten Kate 2002, 249).

The market structure of the sectors using and providing biodiversity is characterized by an asymmetric distribution of resources and technology. The sectors that have the potential to demand and commercialize genetic resources are mainly located in industrialized countries, whereas most of the provider countries can be identified as developing countries (Myers et al. 2000, 855). The ABS concept is a response to this situation, one aiming at participation of provider countries in the economic gains stemming from their biological resources.

ABS internalizes the private commercial value of genetic resources—one of a bundle of values that determine the social benefits of biodiversity. If biodiversity is conserved solely on the basis of the private value of individuals (private marginal benefits: $MB_{private}$), the stock of genetic resources maintained will be much smaller ($X^*_{private}$) than the optimal case, viewed from the standpoint of society (X^*_{social}). If the commercial value of biodiversity is internalized by requiring users of genetic resources to pay for access and share benefits, the stock conserved will be much greater ($X^*_{commercial}$). However, the amount conserved will still be much smaller than the socially optimal amount.

In theory, the ABS concept appears promising. Creation of a market for the product "biodiversity" and trade in biological resources make it possible to protect biodiversity by using it in commercial but sustainable ways. This approach is the opposite of classic protection concepts that call for not using the resources at all. The concept not only addresses biodiversity conservation. Commercialization of genetic resources is regarded as a new source of income, and biodiversity conservation emerges as a joint

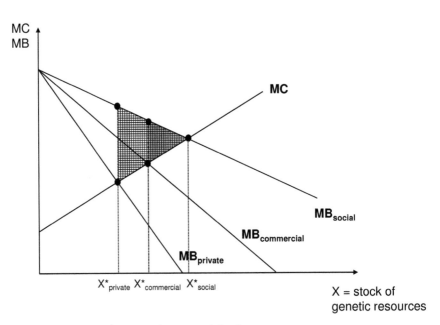

Figure 3.5 Internalization of commercial value.
Source: own presentation.

product. It is anticipated that ABS contracts will provide flows of biotech-nology-related investment and technologies sufficient to promote economic development and permit countries to establish an industry sector related to the use of genetic resources (Reid et al. 1993, 33). New capacity-building and economic developments are closely linked with poverty issues, which have been identified as the major reason for the conversion of biodiversity-rich habitats. Commercialization of biodiversity promises to serve, at the same time, the dual purpose of alleviating poverty and sustaining natural resources (Simpson 1999).

The Bilateral Approach

The CBD has established a bilateral system for the exchange of genetic resources. Under this system access to and the commercial use of genetic resources are regulated and brought into line with access and use costs. A biodiversity-rich country is expected to allow access to its genetic resources in exchange for monetary or nonmonetary benefits, such as technologies in general and biotechnologies in particular (Bonn Guidelines 2001, Appendix II). Under the CBD, the national governments that own genetic material are responsible for regulating ABS. Exchange depends on negotiations between the provider and the user of genetic resources leading to contracts governing access, planned bioprospecting activities, and a benefit-sharing procedure. The contract provides a framework for determining rights and obligations and, in particular, assigning property rights and regulating benefit-sharing in the case that products or processes with new commercial applications are discovered. Shared benefits are usually payments made in advance for the right to explore or royalty payments deriving from the use of material discovered for a given period of time, or both. Contractors obtain, in exchange, the right to patent, or otherwise exclusively exploit, materials discovered. Table 3.4 gives an overview of the potential benefits and costs of users and providers.

Clearly defined property rights constitute the legal basis of contracts between a user and a provider designed to settle questions bound up with ABS. Most of the countries that harbor highly diverse genetic resources are parties to the CBD, and the principle of state sovereignty applies here. If the state has quasi ownership of the genetic resources concerned, it is seen as having the mandate to negotiate with interested parties, and it will be the beneficiary of present and future profits. The local level is involved only to the extent that it is required to give its PIC. The level of the benefits accruing to the local level will depend on national regulations. However, one share of the profits that may be realized through the commercialization of genetic resources, for example, by the pharmaceutical or seed industry, is expected to flow back to the provider of the resources and provide an incentive to continue to conserve biodiversity. Compensation of this kind undercuts the economic rationale of alternate land uses that destroy biodiversity.

Table 3.4   Types of Costs and Benefits Arising out of ABS

Providers' benefits—Users' costs	Users' benefits—Providers' costs
Nonmonetary	**Direct**
Technology transfer	Biodiversity conservation
Free access to technology and products	Access to genetic resources
Co-ownership of IPR	Legal security
Acknowledgement in publications	Nonexclusive or exclusive user rights
Joint research and enhanced scientific capacity	
Participation in planning and decision-making (including research findings)	
Voucher specimens deposited with national institution	
Enhanced conservation capacity	
Monetary	**Indirect**
Bioprospecting fees	New inputs for research on and development of products and processes
Per-sample fees	
Percentage of research budget	Increased profits from new products and processes, protected by IPRs
Royalties as a percentage of net sales or net profits	Technical progress
Development of alternative income-generating schemes	Increase in information and knowledge
Commitment to reinvest in source country	Publications
Specific funds	

Source: based on Columbia University (1999); Bonn Guidelines (2001).

In order to create incentives for biodiversity conservation and assure a continuous supply of genetic material, the benefits reaped from commercialization need to be channeled to the landowner or local community that is in charge of resource management and bears the costs of conservation. In this case, the benefits serve to create a new source of income for these agents, and the result is biodiversity as a joint product. This may serve to underline the important role played by national institutions that define property rights, and thus allocate income opportunities.

One central proposition of property rights theory serves to justify the CBD's bilateral approach. Bargaining solutions are regarded an internalization strategy for externalities. In the so-called "Coase Theorem," Coase (1960) argues that bilateral bargaining based on well-defined and assigned property rights can internalize externalities if a number of assumptions are met, including absence of transaction costs and involvement of fully informed market participants. Viewed in terms of this conceptual framework, property rights contribute to achieving economic efficiency, and it in turn serves to maximize the overall welfare of society. How rights are distributed has no influence on the outcome. If the transaction costs are so high as to prevent bargaining, efficient use of the resources in question will depend on how property rights are assigned. The Coase Theorem, therefore, calls for laws structured in such a way as to remove the impediments to private agreements or to minimize the obstacles to private agreements on resource allocation. It is assumed that the parties are in the best position to know how much they value the property right under negotiation. Ignoring some restrictions (which will be discussed further in the following), bilateral ABS contracts of the kind suggested by the CBD may be interpreted as "Coase solutions" (Sedjo 1992, 208–209; Lerch 1998, 296ff.; Boisvert and Caron 2002, 152).

The Coase Theorem and the assumption on which it is based initiated the development of transaction costs economics, a field that deals with costs that occur when an economic exchange is effected. When the exchange involves multiple agents or agents separated by time or space, transaction costs may be prohibitively high. In that case, the outcome would depend on the specific nature of the initial allocation of rights (Swanson and Goeschl 2000, 76).

The Hobbes Theorem, formulated by Robert Cooter (1982), considers the case that people are seldom rational enough to agree on the division of a cooperative surplus, even when there are no serious impediments to bargaining. The law therefore needs to be formulated in such a way as to minimize the harm caused by failures in private agreements by allocating property rights to the party that values them most (Janssen 1999, 317). Besides, Coase's assumptions on distributive effects are not always applicable. In the case of biodiversity, the way in which property rights are distributed is critical for the outcome of ABS (OECD 2003a, 22). This aspect is examined later, in Chapter 4 of this volume.

Bargaining between the provider and the user of genetic resources can end in a Pareto-optimal allocation of protected biodiversity (X^*) if the marginal benefits (MB) of the user equal the provider's marginal costs (MC) for biodiversity protection. The outcome of such a negotiation is a social surplus (ABC) that can be shared between the participating parties.

In theory, bilateral contracts on ABS appear to be a perfect solution because externalities are internalized, a social welfare benefit accrues, and biodiversity conservation is realized—as joint product. From an incentive point of view, a fee-for-access regime therefore represents an effective system, especially in the case of rare and geographically isolated wild genetic resources of high interest as inputs for research and development.

Nevertheless, Coase had already indicated that there exist transaction costs and other factors that make the bilateral bargaining system ineffective and prevent optimal solutions. Information asymmetry and the relevance of transaction costs, imperfect competition, and uncertainty over the global and intergenerational value of genetic resources are important

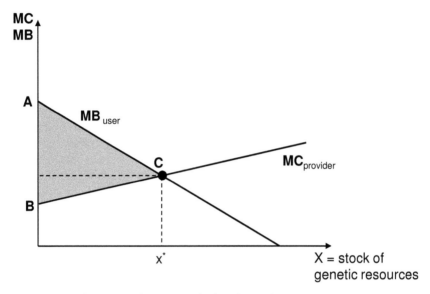

Figure 3.6   The Coase Theorem applied to the trade in genetic resources.
Source: adopted from Janssen (1999, 316).

reasons hampering the achievement of agreements. A closer look is taken at these problems in Chapter 4 of this volume. All these issues and reasons serve to prevent the optimal production of "biodiversity conservation" through bilateral benefit-sharing.

The Role of Intellectual Property Rights

Exclusiveness for IPRs on products derived from collected samples of genetic resources plays a major role in bilateral agreements. But what is the main idea of IPRs?

Today innovations and technologies that promote economic development are becoming increasingly intellectual rather than material in nature. Biotechnological inventions, computers, and chemicals based on renewable resources are examples of goods with a high degree of intellectual content (Bhat 1996, 206). These intellectual goods are based on knowledge that can also be characterized using the two criteria for public goods: nonrivalry and nonexclusivity. Private investments in knowledge do not pay off if the new knowledge becomes public and there are no restrictions on its access once it has been developed. The consequence is the dilemma of public goods: a nonoptimal supply of knowledge and a decrease in research and technical progress (Maskus 2000, 29). IPRs have been established to address the public goods dilemma and provide incentives for research and technical progress. The assignment of IPRs (e.g., patents) grants the recipient a temporary supply monopoly, and this permits her/him to realize a monopoly profit from sales of her/his products. In return, the inventor is required to reveal to the public the information needed to build upon and to commercialize the invention when its IPRs protection has expired. Without this incentive the inventor would most likely keep secret her/his knowledge concerning the invention (OECD 2001a, 13). However, welfare losses are the result of such monopoly rights. Compared with a situation of perfect competition, the price of such a protected product tends to be higher and the amount supplied tends to be lower, in the static sense.

The impact of IPRs depends on the product they protect and the level of economic development of the country concerned (OECD 2001a, 12). Proponents argue that protection is needed especially in the case of knowledge-intensive products that require both a long time for research and development and large investments—and can be duplicated at very low cost. This holds true for the pharmaceutical and the crop-breeding sectors, where development of a new drug/variety may take up to fifteen or more years, as well as for products that can be copied with ease.

On the one hand, IPRs protection, which in effect guarantees returns, is more likely to have a positive impact on the economies of technologically advanced countries. On the other hand, when it comes to economies that are predominantly consumers of protected intellectual property (i.e., low-income countries), the impact may, in the short run, turn out to be negative in terms of lost jobs and decreased production of patented products (Bhat 1996, 207). Proponents of IPRs argue that in the longer term the impact on low-income countries will be positive because they stand to benefit from increased foreign direct investment, more research activities, technological advances, and growth in trade (OECD 2001a, 12). However, IPR protection does not serve to increase investment in traditional technologies because developing countries lack the fundamental prerequisites, including research facilities and human and financial resources (Bhat 1996, 207).

Another negative effect, due to establishment costs, occurs in the low-income countries. Most developing countries do not have an IPRs system in place. These countries need to invest huge financial and human resources to establish an IPRs system. Consequently, these resources are diverted from other uses that might otherwise be used to support economic development (Hilpert 1998).

In the case of agricultural crop protection, Droege and Soete (2001, 161) come to the conclusion that developing countries will maximize their welfare if they protect traditional cultivation methods and demand royalties while rejecting international patent protection. If both protection regimes are in place, industrialized countries will benefit from a higher payoff. Industrialized countries also benefit from a protection regime in developing countries because only in that case will biodiversity be conserved. These countries should therefore give preference to a combination of different regimes. Evenson (1999, 1635) comes to a similar conclusion. Even if IPRs are extended to crops only in developed countries, it will have deleterious effects on developing countries. Janssen (1999, 320) concludes that if biodiversity is an open-access resource in provider countries, IPRs protection will aggravate the already inefficient global provision of biodiversity, whereas if efficient property rights regimes are established to complement IPRs, the decline in biodiversity will be halted.

4 The Effectiveness of ABS
Critical Factors and Measures Used to Address Them

Once the CBD was adopted, provider countries started to develop ABS regimes to implement the convention. Thus far realization of the ABS concept has depended mainly on the performance of provider countries. The process of transposing the international agreement into national legislation is a long and difficult one. Successful cases are rare even when the concept has been implemented, and this has led to discontent in the international community. Complaints have arisen on both sides, provider and user, about the functionality of the approach. The international negotiations seem to indicate that users will have to assume more responsibility in the future. However, no agreement on a future regime has yet been concluded.

The aim of this book is to contribute to the debate by analyzing whether and how the CBD's approach to ABS may be seen as a concept effective in ensuring that biodiversity is conserved and used sustainably, facilitating access to biodiversity, and guaranteeing that the benefits arising from the commercialization of genetic resources are shared fairly and equitably. Having characterized the economic framework of ABS in Chapter 3, we can now move on with the main aim of this book. The present chapter defines the analytical framework (see Figure 4.1) used to measure the effectiveness of the ABS concept, defined as the capability of the ABS regime:

1. to set incentives for the sustainable use and the conservation of biodiversity
2. to facilitate access to plant genetic material
3. to enhance fair and equitable benefit-sharing (prevent misappropriation)

What this means is that an effective ABS regime needs to have the capability to create an environment in which biodiversity is successfully protected in provider countries, in which commercially valuable biological resources in provider countries are used sustainably (i.e., access is requested and granted), and in which the benefits of this utilization are equitably shared between providers and users of the material. If an ABS regime, be it national, regional, or international, has the capability to set incentives, facilitate access, and enhance benefit-sharing, it will be effective.

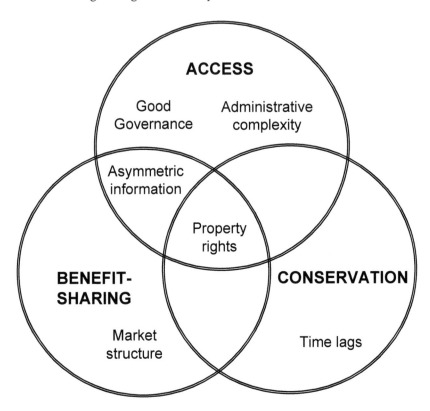

Figure 4.1   Analytical framework for measuring ABS effectiveness.
Source: own presentation.

To measure these capabilities, it is necessary to define their determinants, the so-called critical factors. These critical factors are derived in this chapter using an approach that combines the results from Chapter 3, identification of the economic framework of ABS, with some of the main aspects of new institutional economics theory (i.e., property rights, bargaining solutions, transaction costs, and information failure) and the empirical findings of four ABS country case studies. These are based on the collection and analysis of empirical qualitative data on national and regional ABS regimes in Costa Rica, the Philippines, and Ethiopia. The EU serves as a case study to complement the analytic framework from a user perspective. The structure of this analysis does not reflect the chronology of the research conducted. The findings of the case studies, which are presented in Chapter 5, have already flowed into the analysis in this chapter.

The critical factors identified are property rights and IPRs, information asymmetries, time lags, good governance, administrative complexity, and market structure. They impact on and shape the outcome of the three objectives of effectiveness.

First, biodiversity will only be conserved if incentives are set that are capable of stopping the destructive use of biological resources. Property rights or IPRs must be in place at those levels that are most effective when it comes to maintaining and investing in the asset concerned, and compensation payments must be made in real time if they are to render other destructive uses (e.g., logging) less profitable.

Second, access has two dimensions. There will be access only if users and providers are interested in and able to reach agreement on it. On the one hand, access will only be granted if provider countries can expect benefits. It is therefore necessary to ensure user compliance and to eliminate information deficiencies between providers and users.

On the other hand, access will only be requested if users are unable to find alternative sources. Here ex situ collections and similar alternative sources pose a problem. Besides, access will only be requested if the (transaction) costs involved in obtaining access are not prohibitively high. Transaction costs arise for various reasons. Uncertainty over ownership and good governance tend to lead to difficulties in obtaining PIC and in negotiating and concluding contracts, decreasing demand for access. Complex ABS application procedures also increase transaction costs.

Third, the ABS concept will be effective only if the holders of the resource in question receive fair and equitable benefits. If this condition is to be met, these agents need to be defined and identifiable. Benefits should address the needs of local communities and address the problems arising from time lags. The benefits received need to provide compensation for conservation costs. The distribution of benefits, and thus the CBD's objective of "fair and equitable benefit-sharing," is affected in important ways by the distribution of bargaining power, which in turn is closely linked with market structure. It is essential that compliance with contracts be ensured in user countries.

These critical factors have impacts, positive or negative, on the effectiveness depending on the way they are implemented. This chapter will not yet analyze the case studies in their country-specific context. Instead, the case studies will provide input to develop a general theoretical framework that can serve to analyze a large number of different country-specific cases. Analysis of the effectiveness of the ABS concept will also permit us to derive recommendations on improving ABS governance. Therefore, this chapter will also deal with measures that address the essential critical factors that affect effectiveness.

This chapter will identify and assess various measures, including, e.g., assignment of property rights, compensation schemes, contracts, coalitions, etc., and propose strategies suited to implementing such measures. They are analyzed separately from the critical factors discussed earlier. It is assumed that these measures hold the most promise for addressing the critical factors.

In keeping with the international debate, a distinction is drawn between measures that need to be initiated by provider countries (i.e., provider measures) and measures that need to be implemented in recipient countries (i.e., user measures). Thus far, the focus of ABS implementation has been on provider countries. However, it has become clear to the international community that both user and provider measures together are needed to effectively implement ABS. This is reflected in calls for the development of an international regime. Once the critical factors and potential measures have been scrutinized in theoretical terms, we will go on, in Chapter 5, to apply the analytical framework thus established to four case studies.

Even though ABS has been scrutinized from the standpoint of different fields of research (mainly law), we still lack an adequate theoretical framework for an analysis of the concept's effectiveness. Most of the research conducted thus far has focused either on the general economic framework of ABS, as discussed in Chapter 3, or on individual problems bound up with ABS. Thus far only the OECD has published (in 2003) a more comprehensive approach. This report sums up a number of economic issues associated with ABS; these are issues of a more general nature, and they are not based on empirical findings. The report also regards asymmetric information as a major problem contributing to market failure and the loss of biodiversity, in addition to nonrivalry and nonexcludability. We cannot concur with this assessment. Nonrivalry and nonexcludability must be seen as a general problem contributing to the loss of biodiversity, whereas asymmetric information is a problem associated with ABS. The analysis for this reason identifies information deficiencies as a critical factor. Other issues that the report discusses in brief form include property rights, benefit-sharing, contracting, participation of local stakeholders, and capacity-building. The present book takes the OECD results into consideration, but without adopting the framework proposed there.

This book makes use of existing approaches and publications that analyze these individual aspects. For example, Swanson and Goeschl (2000) analyze the distribution of property rights and its impact on efficiency. Mulholland and Wilman (2003) look into how contracts need to be designed and what payment schemes need to be included to guarantee that risk-averse host countries will provide high-quality genetic material. Gehl Sampath (2005) applies transaction costs economics and economic contract theory to bioprospecting contracts concerning TK and genetic resources.

This chapter seeks to fill the gap by developing and establishing a new analytical framework based on insights from new institutional economic theory, but also based on findings from the case studies. The approach used in this book thus combines deductive and inductive reasoning processes to establish a new analytic framework.

CRITICAL FACTORS FOR AN EFFECTIVE
ACCESS AND BENEFIT-SHARING REGIME

This chapter derives the critical factors based on new institutional economic theory and insights provided by the case studies. The relevant theories include property rights and contract theory as well as transaction cost theory and the theory of imperfect competition. The theories used also provide some indication as to what instruments and measures are well suited to solving problems related to the critical factors.

Derivation of the Critical Factors

Six factors determine the effectiveness of ABS. How have these factors been derived?

To answer the question, we have to recall the results of Chapter 3. Before the CBD was adopted and ABS introduced, there was no market for genetic resources, and the latter were not traded. Users obtained the needed material on their own, without the consent and approval of resource holders. These were thus given no compensation for the resources provided. At the same time, biodiversity loss went on. Economic analysis of biodiversity loss comes to the conclusion that that there are mainly two underlying causes that explain the decline of genetic resources: market failure and policy failure (Swanson 1995, 1–10). The CBD was adopted and ABS was chosen as an instrument to address these problems and establish a market for biodiversity.

The reason why the market for biodiversity fails is that provision of the resource involves externalities and displays characteristics of public goods. Biodiversity is not conserved because it produces positive externalities that are not taken into consideration by private agents. Because the individual's benefits and the private value of producing the good are lower than the benefits gained by society (i.e., social value) in a competitive market, an insufficient amount of biodiversity is provided, from society's point of view. The outcome is not socially optimal. Besides, biodiversity protection is nonexclusive and nonrival and suffers from free riding. This, too, contributes to market failure, and the outcome is an insufficient amount of biodiversity (see Chapter 3, this volume).

The market for biodiversity also fails due to policy and institutional failures in a situation in which appropriate policies and institutions are missing. The market for biodiversity functions well only if policies and institutions provide incentive structures for the agents and their transactions (North 1990, 3–4).

By assigning rights of sovereignty to provider countries and requiring fair and equitable benefit-sharing, ABS establishes a market for biodiversity (OECD 2003b, 48). Theory suggests that ABS is a concept that holds out promise to stop the decline of biodiversity. Following the Coase Theorem, bilateral trade in genetic resources is, under certain assumptions, a bargaining solution that internalizes externalities (Sedjo 1992, 208–209; Lerch 1998, 296ff.; Boisvert and Caron 2002, 152). Theoretically, bilateral trade can lead to a perfect solution, because internalization generates social welfare benefits, and biodiversity conservation emerges as a joint product.

However, the theory seems not to be working in practice. The ABS concept was developed in 1992, and since then its contribution to stopping the decline of biodiversity has been very limited. Many providers and users complain about the approach. Providers criticize the fact that whereas they have not received any benefits, their material is being used without approval. Users argue that ABS has served to impede access and use. These statements run counter to the objectives of the CBD. What we continue to see is market failure.

Nevertheless, the problems that emerge in bilateral negotiations and hamper the trade in genetic resources are not particularly surprising—even without having analyzed the empirical cases. A closer look at the theory gives us a hint as to why certain problems occur and how they can be addressed. The theory offers a number of different explanatory models. Market failure can be caused by externalities, transaction costs and information asymmetries, and imperfect competition due to market form.

Coase (1960) formulated certain assumptions under which his model works. He already indicated that there are transaction costs and other factors that make the bilateral bargaining system ineffective and prevent optimal solutions. He therefore either excluded them or stressed the need for their existence. He assumes that property rights are well defined and the costs of transaction are zero, which implies that all agents in the market are perfectly informed.

These assumptions do not hold for the case of ABS. Even under ABS, the market for genetic resources is not perfectly competitive (Gehl Sampath 2005, 65). It is possible to identify certain imperfections that distort trading activities or cause market failure. This statement may seem quite surprising in view of the fact that the ABS concept was adopted to eliminate existing market failure. The ABS concept itself is responsible for some of the problems that arise, although some are reasoned in the predetermined conditions of ABS and the environment in which the ABS concept is applied.

Property Rights Theory

Property rights play an important role because ABS creates a market in which genetic resources are traded against compensation. Exchanges of this kind also involve a transfer of property rights, as described by Coase. The question of the assignment, distribution, and strength of property rights is the most relevant issue. According to the theory, private property rights contribute to an efficient allocation of resources and increase social welfare (Alchian 2007; Richter and Furubotn 1996, 81). As long as externalities continue to exist, because property rights are not well defined, the market for genetic resources is bound to fail.

The OECD report (2003a, 27–28) stresses the importance of property rights and the way national governments translate the principle of national sovereignty into some other form of property rights. It proposes the forms of public property or public interests; the latter form leaves room for private property rights. Swanson and Goeschl (2000, 77) analyze the case of crop genetic resources and come to the conclusion that is makes sense to locate property rights, for efficiency reasons, at those levels that are more effective in maintaining and investing in the asset concerned. Looking at the value chain, it is evident that there are potential rights holders at all stages of the production process. The levels may include providers—local-level private or communal landowners and/or governments—and users such as companies and researchers/research institutions, depending on the level at which the material is processed. Swanson and Goeschl use the International Union for the Protection of New Varieties of Plants (UPOV) Convention as an example to show that IPRs systems do not have a positive impact on the supply of genetic resources to the plant industry. The systems have created incentives to invest in research and development in the plant-breeding sector (i.e., at the end of the value chain), but they have not generated investments in local farmers who conserve local landraces, maintaining crop diversity. The reasons are that local farmers have yet to receive benefits from the use of their varieties. Hart and Moore (1990) speak of property rights failure when the best investor in an asset is not the holder of the property rights to it.

The case studies serve to underline that the concept of property rights is not necessarily well defined in ABS. The CBD allocates property rights to states but not to landowners or resource holders. It is the task of government to determine how property rights are distributed within a given country, and a government will not necessarily distribute a share of the benefits to the resource holders. The most adequate response to this critical factor must therefore be seen in the assignment of property rights.

Contract Theory and Transaction Costs

The reason why contracts are the heart of the exchange of genetic resources and benefits is that contracts reallocate rights among the contracting parties (Barzel 1997, 33). Contracts document the exchange of relative property rights between persons. Relative property rights are property rights that are assigned to a certain person, the contract partner. Absolute property rights are rights over property that everyone is obliged to respect (Richter and Furubotn 1996, 79ff.).

The incentive structure of contracts is very important when it comes to compliance. It may be difficult to create an appropriate incentive structure if the transactions regulated by the contract do not take place at the same time. Time lags of this kind are very relevant for ABS because the time at which genetic resources are acquired does not coincide with the time at which benefits are generated. Besides, transaction costs are significantly relevant for contracts. The main problems that may arise out of transaction costs and the time lag between the conclusion and the execution of a contract are: (i) asymmetric information and (ii) transaction-specific investments related to the frequency and uncertainty of transactions (Richter and Furubotn 1996, 92).

Williamson (1985, 52) identifies asset specificity, frequency, and uncertainty as important characteristics of transactions that have a decisive impact on transaction costs. An asset is specific if it is worth much more within a certain transaction than outside of it. Parties cannot simply switch to another partner once investments have been made. Williamson (1983, 526) distinguishes four types of investment specificity: site specificity (i.e., physical proximity), physical specificity (e.g., investment in machinery), human asset specificity (e.g., learning by doing), and asset specificity due to expectations of high demand. However, the trade in genetic resources is not characterized by asset specificity. Wild and previously undiscovered genetic resources collected for screening purposes usually have no specificity. A provider country can offer its resources to any company interested in using them, and companies are free to approach any provider country. Site specificity may be relevant in cases where a pharmaceutical company asks for a specific plant in a specific country or region. Long-term relationships between companies and countries (e.g., in the case of Costa Rica) may be characterized by human specificity. However, the case studies do not indicate that asset specificity is a factor important enough to warrant closer investigation. This factor has therefore not been selected as a critical factor.

Frequency also has an impact on transaction costs. If transactions are frequent, the parties will invest in a governance structure designed to decrease transaction costs and make transactions efficient (Gehl Sampath 2005, 69). Only a limited number of the ABS agreements concluded thus far have led to frequent exchanges. However, the parties do tend to invest in governance structures in cases involving a frequent, long-term partnership. Frequency is therefore not a critical factor. Conditions of uncertainty may affect users and providers differently and may also result in information asymmetries. These information asymmetries entail the risk that one contracting party may take advantage of the other's relative lack of relevant information, i.e., to engage in opportunistic behavior.

Transaction costs may be (i) search and information costs; (ii) bargaining and decision costs; and (iii) monitoring, renegotiation, and enforcement costs. Search and information costs comprise the costs generated by the search for a contractual partner. As a rule, contractual partners are faced with bargaining and decision costs in the course of their negotiations. This process calls for consultations. Monitoring, renegotiation, and enforcement costs result from the need to monitor contract performance, to renegotiate conditions, and to enforce a contract (Richter and Furubotn 1996, 52).

In the case of ABS, the three cost categories assume the form of uncertainty and asymmetric information, a situation often aggravated by opportunistic behavior. The reason for uncertainty is that the parties to a contract are unable to predict the future. They are forced to make decisions without knowing what consequences they may have. If contracts can be adapted to new or unexpected situations, the result will be better allocation. Uncertainty is closely related to information. Levels of information may differ among the contracting partners. One party is very likely to have more knowledge than the other concerning given issues relevant for a contract. Opportunistic behavior may occur both before and after a contract has been concluded. Because the parties have an incentive to behave opportunistically once a contract has been concluded, the theory suggests that ex ante measures are needed to ensure the efficiency of allocation, including, for example, screening or signaling. Mechanisms of this kind enable the uninformed party to acquire additional information (Richter and Furubotn 1996, 92). Screening allows the uninformed party to induce the other party to reveal its information, and signaling allows the informed party to signal its willingness to comply. Any measure that provides additional information to the uninformed party is suited to address the problem of asymmetrical information.

Providers and users have search costs because before they can conclude a contract they need to look for appropriate partners in whom they can trust. During the bargaining process, users and providers are faced with asymmetric information. Providers have no information about the benefits users expect. Users lack information on the exclusiveness and the quality of the material concerned. Both users and providers are faced with monitoring costs bound up with asymmetric information. Providers are unable to observe the use made of the material once it has left their territory, and users are unable to observe how the shared benefits are used and whether the provider countries invest them in biodiversity conservation.

Most of the transaction costs involved in ABS are due to asymmetric information. Asymmetric information has for this reason been derived as a critical factor. There are also some other, additional sources of transaction costs that need to be mentioned. Search costs can arise due to the difficulties users have in identifying reliable and suitable providers. In the German user survey, users state that they have difficulties finding appropriate partners due to lack of support and information. This means that their search costs are high. Bargaining and decision costs are also affected by the institutional arrangements in place in provider countries. In the German user survey it is noted that some users find ABS-related administrative procedures time-consuming, bureaucratic, and complex (Holm-Mueller, Richerzhagen, and Taeuber 2005, 46). The case studies also provide some interesting insights regarding these issues. The regulations in place in the Philippines have proven very complicated and bureaucratic. Many Philippine stakeholders agree that this is the reason why no ABS has taken place thus far, and the country's ABS regulations have recently been improved. In the case studies, the problem of administrative complexity and associated transaction costs appears highly relevant. Administrative complexity was therefore chosen as an independent critical factor, and not subsumed, together with asymmetric information, under the category "transaction costs." Besides, the three categories of transaction costs are not equally relevant.

Whereas transaction costs are very important, the environment in which transaction costs arise is essential as well. According to Davis and North (1971), the new institutional economics breaks down into two parts: the institutional environment and the institutions of governance. Williamson (1991) argues that the institutional environment consists of a set of parameters (i.e., political, social, and legal) that establish the basis for economic transactions (i.e., production, exchange, and distribution). If the parameters are changed, the result will be shifts in the comparative costs of governance. In the case of ABS, good governance is such an institutional environment. Good governance comprises, for example, political stability, control of corruption, rule of law, and accountability (Kaufmann, Kraay, and Mastruzzi 2006, 4). Good governance has for this reason been chosen as another critical factor.

Imperfect Competition

It is evident that the market for genetic resources suffers from imperfect competition for reasons bound up with market structure. A market that operates under conditions of perfect competition is characterized by four conditions: (i) numerous participants (i.e., many buyers and sellers); (ii) freedom of exit and entry; (iii) perfect information; and (iv) homogenous products (Baumol and Blinder 1994, 222). The second and fourth conditions are not relevant to the case of ABS because they are given. Anyone is free to enter and exit the market, and at the collection stage wild genetic resources are homogenous goods because their quality and potential are unknown. The third condition is not given because neither users (i.e., buyers) nor providers (i.e., sellers) are perfectly informed. This problem was mentioned in the previous section. Nor is the first condition is given. If sellers and buyers are not able to participate on equal terms, we can differentiate between four forms of market participation: (i) monopoly, with only one seller; (ii) oligopoly, with a small number of sellers; (iii) monopsony, with only one buyer; and (iv) oligopsony, with a small number of buyers.

What we observe in the case of ABS is a small number of relevant buyers that acquire genetic resources for commercial purposes, whereas the number of sellers is quite large. Mergers in the pharmaceutical and agricultural sectors have created large life science companies that dominate the market (Braga 1996, 360). In keeping with the different categories outlined earlier, the market for genetic resources is characterized by oligopsonistic competition. The users in the market have a strong bargaining position and considerable power. For the process involved in negotiating ABS contracts, market structure is particularly relevant. Measures that serve to strengthen the position of the weaker party may be seen as an adequate response. Due to its importance, market structure was chosen as a critical factor.

The six critical factors are analyzed separately in the following sections. The findings from the case studies have been are included in the analysis, which they have deepened and broadened.

Property and Intellectual Property Rights

The strength and distribution of property rights are the most critical factors for ABS governance because property rights impact on all three elements of ABS effectiveness: conservation, access, and benefit-sharing. Property rights enable property owners to market their resources. Only if the agents responsible for conserving biodiversity have adequate property rights over their biological resources will they be able to grant access, and be in a position to receive the benefits that, in the next step, set incentives for biodiversity conservation.

In keeping with genetic vocabulary, we can break biodiversity down into two parts: the phenotype, that is, the tangible biological material, and the genotype, that is, the genetic and biochemical information contained in the resource. There are differences in the way property rights are assigned to these two forms of biological material. Tangible resources (e.g., plants) in general are subject to private property rights, in the form of landowner rights, or to communal property rights, in the form of state or community property rights. Intangible resources like the products of research and development can be protected by IPRs, e.g., through patents or plant breeder rights (Sedjo 2000, 111).

Property rights are transferable. In most cases companies or research institutions that sign ABS contracts with provider countries receive property rights for the tangible material they have purchased in exchange for access, sample fees, and up-front payments. These property rights are usually restricted by stipulations regarding utilization. In the case that a product is successfully researched, developed, and commercialized, the inventor may receive IPRs for the intangible material. The contribution of provider countries to the invention is compensated for in the form of royalties and milestone payments (the latter are made if a sample has evolved, in the research and development process, into a more valuable substance) or other nonmonetary transfers that have impacts on national research and development, local economic development, and capacity-building (see Chapter 3, this volume; Columbia University 1999, 75). One necessary condition for the effectiveness of the ABS concept is that the benefits, be they monetary or nonmonetary, be able to compensate for costs incurred in connection with conservation activities and to set an incentive for conservation.

However, the absence of clear property rights at the resource manager level can impede efforts to realize profits, and consequently to achieve biodiversity protection, because there are no incentives in place for conservation. At this level the CBD does place much weight on property rights. Apart from affirmation of a state's sovereignty over its biological resources and emphasis on the existence of IPRs, the CBD does not call any other allocation of property rights. National governments are responsible for the definition and assignment of property rights. Whether or not national governments transfer their authority and rights to other stakeholders depends on national legislation.

As regards economic theory, Coase opened the discussion on the new discipline of "transaction costs economics," and he questioned the impact of the initial allocation of property rights. There exist different forms of property rights systems for biological resources. The status of these rights and changes to these rights may generate changes in the value of the property concerned (OECD 2003a, 28). In the case of state-owned property, the government in the first place manages a country's biodiversity and is responsible for its provision. The government will receive benefits if it is able to enforce its property rights vis-à-vis biodiversity users. Sharing benefits with individuals or communities who have contributed to the existence of biodiversity in the past, or even in the present, may be important in terms of equity and fairness (Bonn Guidelines 2001). It is not, however, important from an incentive point of view (and for this reason the present analysis does not consider the equity dimension). However, if the local level is in charge of the management and the supply of the resource, it is essential that it be able to participate in the benefits arising out of the use of genetic resources provided. The CBD demands only that the PIC of the local stakeholders be secured. This consent is a rather weak form of participation and can be organized with local agents without any form of benefit-sharing. In this case, i.e., without any marked participation in the benefits, agents will tend to come up with a very low estimate of the value of wild genetic resources, even if the private UV of these genetic resources is high for companies in user sectors. If local-level participation consists not only of PIC but also of benefit-sharing, this is very likely to set the incentives needed to conserve and make sustainable use of genetic resources.

The relation between property rights and biodiversity values depends on the process stage of genetic resources in the production chain, and this plays an important role for the effectiveness of the ABS concept (see Figure 4.2).

Comparison of the property rights allocated on the basis of international regulations to the various stakeholders involved (i.e., individuals, local communities, government, intermediary, companies, and researchers) leads to the conclusion that the strength of the property rights of the concerned party will increase level by level, as will as their economic market value. In gaining IPRs for developed, marketable products, companies and research institutions acquire strong property rights for high-value goods. Governments have also strong rights over their biological resources, and these are reaffirmed in the state sovereignty principle set out in the CBD. According to this principle, on the global level the governments of provider countries are in a better position than local landowners to negotiate with users and to secure greater benefits in ABS contracts. However, the government needs

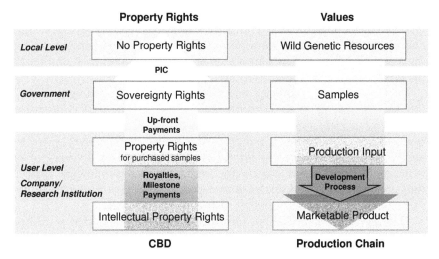

Figure 4.2   Distribution of property rights and values among stakeholders.
Source: own presentation.

to transfer these benefits to the local level (Barrett and Lybbert 2000, 296). As already mentioned, the convention does not allocate rights to the local level. If national governments fail altogether to regulate the property rights situation in their countries, the open-access status of genetic resources will continue in effect; degradation will go on. Resource holders will have an incentive to conserve nature only if national legislation fills this gap left open by the CBD. Thus, strong IPRs, such as patents and plant breeder rights on the user level for the marketable product, will not be sufficient to ensure biodiversity conservation. Conservation incentives in the form of rights or benefits need to be set for the economic agents who decide on the use of the biological resources. If these are local agents, national legislation is needed to ensure that they benefit from any ABS contract.

Information Asymmetries

Besides property rights, information asymmetries are the most important critical factor that affects the access and benefit-sharing element of effectiveness. Even in the access phase, information asymmetries can be identified as a major cause of unsuccessful negotiations, resulting in insufficient contracts entailing meager flows of benefits, or leading to the breakdown of talks.

It is possible to break down information asymmetries into pre- and post-contractual principal–agent problems. In the presence of two-dimensional asymmetric information, each bargaining partner has private information on her/his activities (OECD 2003a, 16). This is the case in bilateral ABS contracts between users and providers of genetic resources. If an intermediary is involved, the transaction is more complex. In this case user and provider do not negotiate directly. Property rights, genetic resources, and information, but also information deficiencies, are channeled through the intermediaries. The existence of intermediaries serves even to intensify the problem of asymmetric information.

The problem of asymmetric information is also described by the OECD (2003a, 16) and by Gehl Sampath (2005, 75–76). The OECD notes that users have private information on their potential interest, the costs of research and development, and the availability of alternatives. Providers have private information on the reliability, quality, and diversity of the material. Whereas these aspects are considered in the following analysis, they are aggregated and analyzed in depth. Consideration is given to how these asymmetries arise and what their consequences are.

Gehl Sampath derives three forms of transaction costs that arise from asymmetric information: search and information costs, bargaining and decision costs, and monitoring and enforcement costs. She regards the problem of uncertainty about product quality as part of search and information costs in the market for genetic resources, one that, whereas less important for pharmaceutical drugs, assumes more importance when it comes to botanical medicines. Bargaining and decision costs arise from uncertainties in the drug research and development process, legal uncertainties, and renegotiations. Monitoring and enforcement costs arise in connection with the two-sided principal–agent relationship between a company and the provider country as well as between government and local communities in the provider country (Gehl Sampath 2005, 76ff.). The classification proposed has not been used for the present study because not all of the criteria are used identically. For example, legal uncertainty (as one component of good governance) is here considered as part of the transaction costs environment and not as an element of transaction costs, and lack of knowledge regarding quality is identified here not as search costs but as costs that arise during the bargaining process.

Pre-Contractual Information Deficiencies

Pre-contractual problems occur because providers are faced with information deficiencies that affect a planned exchange of genetic resources for benefits before a contract has been concluded. Providers lack information on the potential benefits of the genetic resources provided. Users have an incentive to conceal their information regarding the benefits they expect to receive from genetic resources. The benefits of commercialization, and not the costs of conservation, are the important factor in the negotiations. Providers' costs consist of opportunity costs and costs for protection measures. These are important for any conservation concept because resource holders are usually compensated for providing environmental services based on their costs. However, the CBD's ABS concept is based not on the costs that arise through biodiversity conservation but on the benefits arising out of commercialization. This is reasoned in the CBD's goal not only to conserve biodiversity but also to achieve equity. When the CBD was adopted, expectations regarding the monetary profits arising from the commercial use of biodiversity were high. Genetic resources were even referred to as "green gold." ABS negotiations, therefore, focus on the benefits and how they are shared (Barrett and Lybbert 2000, 294).

If a potential user supposes or even knows that commercialization of genetic resources is likely to entail high benefits, she/he will have an incentive to conceal her/his willingness to pay in order to reduce the compensation due to resource providers and to reap a profit. On the other hand, providers suspect that high benefits are acquired through research on and development of genetic resources. In the end, expectations regarding ABS contracts may diverge so sharply that negotiations fail.

Post-Contractual Information Deficiencies[1]

Post-contractual problems arise in the form of two-dimensional moral hazards on the provider and the user side. First, information deficiencies and missing control mechanisms on the provider side can result in overregulation in the form of highly restricted access. This overregulation increases user transaction costs and prevents successful negotiations on ABS.

Providers experience moral hazards regarding the use of the material collected. For provider countries it is important to ensure that in return for access to biological material, companies meet their obligations arising out of bilateral agreements regarding the acquisition of material, liability, and payments (Reid et al. 1993, 38). The capacity of national institutions to monitor the use of the material provided is very limited, though. The final utilization of genetic resources, advanced research and development, as well as marketing of the products take place outside of the provider country. Providers are unable to observe the research and development activities of users as soon as the latter have left the country with the samples of genetic resources they have collected, even if contracts have been concluded. Bioprospecting activities defy any control by the country of origin due to the prohibitive transaction costs involved. There exist numerous possibilities to cross borders and to exit a country, especially in countries like, for example, the Philippines, which has more than seven thousand islands. National governments are not even able to monitor all ongoing contractual bioprospecting activities in their territories. The matter becomes even more difficult if the material has been transferred to another country. Acquired resources may be passed on to another company without the provider's consent or the user may develop products and processes without declaring this to the provider country. In this case, potential benefits are lost. In addition, IPRs, for example, patents, and plant breeder rights are generally issued not in provider countries but in industrialized countries, which have the biggest sales markets. Providers are unable to observe these markets.

Negative experiences or worries on the part of provider countries can lead to very strict and complicated overregulation, making access almost impossible and prompting interested foreign parties to move their investigations to another country with a more bioprospecting-friendly climate. The unapproved acquisition of genetic resources has led to a bad image for users and bioprospecting alike, resulting in low acceptance in provider countries or with NGOs in industrialized countries. "Biopiracy" is the expression often used to describe the illegal acquisition of biological material. In many countries environmental and indigenous groups object to the implementation of the ABS concept, because they feel that the present legal and policy environment fails to ensure PIC and fair and equitable benefit-sharing (A Laird and ten Kate 2002, 243). One of the main points criticized is that the CBD promotes IPRs as a basic element of benefit-sharing, whereas indigenous rights and TK, often inputs for biotechnological innovations, are not protected. The critics propose the introduction of an additional property rights system (*sui generis* rights system), for example, intellectual community rights that provide communities the opportunity to protect their resources and knowledge.

It is not only commercial users who suffer from biopiracy. Today the term *biopiracy* is very broadly defined and refers to almost any commercial activity associated with genetic resources. Consequently, researchers and companies regard the term as a serious impediment to research. Their fear is that they could be stamped as biopirates and see their image tarnished (Wynberg and A Laird 2005, 31).

Any strict legislation implemented by provider countries tends to have negative effects on the research conducted at local universities and research institutions in the countries concerned (Richerzhagen and Virchow 2007, 76). Some countries do not distinguish between academic and commercial research and interests, and they apply the same standards for both purposes. This also tends to lead to very restrictive regulations, which may cause essential research to grind to a halt (Dávalos et al. 2003, 1520).

The second case of moral hazard is that experienced by users. Users lack information on (i) the quality of the material provided and (ii) the exclusiveness of the material. A third factor that may cause concern for users is misallocation of the benefits received (iii). This factor is only relevant if users depend on long-term, continuous provision of material.

   (i) Users lack information on the quality of the genetic resources provided. Mulholland and Wilman (2003) analyze this dimension of information deficiencies more closely. In their view, users are unable to perfectly monitor host-country inputs into the drug-discovery process, because host countries control access not only to the resources provided but also to information on the quality of the material. The authors suggest that companies need to design contracts that provide incentives for host countries to deliver an amount of bioprospecting

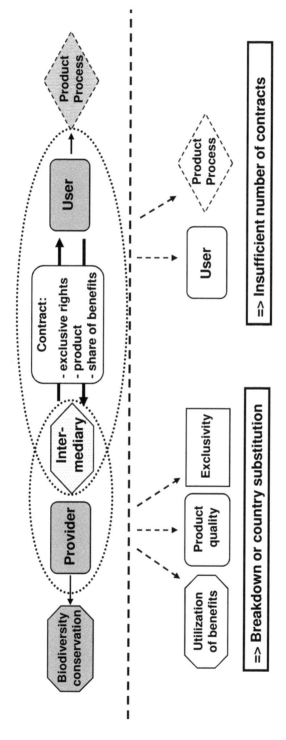

Figure 4.3 Two-dimensional information deficiencies. Source: own presentation.

output that maximizes the company's output. This proposal is discussed later in this chapter in the section titled "Screening based on contracts." Surprisingly, whereas this case of asymmetric information is important, it has not proven very relevant in empirical terms. In all the interviews conducted as well as in the user study (Holm-Mueller, Richerzhagen, and Taeuber 2005) users complain more about their lack of knowledge regarding regulations and weak institutional infrastructure. However, additional information may be a reason to pay more to providers. Furthermore, companies obtain material from intermediaries, but these second-level providers are often not based in the host countries. They are brokers in the international markets. It therefore seems appropriate to take a closer look at the problem, whereas Mulholland and Wilman (2003) see the problem as given and focus more on the solution (i.e., contract design).

The market for genetic resources suffers from underconsumption due to adverse selection. Users can receive a variety of benefits from the use of genetic resources, but these benefits are valuated differently by users. Valuation depends on the specific characteristics that determine the quality of bioresources. Users are willing to pay for these benefits only if they can be sure that they exist. This is why information on these characteristics provided to the user also serves as a criterion for quality. Passport data on genetic resources, including, for instance, indication of their origin, the location where they were collected, description of specific biological traits, but also a legally binding guarantee that PIC was obtained, may serve as such criteria for quality.

As long as users are unable to differentiate quality levels of genetic resources, they will not be willing to pay more for "better" genetic resources. Users who obtain genetic material through brokers are forced to trust these intermediaries. A company or research institute cannot check whether PIC has been appropriately obtained and whether an ABS agreement has been concluded. Other characteristics, such as origin and known traits, may also be concealed. If the material is obtained directly from the country of origin and not collected by the users themselves, the latter have no choice but to trust the information given by providers. For example, they have to trust that the PIC of a local community has been obtained and the geographical indication is correct.

A user who cannot identify the quality of genetic resources will place less value on the material. Consequently, an uninformed user's demand for such material will be lower, and she/he will tend to purchase less of it, than an informed user. In Figure 4.4 the demand curve for the uninformed user ($D_{uninformed}$) is lower than the demand curve for an informed user ($D_{informed}$), and the quantity traded is lower ($Q_{uninformed}$) because of the existence of information deficiencies.

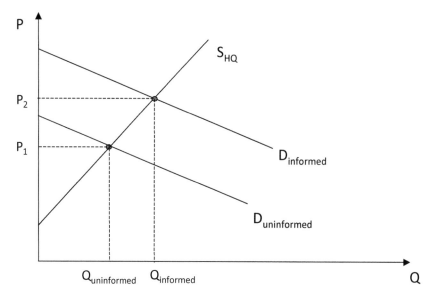

Figure 4.4 Informed and uninformed users in the market for genetic resources.
Source: adopted from Borooah (2003).

This situation leads to underconsumption and declining consumer
and producer rents. The factor consumer rent measures the difference
between the amount users are willing to pay and the amount they actually pay. Producer rent measures the difference between the amount
providers are willing to accept and the amount they actually receive.
Both rents would be higher if the user received additional information
on the good. If users were informed on quality, they would be able to
differentiate between genetic resources of high and low quality. Consequently, more resources would be demanded.

In economic theory, goods can be classified in terms of the level of
a consumer's lack of information regarding a product's quality and
the level of information needed to identify quality (Nelson 1970). A
product's quality needs to be identified on the basis of the product itself. A good has search attributes if it is a product with features easily
observable before purchase. It in this case has low pre-costs for detection and thus allows users, for example, to differentiate a specimen
(i.e., plant, animal, insect, etc.) by means of simple inspection. If the
cost of the inspection exceeds the marginal benefit of the additional
information obtained, users will reject the specimen. In the case of
experience attributes, users can detect certain product qualities only
after they have bought and used a product. The reason why goods
with experience attributes have high pre-costs and low post-costs of
detection is that the relevant information can be obtained only as a

by-product of use, i.e., after the good has been purchased (Nelson 1970). However, this information serves as the basis for decisions regarding repeated purchases. Credence attributes are attributes that consumers are unable to valuate even after purchasing the product. They thus have high pre-costs and high post-costs of quality detection. The consumer has to rely on third-party judgments, or they are forced to trust the provider as regards the quality of the goods in question (Darby and Karni 1973). The last category, Potemkin attributes, describes process-oriented qualities that are hidden for third parties as well as for customers at the end-product level. It is impossible to detect them at the product level, even when a third party is involved (Tietzel and Weber 1991; Spiller 1996).

Genetic resources mainly have experience attributes regarding their quality in terms of commercial potential. The material has to undergo some research before the user is finally able to evaluate its potential and decide whether the product will be marketed. This is why material that has already been tested and processed by the provider has more value to the user than material obtained without any prior scientific analyses. It has been observed that demand for genetic resources is much higher in provider countries, like, e.g., Costa Rica, that provide not raw material but processed samples (Richerzhagen and Holm-Mueller 2005, 453ff.). However, making additional information available entails additional costs for a provider. For example, collection in provider countries may need to be conducted more systematically. In particular, advanced scientific knowledge and skills in documentation, cataloguing, and databasing are needed in order to provide such information.

Nevertheless, it is not possible to detect all quality characteristics after utilization. In many cases it is not even possible to identify the origin of the material. In this case, origin is a Potemkin attribute. The user can only trust the provider or intermediary's statement that material has in fact been obtained as indicated. If detection is possible, it is often associated with high costs and calls for the involvement of a third party. For example, microbial collections are frequently asked

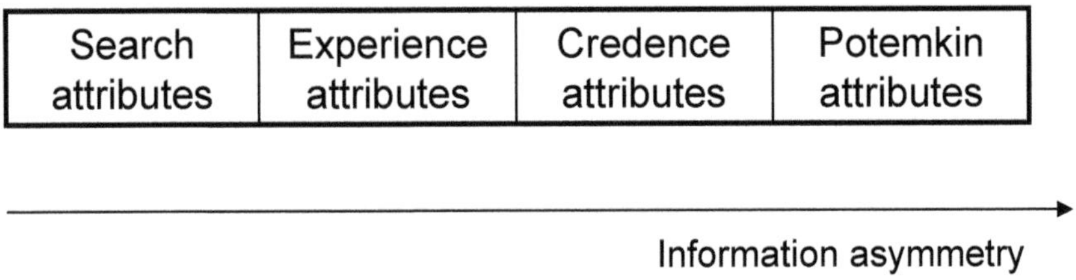

Search attributes	Experience attributes	Credence attributes	Potemkin attributes

Information asymmetry

Figure 4.5 Information asymmetry in markets.
Source: adopted from Jahn, Schramm, and Spiller (2004).

to assist users in identifying the origin of material they have used. In this case origin is a credence attribute.

Proof that PIC has been obtained is a Potemkin attribute, one that cannot be revealed even with the support of a third party. No analysis of genetic material can identify whether PIC has been obtained. Users that were not involved in the PIC and ABS process have no choice but to trust their intermediary or provider.

(ii) Users have information deficiencies related to exclusive rights. In general, the user needs access to genetic resources that is both legal and secure, but also exclusive. Signing an ABS agreement gives users exclusive rights for a particular region and a certain period of time. The user, however, has only limited information on and control over whether the provider country offers the same samples of genetic resources to other competing users. For lack of information or certainty, users will often respond by choosing a different country if other countries offer the same resources (Richerzhagen and Virchow 2007, 76).

(iii) Users lack information on how the shared benefits are allocated. According to the idea underlying the CBD and the Bonn Guidelines (Bonn Guidelines 2001), the benefits arising out of bilateral agreements should be allocated for biodiversity conservation measures in the provider country. Often short-term national interests in biodiversity-rich countries diverge from the objective of long-term conservation and sustainable utilization of genetic resources. Due to these short-term interests, the benefits (in terms of royalties or up-front payments) derived from access to and utilization of genetic resources may not be reinvested in biodiversity conservation but allocated to other national activities. This may place the long-term security of genetic resources at risk. In this case, a problem of asymmetric information exists as well. It is assumed that benefit-sharing is regarded—at least in part—as an incentive for further conservation and secured utilization of genetic resources, and it is assumed that users with a long-term interest in bioprospecting are interested in the appropriate use of the benefits, and that this will guarantee the conservation and further use of genetic resources. However, other users with an interest in the conservation of biodiversity are unable to influence the allocation of benefits at the national level in the provider country. It appears that the crucial point of any bilateral ABS agreement is the risk that the provider country may misallocate the benefits it receives, in this way jeopardizing the conservation and sustainable utilization of genetic resources. Practical conservation efforts or concrete threats to biodiversity are centered on at the local level, where the influence—and sometimes the interest—of national decision-makers is limited. Hence, states are not always in control of maintaining and providing genetic resources, especially if they lack adequate laws and institutions for genetic resources management. In this case the user will, in specific situations, be faced with a case of moral hazard.

Time Lags

Time lags have strong effects on the objective of conservation. Time lags between the collection and provision of promising samples and the development of a marketable product make it very difficult to achieve a fair and equitable benefit-sharing and to set incentives for conservation (Barrett and Lybbert 2000, 296–297; Dutfield 1999, 2). There is a huge measure of variation between industry sectors when it comes to the costs and the time it takes to develop a marketable product from a natural sample as well as in terms of the probability that a successful product will emerge. In the pharmaceutical sector, ten to fifteen years of research and development are needed to discover and develop a drug. Whereas the costs of this process vary, they tend to range between US$231 million and US$500 million. The probabilities of success vary from one in five thousand to one in ten thousand. In the botanical medicine sector, the process may take less than two years and the costs can amount to less than US$1 million. However, botanical medicine is still regarded as a niche sector. In the agricultural sector, it can take from eight to fifteen years to develop a new variety, and the costs range between US$1 to US$2.5 million for a traditional variety and US$35 to 75 million for transgenic characteristics. A new chemical pesticide can take from eight to fourteen years to develop and can cost US$40 to 100 million, whereas a biocontrol agent can be developed within two to five years and cost US$1 to 5 million (ten Kate and A Laird 1999, 10).

Benefit-sharing is the incentive set for conservation, and it depends heavily on the successful development of products and the accumulation of profits. Experience shows that users of genetic resources are unwilling to pay sufficient compensation as long as no product has been developed and distributed in the market. However, if they are to prove effective, income substitutions designed to alter economic activities and induce people to refrain from biodiversity-damaging actions have to be paid directly, not fifteen years later on. Otherwise, benefit-sharing will fail to institute an incentive to conserve biodiversity. Therefore, time lags are highly critical for ABS.

Good Governance in Provider Countries

Good governance in the provider country plays an important role for the transaction costs that arise in the access phase of ABS. This is also noted by a German user survey that asked potential users about the main problems they face acquiring genetic resources (Holm-Mueller, Richerzhagen, and Taeuber 2005, 46).

Governance in general is a concept that has been developed and applied by two disciplines: political science and economics. Whereas political science concentrates on altered forms of interaction and coordination mechanisms between the state and society, economics examines the ways in which market events are affected by institutional arrangements and how economic activities are embedded in society (Brunnengraeber et al. 2006, 8). The latter approach has been selected for the present analysis. As already mentioned, the governance debate in economics has its roots in the new institutional economics. Here governance is viewed as the institutional environment in which transactions take place, and this approach can also be applied to ABS.

Good governance is a strong factor involved in the environment of economic ABS transactions. As a concept, good governance is narrower than governance in general, and it is found mainly in the field of development policy. The term refers to specific conditions on which international financial and development institutions, including, e.g., the World Bank, the International Monetary Fund (IMF), or national ministries, condition the development cooperation they provide. The World Bank Governance Indicators cover 213 countries and territories and measure six dimensions of governance from 1996 to the end of 2005: voice and accountability, political stability and absence of violence, government effectiveness, regulatory quality, rule of law, and control of corruption.[2] These factors also shape the environment in which negotiations and bioprospecting are carried out. Detailed analysis of these indicators is beyond the scope of this book. However, the World Bank figures are used as reference points to indicate where the case study countries stand and to analyze their institutional environments.

The case study on Ethiopia shows that lack of such good governance, as well as of political stability, long prevented the development of an ABS regime. Many provider countries are developing countries with unstable political systems. The general political situation also has an influence on the status of countries as providers. If possible, users will access countries—and their resources—that signal reliability and provide political security. Besides, many countries still have not implemented the CBD and its ABS obligations. These countries are unable to provide legal security to users regarding the utilization of genetic resources. If they have been implemented in the first place, their regulations and procedures tend to be unclear. They often fail to create focal points for users, and in many cases legal access entails high transaction costs. Under such conditions users may seek to obtain unapproved material, or even discontinue collecting and research activities in the country concerned. A company that distrusts the level of legal security given in a country will tend to respond with country substitution and move to a country with a set of transparent regulations or—in a few rare cases—move to a country without any access legislation (Richerzhagen and Virchow 2007, 76). Countries that have no ABS legislation and that harbor resources similar to those found in neighboring countries that have implemented ABS regulations and charge for access provide interesting legal loopholes. This is one legal way for users to circumvent the ABS obligations of the CBD. If genetic resources are accessed in these countries, no conservation incentives will be established. Nevertheless, lack of an ABS regulation has negative impacts on the demand for access. The developing process of regulations can also be difficult for users. Dávalos et al. (2003, 1519) regard the period during which a country develops ABS legislation as the hardest and most insecure for users interested in obtaining access.

Insecurity regarding national property rights may also prove to be a problem. Even if an ABS regime is in effect, absence of or uncertainty about ownership in a provider country leads to difficulties in obtaining PIC, in negotiating on ABS, and in concluding contracts, and it raises the transaction costs of users. An ABS regime will be embedded in the national political and legal system of the respective country. These are the main factors that influence the state of implementation and the efficiency of ABS regimes, and with them the bioprospecting climate as well.

Administrative Complexity

Administrative complexity is another form of governance: governance concerned with the reduction of bureaucratic procedures in administrations and adjustment of these procedures to the needs of "customers" (Brunnengraeber et al. 2006, 3). Administrative capacity is closely linked with institutional capability and transaction costs in the access phase.

Institutional capability is a major condition needed for an effective ABS regime, and it can be a weak point, especially in developing countries. The case study on the Philippines shows that administrative complexity has a major impact on the access process and user transaction costs. Competent, multifunctional institutions are required to design and allocate rights, to manage conservation areas, to coordinate activities, to negotiate ABS contracts, to monitor compliance, and to sanction misappropriation related to the use of genetic resources. Many developing countries lack such institutions. Adequate funding is needed to establish and maintain them. For many countries the establishment of an ABS regime is a challenge, and one associated with high costs and transaction costs arising, for instance, from additional needs for consultation, work, extra staff, and creation of institutions (Liebig et al. 2002, 72). Implementation of the CBD, which affects many different areas, calls for legal and technical capacity. The concern of provider countries that they may not be able to cope with the complexity of the ABS issue, and their fear of being exploited, may also result in an overregulation of ABS (Richerzhagen and Virchow 2007, 76). Developing countries often develop and implement very strict laws whose scope is often beyond their actual needs. Many companies regard ABS legislation in some countries as unclear, bureaucratic, time-consuming, and expensive to comply with and have plans to relocate their research activities (ten Kate and A Laird 1999, 7). At the policy level, this problem has already been addressed. For example, the Bonn Guidelines (2001) were adopted by the members of the CBD as an instrument to guide both providers and users through the ABS process. The guidelines stress the importance of national focal points in informing applicants about specific ABS procedures (Bonn Guidelines 2001, IIA/13).

Market Structure

Market structure mainly affects benefit-sharing, and in particular negotiations on benefits, because bargaining power is not equally distributed between users and providers. Benefit-sharing can be fair and equitable only if the negotiations are conducted by equal partners.

One characteristic of the bioprospecting market is its diverse structure. The market is dominated by a small number of large buyers and the competition in it can thus be described as oligopsonistic. In the past years mergers between agro-chemical, agro-seed, and pharmaceutical firms have created large, global life science companies and strengthened their position in the market (Braga 1996, 360). Some examples are listed in Table 4.1.

Apart from these companies, there are also a large number of small biotech firms in the market, although their influence appears to be limited. There is a growing tendency for large, established pharmaceutical, agricultural, and other life science companies to cooperate with smaller, start-up biotechnology research companies. This arrangement permits large

Table 4.1 Mergers in the Pharmaceutical Sector

Rank	Company	2002 prescription sales (US$ billion)	Merged entities (sample)
1	Pfizer	41.2	Warner-Lambert, Pharmacia, Parke-Davis, Searle, Upjohn
2	GlaxoSmithKline	28.9	Burroughs Wellcome, Smith, Kline, French, Beckman, Norcliff Thayer, Beecham, Sterling
3	Merck	20.0	Merck Sharp & Dohme
4	Johnson & Johnson	28.6	Roc, MacNeil, Janssen
5	AstraZeneca	8.1	Astar, IC1/Zeneca, Stuart
6	Novartis	16.6	Sandoz, Ciba-Geigy
7	Aventis	14.3	Rhone-Poulenc, Hoechst, Connaught Labs, Merieux
8	Bristol-Myers Squibb	14.3	Mead-Johnson, DuPont Pharmaceuticals
9	Roche	12.5	Hoffman-LaRoche, Nicholas, Synex
10	Wyeth	11.7	American Home Products, Ayerst, Lederle

Source: Oligopoly Watch (2007).

companies to obtain the innovative research critical to the development of new products. They then use their financial and technological capacity to manufacture and market the products. This in turn allows biotechnology research companies to acquire additional revenues to fund expensive research efforts (Hill 1999). Due to this relationship, large life science companies continue to dominate the market for genetic resources. However, the flow of genetic resources passes through many stations. These developments enhance the bargaining position of users and point to another category of problems: it is essential, though often difficult, to keep track of the movement of genetic resources between users; indeed, there is no other way to ensure that benefits are shared fairly and equitably.

Due to evolutionary migration in many regions, genetic resources tend to be very similar in neighboring countries and widely distributed in geographic terms. Companies always have the option to threaten to move their research activities to another country. In addition, companies often have better negotiating skills and legal support in ABS negotiations than provider countries. This results in an unbalanced bargaining process.

The position of provider countries is often weakened by the argument that the importance of natural product research and development in traditional user sectors like pharmaceuticals and biotechnology has recently shown signs of decline. However, in other sectors, including horticulture and botanical medicine, research and development continue to generate significant demand for genetic resources (European Community [EC] 2002, 34).

The study on users of genetic resources in Germany, by Holm-Mueller, Richerzhagen, and Taeuber (2005), shows that genetic resources are still of great importance today—and will continue to be in the future. A majority of respondent users do not consider activities in the field of genetic resources as the most important field in which their company or institution is active. German companies and institutions indicate that it has become more difficult for German users to gain access to genetic resources since the CBD entered into force. In particular, users based with ex situ collections, universities, and other research institutions and users working in the horticultural sector belong to this group. However, the majority of the users report an increased or constant use of genetic resources in the last five years and since the CBD entered into force. According to the results of the study, genetic resources will continue to play an important role in the future. The majority of users responded that their use of genetic resources is likely to expand in the future, or at least to continue at a constant level.

Wynberg and Laird (2005, 9–10) come to a similar conclusion. In the 1990s the potential of natural products was overshadowed by other chemical approaches (e.g., combinatorial chemistry) and the introduction of high-throughput screening using synthetic libraries. In addition, advances in molecular biology, cellular biology, and genomics, along with a declining emphasis among pharmaceutical companies on infectious disease therapy, worked in favor of a downturn in natural products research. The trend is now reversing due to new technologies and the failure of these other approaches to deliver the success they seemed to promise.

The existence of ex situ collections is also an important aspect of benefit-sharing (Mulholland and Wilman 2003, 419). Many users acquire research material from gene banks and other collections and not through their own collecting activities in countries of origin. If material has been stored for a long time, it can often be very difficult to determine the country of origin and the appropriate recipient of shared benefits. Even though most material from ex situ collections is only accessible on the basis of MTA, which make it possible to track the transfer of material and to define terms for benefit-sharing, weak progress in the implementation of ABS regulations still makes it possible to access some material without any commitment to share the benefits. Genetic material acquired before the CBD came into effect is excluded from ABS regulations. However, national governments can seek to close this gap by adopting appropriate regulations.

MEASURES ADDRESSING THE CRITICAL FACTORS IN PROVIDER AND USER COUNTRIES

Having defined and analyzed the critical factors and assessed how they affect ABS effectiveness (conservation, access, and benefit-sharing), this book will now go on to identify and analyze measures that are designed to address the critical factors and that may be seen as potential solutions. Provider and user countries can establish measures and make use of certain instruments to address the critical factors within their territory or beyond it. The international discussions on provider and user measures indicate that analysis of measures also distinguishes between these two categories. In most cases responsibility for the implementation of the measures rests with either the provider countries or the user countries. However, some of the measures require efforts by both providers and users. The critical factors have been identified in earlier in the chapter. These are property rights, information asymmetries, time lags, good governance, administrative complexity, and market structure.

Provider Countries

Provider countries can initiate measures to address problems indicated by the critical factors. Assignment of property rights, development of compensation schemes that give consideration to the time lags between the discovery of material and the development of a product, efforts to strengthen capacities and institutions, screening of users based on contracts, efforts to build trust and reputation, and the formation of coalitions have the potential to alleviate some such problems. Use of these instruments will not lead to a "one problem/one instrument" solution, nor are the instruments discussed here exhaustive in nature. However, there is evidence that such measures may be regarded as the most feasible and effective instruments. It is important to bear in mind that only a mix of these instruments can prove effective and provide support for an ABS regime. Both the selection and the intensity of measures should always depend on the specific configuration of the critical factors and be adapted to the specific situation in the respective country.

Assigning Property Rights to Resource Holders

Property rights have been characterized as the strongest critical factor. The possibility to apply for patents creates a strong (intellectual) property right at the end of the production chain and an effective instrument to ensure the accumulation of profits. The benefits arising out of the use of genetic material should be shared with providers with a view to establishing incentives. However, in order to implement the ABS concept, resource holders need to be legally entitled to compensation for their conservation activities as well as for their efforts to stop destructive activities, e.g., deforestation. The CBD assigns sovereignty rights over genetic resources to countries and leaves it to national governments to set incentives based on national property rights systems. To fulfill the concept's objective, governments of provider countries are required to assign property rights to land and resource holders that allow them to participate in benefit-sharing arrangements. As the theory suggests, the respective government should be able to participate in or monitor negotiations and the benefit-sharing process to ensure that ABS contributes to conservation. In cases in which material is obtained on state property, the government should be involved in the negotiations and figure as the beneficiary.

If the national property rights system does not assign property rights to resource holders, a national trust fund of the kind proposed by Moran (2000, 143) may prove to be an appropriate instrument. Trust funds of this kind should acknowledge the sovereign rights of provider countries, but this should not be allowed to undermine the independence of a trust fund. The proposal for a trust fund is presented and discussed in the following section.

Some countries have not established private ownership concepts regarding, for example, land or biological resources. If these countries do not intend to alter their property system, and biological resources remain in the public domain or are vested with the state, the national ABS regime needs to ensure that incentives are still set.

Compensation Schemes and Funds

Looking at the matter in terms of incentive, one very important consideration is the time frame in which benefits are shared and compensation is paid. The time lags between the collection of samples and the development of a marketable product therefore represent another critical factor, one that adequate compensation schemes or funds can address. Research and development as well as product approval and patenting processes are very time-consuming. If benefit-sharing takes place fifteen years after collection, no immediate conservation incentives will be set. Only if compensation is paid at the time when resources are being managed and conserved will the desired effect be reached. Adequate compensation mechanisms, in the form of appropriate compensation schemes and funds, need to be developed and applied in ABS contracts, because they help to overcome the actual time lags. A biodiversity tax has also been proposed as an instrument that can provide additional funds to overcome the financial gap.

As far as monetary compensation is concerned, there are different forms of possible compensation. Mulholland and Wilman (2003) distinguish between three forms: an advance payment (up-front payment), a price per sample (sample fee), and a royalty rate based on a successful outcome. In their paper they come to the conclusion that royalty payments do not represent an adequate payoff for risk-averse host countries, one that serves to set incentives for the optimal provision of biodiversity and related information.

In practice, all three forms of monetary benefits are widely used and identified in the provider country case studies, although nonmonetary forms of compensation also play an important role here. Sample fees are based on market activities and only cover supply costs, including, for example, field collection, documentation, packaging, processing, and shipping. Usually these fees will be in line with the price that is asked by collections for providing material. Up-front payments represent an impediment to users because they are a risky investment. Users are expected to make a prior concession, even though they cannot be sure that the sample they receive will lead to a marketable product or patent. Some up-front payments are used to cover operational costs. Others involve a trade-off in terms of lower royalty rates, although they do involve some up-front benefits for provider countries. For users this form of payment has the lowest priority. Royalties are closely linked to outcomes. The percentage of royalties (in most cases related to the gross profit anticipated for a particular product) can be fixed in the initial ABS contract or be made subject to negotiations to be conducted once the research and development process has progressed. The level of royalties may be influenced by various factors, including, for example, information provided with the samples, the novelty or rarity of the species concerned, and the relationship between final product and collected material (ten Kate and A Laird 1999, 66). There is one additional form of payment, so-called milestone payments keyed to the stages of the research and development process. For example, they may fall due if the user identifies an active compound or applies for a patent based on the use of the material collected.

Whereas nonmonetary benefits may be greater in terms of diversity, they require a higher level of cooperation between users and providers, one that goes beyond a pure exchange of genetic resources for monetary compensation. From a development policy perspective, such benefits are very useful because they have great capacity-building potential. They include joint publications, training and joint research, and technology and knowledge transfer. Up-front payments and nonmonetary benefits transferred shortly after the conclusion of an ABS contract may serve to bridge the gap opened up by time lags. Milestone payments and royalties as a rule come too late to set an incentive for conservation. Nonmonetary benefits also provide benefits that can set certain conservation incentives. Providers need to consider their importance during the negotiations. However, they cannot provide sufficient benefits on their own.

The case studies and the existing literature show that it is difficult to estimate the actual level of benefit-sharing. Most of the details of ABS contracts and partnerships—especially compensation levels—are confidential. Some published contracts and user data indicate that monetary benefits include sample fees, up-front payments, and milestones and royalties, which usually range from 1 to 5 percent on net sales.

However, thus far benefits have been paid only in a few cases where genetic resources have been used for commercial purposes. It has been estimated that even if only a 2 percent royalty were charged on all genetic resources used for research and development in the agricultural and medical plants sector, the users of genetic resources would owe more than US$300 million in unpaid royalties for crop seeds from farmers, and more than US$5 billion in unpaid royalties for medical plants (Anuradha 2001, 32).

Biodiversity Trust Fund

Besides the direct compensation payments agreed on by users and providers, establishing a fund can contribute to realizing a benefit-sharing system. The fund solution was long ignored in the international CBD negotiations. More recently, with a view to the international regime, this idea has been brought up again and the establishment of a trust fund designed to regulate transboundary situations is now under consideration. However, no practical proposals are available on how best to implement such a mechanism. A biodiversity trust fund can address the problem of time lags, because it can accommodate the long-term time frame of bioprospecting projects and the time lag between collection of material and development of a product. Furthermore, a fund would also address problems arising from information deficiencies. Embedded in national and international law, a trust fund can be used to manage and allocate benefits arising out of the use of genetic resources. Transparently governed by a board of stakeholder representatives, including governmental and NGOs, scientists, industry, and communities, a fund of this kind can be a successful instrument in establishing trust among the partners involved. This would call for an initial payment by a group of users or even all users using genetic resources. The payment may be interpreted as compensation for all material that has until now been used for free. Once a trust fund is established, users who have concluded ABS agreements with providers can transfer monetary benefits on the agreed date: up-front payments in the beginning, milestone payments and royalties later on.

A trust fund can even address the property rights problem and offset the lack of a set of national regulations on the distribution of benefits to resource holders. Thus far the distribution of benefits has depended on national legislation, local governments, and a country's property rights system. These regulations do not always ensure that incentives are set (Barrett and Lybbert 2000, 295). By channeling benefits in a controlled and consistent matter agreed on by the governing board, independent government decisions, a trust fund can alleviate the problem arising from user information deficiencies. A trust fund can ensure that benefits are distributed to the areas from which the material was collected and to those who have contributed to its conservation and provision. If private or public donors are willing to contribute initial payments to create a start-up fund, this will make it possible to directly compensate resource holders for their conservation activities. Royalties and milestone payments can flow into the fund at a later date, compensating other resource holders. Initial payments would only be necessary for the first generation of ABS agreements. Later on, payments that fall due in connection with the commercialization of genetic resources can be used to compensate current resource holders and providers. The fund may have the function of an intergenerational contract. A trust fund would serve to suspend the direct relationship between provider and user. It can be established at the regional, national, or international level, but it needs to be applied at the same level at which the ABS regulation takes effect. In the case of regional ABS laws, this should be at the regional level, in the case of national ABS laws, it should be at the national level. From an efficiency perspective, a regional or international fund would be the better choice.

The trust fund could also be integrated into an international multilateral system such as the ITPGRFA. The ITPGRFA establishes a separate regulatory framework for genetic resources based on their specific characteristics, especially the need to identify the country of origin and the need for unrestricted access to a wide genetic base for future crop improvements. The treaty is a legally binding instrument, one that aims for the same objectives as the CBD (ITPGRFA 2001, Article 1.1). It recognizes the sovereign rights of states over their own genetic resources and the rights of national governments to decide on access to those resources resting with national governments (ITPGRFA 2001, Article 10.1). However, the ITPGRFA establishes a system that differs from that defined by the CBD, and it is by far more detailed and concrete than the CBD.

The treaty's key component is the multilateral system of ABS, which includes all plant genetic resources for food and agriculture listed in the treaty annex. Genetic resources held in the ex situ collections are also included. The list comprises thirty-five crops, including most major food crops (e.g., cereals and grain legumes), and some eighty forages. The selection of crops is based on criteria bound up with food security and interdependence. However, a number of crops that might be covered by the criteria are not included, among them soybeans and sugarcane. The list reflects the specific interests of the negotiating parties (Moore and Tymowski 2005, 15).

Whereas in the framework of the multilateral system parties to the international treaty give up their individual sovereign rights to negotiate ABS terms under MAT and PIC, the exchange of genetic resources is based on standard terms. Access should be provided to legal and natural persons under the jurisdiction of any contracting party and solely for the purpose of utilization and conservation for research, breeding, and training for food and agriculture, provided that this purpose does not include chemical, pharmaceutical, and/or other nonfood/feed industrial uses (ITPGRFA 2001, Article 12.3). In these cases the bilateral system of the CBD is applied. Access to genetic resources is provided in accordance with national ABS legislation, or, in the absence of such legislation, in accordance with such standards set by the treaty's Governing Body (ITPGRFA 2001, Article 12.3). The last point is quite interesting because the CBD provides no solution for cases in which countries have not implemented any ABS regulations, whereas the ITPGRFA regulates cases of legal insecurity. The Governing Body is composed of all contracting parties, and its responsibilities range from advancing the implementation of the treaty to administering its budget and establishing cooperation and maintaining exchange with other relevant organizations.

Access is formalized through standard material transfer agreements (SMTA) containing the main provisions on ABS in the treaty. The SMTA conditions continue to hold even when the material has been transferred (ITPGRFA 2001, Article 12.4). Aside from the sharing of nonmonetary benefits (e.g., exchange of information, access to and transfer of technology, capacity-building, benefits from commercialization), benefits from commercialization are shared by being deposited in a trust account managed by the Governing Body. Under the SMTA, the recipient has the possibility to choose between two types of payment. The first is based on a broad definition of products and requires benefit-sharing payments of 1.1 percent of sales of all products from genetic resources that incorporate material obtained from the multilateral system and to which access is restricted by IPRs. Alternatively, recipients can choose to make payments of 0.5 percent on all commercial products of a certain Annex I crop, regardless of whether access to these is restricted and whether they incorporate material from the multilateral system. This latter option enables the multilateral system to generate income right away, because it applies to products that are already in the market, whereas the first option applies only to new products that will not be ready for commercialization for another seven to fifteen years. In addition, the parties reached agreement on a funding strategy, on the rules of procedure, and on compliance. Decision was also reached on the establishment of a compliance committee that operates with provisional compliance procedures and mechanisms (International Centre for Trade and Sustainable Development 2006; Earth Negotiations Bulletin 2006, 12).

Biodiversity Tax

A biodiversity tax of the kind proposed by Parry (2004) would be another possible compensation mechanism. It would be independent of compensation schemes established in bilateral ABS agreements. This approach abandons the task of seeking to trace all the uses of genetic material to identify benefits and beneficiary. Instead, users of genetic resources would be required to pay 3 to 5 percent of their profit ratio on all products sold in the market and based on collected natural material. A global, voluntary agreement could provide the legal framework. A smaller tax should be paid for products derived from knowledge and gene databases. A global institution like the GEF is seen as an adequate management authority to channel incoming payments to conservation projects. This would detach benefit-sharing from access agreements. However, the question that remains is how to monitor the actual use of genetic resources.

Institutional Capacity-Building

Both administrative complexity and political and legal insecurity are critical factors with relevance for transaction costs. If transaction costs are too high, users will refrain from applying for access. The creation and the strengthening of institutional infrastructure must therefore be seen as an important instrument to decrease transaction costs and facilitate access.

Any ABS regime will rely on institutional infrastructure and capacity. It is impossible to create or maintain a regime if the implementing institutions needed are missing, or if they are too weak or overburdened. An institution responsible for ABS-related issues in a country needs sufficient time and capacity for efficient implementation. Government departments will most likely already be operating at full capacity. Institutions responsible for negotiations, collection and provision, conclusion of the contracts, etc., need to have the ability to multitask. According to the Costa Rica case study, it must be seen as an advantage if the ABS institution in a provider country is detached from government bureaucracy and procedure and has a dedicated interest in ABS activities. A research institution dealing with biodiversity is a good option here. It will already be in possession of expertise and resources. An efficient focal point of this kind can attract more users and strengthen a country's bargaining position.

Coalitions

The unequal bargaining power of providers and users has been identified as a critical factor for fair and equitable benefit-sharing. For many years the idea of a biodiversity cartel has been proposed as a means of countering this imbalance (Vogel 2000). Cartels are usually a combination of independent (business) organizations formed to regulate production, pricing, and marketing of goods by members as well as to limit competition. In general, cartels are economically unstable due to the incentive members have to cheat and sell more or to sell at a lower price than agreed. Each member has to agree to produce a certain amount to control the price. Once the price has risen, it becomes tempting for each member to offer secret discounts in order to secure some of the profits that normally go to other members. For this reason, members usually monitor each other and transparency is needed. There is no way to ensure this if the goods and prices concerned vary and it is virtually impossible to compare them (Baumol and Blinder 1994, 294).

What shape might be given to an oligopoly over natural resources and the TK related to them? The idea is that a cartel of all biodiversity-rich states would agree on a price (fixed royalty rate) and not on output, as in the case of other cartels, including, for example, the Organization of the Petroleum Exporting Countries (OPEC). The benefits received from ABS contracts would then be shared among all countries that theoretically are able to provide the same resource. However, the question remains whether an international cartel can effectively contribute to the realization of the CBD's objectives.

Looking at the biodiversity market, we find that one group of countries has already initiated a coalition: the Megadiverse Group. This coalition could be developed into a cartel. In 2002, seventeen countries rich in biological diversity and associated TK formed a group known as the Like-Minded Megadiverse Countries (LMMC). These countries are Bolivia, Brazil, China, Colombia, Costa Rica, Democratic Republic of Congo, Ecuador, India, Indonesia, Kenya, Madagascar, Malaysia, Mexico, Peru, Philippines, South Africa, and Venezuela. The group was formed as a mechanism for consultation and cooperation aimed at promoting common interests related to the conservation and sustainable use of biodiversity. The LMMC Group holds nearly 60 to 70 percent of all biodiversity, that is to say, the member countries already hold a large market share. Besides, the LMMC is widely recognized as an important negotiating bloc in the CBD and other international fora. Nevertheless, the course of international negotiations has made it evident that the group is highly diverse and not in agreement, especially regarding its objectives and approaches. At present it is more a voice of biodiversity-rich countries, one that formulates positions and raises concerns, than a concerted economic body.

Enforcement of a cartel may entail high costs, especially if the product concerned is not homogenous, the market is not concentrated, prices are invisible, and there are only a limited number of buyers, as in the case of genetic resources. Monitoring of members' selling activities and attempts to cheat is more difficult when heterogeneous products are involved (Baumol and Blinder 1994, 294). It is impossible to set one fixed royalty rate for all genetic resources that can be sold as raw plant material, processed samples, or DNA and to monitor cartel members' trade in these resources. Due to the confidential character of many ABS contracts, prices are not transparent at present.

Market concentration and organization on the supply side, in the form of associations or like-minded groups, could serve at first to facilitate negotiations on a cartel agreement and later serve to support monitoring and control, but the supply side of genetic resources is not concentrated. Resources can be obtained from locations around the world. However, the existence of the Megadiverse Group could definitely facilitate negotiation of an agreement among members. On the other hand, concentration on the demand side works counter to disclosure of fraud. Due to its characteristics, the cartel concept is not a promising instrument for strengthening the bargaining position of provider countries.

Screening Based on Contracts

Two problems of asymmetric information exist that can be addressed on the basis of contract design. These information deficiencies present an obstacle to an efficient outcome of ABS negotiations and agreements. They have effects on access to genetic resources and benefit-sharing. First, there is private information that users have regarding expected benefits. This is a pre-contractual problem. In any case, users have an incentive to hide their information on the amount of benefits they expect in order to negotiate a lower price for genetic resources. Second, providers (and/or intermediaries) will also have private information on the quality of the material provided.

Screening of partners on the basis of specific contract design is an instrument that can be used to address the principal–agent problem. The uninformed party (principal) uses screening to set incentives to which the better-informed agent may respond by acting in keeping with the principal's interest in maximizing profit. In the case of ABS, these incentives are contracts. Screening is carried out before contracts are concluded (i.e., ex ante). Other forms of screening involve efforts to obtain additional information through third parties. However, this aspect is not considered in the present study.

We analyze two models here that apply this instrument to two cases: (i) users' private information on benefits and (ii) providers' private information on quality. Even though this section deals with provider countries and the opportunities they have to address certain problems, a user measure ([ii] providers' private information on quality) is also analyzed in this connection.

(i) Users' Private Information on Benefits

The following model, which is based on Illing (1992), is used to illustrate the problem of asymmetric information in ABS negotiations and to show how specifically designed contracts can alleviate the problem. Illing analyzes the validity of the Coase Theorem in the presence of private information about the cost function of a polluter as one kind of transaction costs. He shows that under asymmetric information distribution of property rights has a predictable impact on efficiency, with allocation distorted toward the party that holds property rights. Considering this result, Illing draws the conclusion that the predictions of the Coase Theorem do not apply in a bargaining situation under asymmetric information. In the case of ABS, the presence of private information on the benefit function of a commercial user (e.g., pharmaceutical company) needs to be considered. Illing's approach is therefore applied to the problem of information deficiencies on part of the provider regarding the benefits of users.

THE MODEL

There are two bargaining partners: Y and Z. Y stands for a provider country of genetic resources and Z represents a user of genetic resources. The land use activities of Y will influence the existing amount of areas x (in hectares), which are rich in biodiversity, in a positive or negative way, imposing an externality on Z, or her/his profit $B(x)$. By refraining from activities with a negative influence on these areas or by taking preventive actions, Y can increase x. However, this entails costs $C(x)$ for Y. It is assumed that $C(0) = 0$; $MC = C'(x) > 0$; $C''(x) > 0$; $B''(x) < 0$. Following the state sovereignty principle of the CBD, and assuming that the provider country considers genetic resources as state property, Y owns all biological resources and biodiversity within her/his country. Without any compensation, Y thus has no incentive to take steps against the loss of areas rich in biodiversity, and status quo q of biodiversity is either maintained or decreases as a result of continuing degradation. However, commitments associated with international agreements and environmental projects impose a minimum amount of conservation, so that $q > 0$.

According to economic theory, it is not efficient to conserve the status quo of biodiversity. If the conditions of the Coase Theorem (i.e., exclusive property titles are defined and transferable, no transaction costs exist, and perfect information is ensured) are met, a negotiated solution among the different users will result in a Pareto-optimal allocation of biodiversity. In this situation the provider country Y and the user Z have an incentive to bargain and trade at least temporary property rights, because both parties can improve their situation by gaining a share of the rents arising from a more efficient level of biodiversity. Whereas allocation is independent of the definition of property rights, distribution of income is not. However, in this analysis income effects are excluded for now. The Pareto-optimal allocation is achieved if both parties agree on an optimal amount of biodiversity rich areas x^*, following the condition $MB(x^*) = MC(x^*)$. Here the total surplus $[B(x) - C(x)]$ for the contracting partners reaches a maximum. In the presence of asymmetric information this result may change. As soon as one party has private information about her/his benefit or cost function, allocation will be distorted. For the present analysis it will be assumed that the benefit function of Z for an increased amount of biodiversity-rich areas is B_L (low benefits) or B_H (high benefits), and following the first-order condition, the efficient levels of biodiversity are x_L^*; x_H^* with $x_H > x_L$. Both contracting partners are risk-neutral. The following holds for all amounts of biodiversity x: $B_L(x) < B_H(x)$; $B_L'(x) < B_H'(x)$ $\forall$ $x > 0$. Z knows her/his benefit function, whereas Y knows only the probabilities that high and low benefits will be realized p_L; p_H where $p_L + p_H = 1$.

ASYMMETRIC INFORMATION AND SCREENING

A bargaining game between the two parties is analyzed in what follows. Y owns the property rights to biodiversity. The status quo is $q > 0$. In the first stage, Y makes an offer. Z can accept or reject it. Then the game ends.

Not perfectly informed about the true benefits of Z, Y has to choose another strategy. If Y offers only a contract with a compensation payment equal to the average expected total benefits, only Z with B_H will accept the offer. In this case it would be optimal for Y to offer two contracts $Ri = [\hat{x}i; T(\hat{x}i)]$: one for a low-benefit user (B_L) and one for a high-benefit user (B_H). Depending on each contract, a specific level of biodiversity-rich areas x with corresponding compensation payments $T(x)$ will be realized. $R_L = [x_L^*, T(x_L^*) = (B_L^*)]$ and $R_H = [x_H^*, T(x_H^*) = (B_H^*)]$ with efficient outcomes are x_L^* and x_H^*. If Y offers these contracts, Z, as a high-benefit user, has an incentive to underestimate her/his own benefit and her/his willingness to pay in order to keep the price down and reap a profit (BCD): $B_H(x_L^*) - B_L(x_L^*)$. If Y wants to avoid this situation, she/he must design the contracts in such a way as to ensure that a low-benefit user and a high-benefit user will each choose the contract designed for her/his specific type.

The optimization problem of Y is to maximize the payments she/he may receive, minus accruing conservation costs.

(1) $\max_{x_i, T(x_i)} p_L T(x_L) + p_H T(x_H) - p_L C(x_L) - p_H C(x_H)$

It is assumed that maximization of a provider country's profits will lead to a higher protection level for biodiversity.

I. Participation constraint

(2l) $B_L(x_L) \geq T(x_L)$

(2h) $B_H(x_H) \geq T(x_H)$

The conditions (2) ensure participation (individual rationality). It must be more attractive for both types of company (B_H, B_L) to accept the contract than to reject in favor of the status quo. However, a high-benefit company can always claim to be a low-benefit company to obtain an extra benefit: $B_H(x_L) > B_L(x_L) > T(x_L)$. Hence only condition (2l) is plausible and consequently binding: $B_L(x_L) = T(x_L)$.

II. Incentive compatibility

(3l) $B_L(x_L) - T(x_L) \geq B_L(x_H) - T(x_H)$

(3h) $B_H(x_H) - T(x_H) \geq B_H(x_L) - T(x_L)$

The conditions (3) ensure incentive compatibility. A low-benefit user will never claim to be a high-benefit user in that this would reduce her/his total benefits—after paying T(xi). Hence only condition (3h) is plausible and consequently binding $B_H(x_H) - T(x_H) = B_H(x_L) - T(x_L)$. The optimization problem with constraints can then be transformed into the following unconstrained maximization problem.

(4) $\max_{x_p, x_b} p_L[B(x_L) - C(x_L)] + p_H[B(x_H) - C(x_H)] - p_H[B_H(x_L) - B_L(x_L)]$

Under asymmetric information, Y's optimization problem has changed. Y is no longer interested in maximizing the payments she/he may receive—minus accruing conservation costs. Rather, Y needs to pay heed to the costs required to ensure that a high-benefit user (B_H) does not claim to be a low-benefit user (B_L). By forgoing a payment $B_H(x_L) - B_L(x_L)$, Y gives Z, a high-benefit user, an incentive not to claim to be a low-benefit company. The probability that these payments will have to be made is p_H.

The first order conditions are:

(5l) $p_L \left[\dfrac{\partial B}{\partial x_L} - \dfrac{\partial C}{\partial x_L} \right] = p_H \left[\dfrac{\partial B_H}{\partial x_L} - \dfrac{\partial B_L}{\partial x_L} \right]$

(5h) $\dfrac{\partial B}{\partial x_H} = \dfrac{\partial C}{\partial x_H}$

It is assumed that $\hat{x}_L$ is the solution of equation (5l). If Z can realize high benefits, the efficient outcome will be $x_H = x_H^*$ even in the presence of asymmetric information. Y cannot acquire the first expected surplus because she/he needs to give consideration to the information rent $B_H(x_L) - B_L(x_L)$ (BCD). Hence $T(\hat{x}_H) = T(x_H{}^*) - B_H(x_L) - B_L(x_L)$. This is only a redistribution in favor of the informed party Z.

If Z is a low-benefit user, allocation will be distorted. To simplify matters, it is assumed that $p_L = p_H = 0.5$. Y still can acquire a surplus (ABFG), but the amount of biodiversity offered is inefficiently low because $\hat{x}_L < x_L{}^*$. According to (51) and the constraints of the benefit function, $p_H \left[\frac{\partial B_H}{\partial x_L} - \frac{\partial B_L}{\partial x_L} \right]$ is positive, as is $p_L \left[\frac{\partial B}{\partial x_L} - \frac{\partial C}{\partial x_L} \right]$. This can only be the case if $\hat{x}_L$ is smaller than efficient outcome $x_L{}^*$ and MB > MC. Y will take a loss of surplus only if she/he is not worse off in this case. Y will deviate from the contract if her/his expected marginal loss of surplus (FG) is equal to the expected marginal savings of payments (EF) it had previously forgone. CDEF stands for savings and CFG represents loss of surplus of Y.

Thus, in the presence of private information payment of an information rent to a high-benefit user does not result in a Pareto-optimal contractual offer to a low-benefit user, whereas the information rent prevents a high-benefit user from claiming to be a low-benefit user.

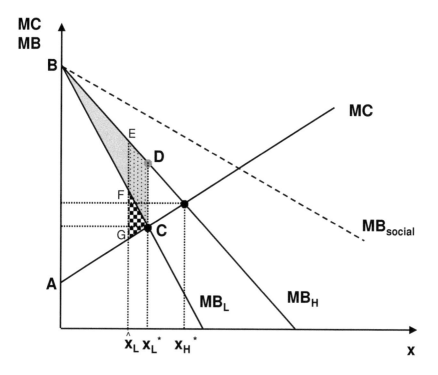

Figure 4.6 The Coase Theorem under asymmetric information.
Source: adopted from Illing (1992).

The Coase Theorem is only valid if certain information structures are present. If a provider country is not completely informed about a user's expected benefits, the result will not be consistent with the predictions of the Coase Theorem. First, if the partner is a high-benefit user, the outcome will be Pareto-optimal, but the distribution of benefits will have changed compared to a bargaining situation in the presence of complete information. The provider country does not receive the whole surplus and the high-benefit user receives an incentive payment. Provider countries are not able to solve the problem of asymmetric information, but they can alleviate it. They can offer different contracts for different types of company and in this way screen users. By giving consideration to the participation constraint and incentive compatibility, providers can maximize their revenues. This maximization has a positive impact on the conservation of biodiversity. Thus, in the presence of asymmetric information screening applicants on the basis of a specific contract design can improve the situation. Second, if the partner is a low-benefit user, the outcome will not be Pareto-optimal, as already shown in the model. Even though the provider may obtain the whole surplus, the amount of biodiversity protected is too low and the allocation of the resource is not efficient. In both cases the provider's benefits are smaller than they would be in the presence of complete information, because the benefits are distributed in favor of the informed party and because the resources are misallocated.

Providers' Private Information on Quality

Mulholland and Wilman (2003) analyze information deficiencies on the user side. In their view, providers have private information on their inputs into companies' drug-discovery processes because they control access both to the resources and to information on the quality of the material. In this case the authors suggest that companies need to design contracts that provide incentives for the host countries to deliver an amount of bioprospecting output that maximizes their own output. In the model it is assumed that provider country agents are typically poor and risk-averse developing countries and that users are risk-neutral principals. Compared to the case analyzed in the previous chapter, risk aversion plays an important role here. If both principal and agent are risk-neutral, the principal will design the contract in such a way as to shift the risk to the agent. If the agent is risk-averse, the two parties will have to share the risk.

Host countries will only sign a contract that provides them with enough expected utility to overcome their reservation utility. Their expected utility will depend on the payoff they expect to receive and the utility that they expect to obtain as a function of these payoffs. To convince a host country to sign a contract, the principal must offer adequate payoffs. For the principal there is a trade-off between providing the agent with full insurance and full incentive compatibility (Varian 1992, 441ff.).

In the Mulholland and Wilman model, users request biodiversity resources and access to information. The production process is assumed to be random due to the unpredictable outcome of research and development. They regard time lags between collection and outcome and ABS contracts as an instrument that provides insurance. They model the contract on a principal–agent relationship. In their model the provider country controls both access to the resources and related information on their potential. Bioprospecting output Q is a function of stock of biodiversity Z and the stock of information related to pharmaceutical potential G. Biodiversity stock Z depends on the conservation measures undertaken by host country I to prevent destruction or degradation of biodiversity, which occurs at the rate δ.

$$Z = I - \delta Z$$

Information stock G depends on the agent's efforts during the collection and processing procedure (e.g., screening and identification), which are e. The degradation rate of the information stock is ε.

$$G = e - \varepsilon G$$

The function for bioprospecting revenue is R (G, Z) = πQ (G, Z). π is the competitive price.[3] Because it is necessary to consider a random variable ω that is not influenced by the principal or agent but that is a state of nature, the bioprospecting revenue is W (ω, G, Z) = ωR (G, Z). As already mentioned, the production of W, which is carried out by the agent, cannot be fully observed by the principal. The agent therefore has an incentive to provide less e, G, I, and Z.

The pharmaceutical company, as a risk-neutral principal, aims to design a contract that induces providers to produce an amount of resources and information that maximizes her/his output. The contract therefore needs to fulfill the incentive compatibility to induce the provider, as an agent, to behave in the desired way. The participation constraint guarantees that the agent will be not worse off than she/he would be if she/he had chosen another option. Sample fees, advance payments, and the royalty rate are considered potential payoffs. The principal can choose the level of any of these payments. However, empirical data show that in the classic case (i.e., provider country negotiates with user) contracts are usually the result of a bargaining process between users and providers and that provider countries can influence it. Nevertheless, it has to be kept in mind that today more and more intermediaries are entering the market. This reduces the frequency of occurrence of the classic situation because host countries are not necessarily involved in the negotiations and transfers. In the model royalty rate α is chosen by the principal and paid to the agent from profits from any products developed. It is based on an observed successful outcome, but price Pe and advance payment Φ (G, Z)[4] depend on variables G, e, Z, and I, which are not perfectly observable.

The authors come to the conclusion that if the principal uses royalties in the payment schedule for a risk-averse agent, the marginal benefits will be reduced, and the result will be lower levels of I, e, G, and Z. With regard to the participation constraint, the agent's risk aversion reduces the payment share of the royalty rate. It is for this reason more costly for the principal to meet the participation constraint than it would be by other means. Sample fees and advance payment acknowledge the agent's risk. One suggestion here is to earmark advance payments for investments in G and Z. What this means is that host countries will use their compensation payments for conservation measures or for training and technology development. These conclusions are also highly relevant for the compensation schemes discussed in an earlier section of this chapter. Empirical evidence shows that users chiefly prefer to compensate providers in the form of royalties. But only if the agent is risk-neutral can royalty payments provide incentives for the optimal level of G, Z, e, and I. These insights need to be considered, especially in the design of model contracts.

Reputation-Building

In the access phase transaction costs are high due to information deficiencies. Providers have private information on the allocation of benefits received as well as on the way in which the material provided is handled, and especially as regards the exclusivity of material provided. The case study on Costa Rica indicates that the ways in which provider countries deal with such private information is important for their attractiveness. They can in this way signal that they are reliable partners despite their informational advantage.

Reputation-building is quite a strong form of signaling and can alleviate the problems arising from uncertainty and information deficiencies on both sides, on the part of the providers and the users. However, this section considers only signaling on the provider side. The section in this chapter on user measures deals with the user perspective.

According to Spence, "Market signals are activities or attributes of individuals in a market which, by design or accident, alter the beliefs of, or convey information to, other individuals in the market" (Spence 1974, 1). A characteristic signal is one that is observable and can be influenced by the individual through his behavior and action. Provider countries that have implemented ABS regulations and regard themselves as reliable partners that deserve the trust of users can signal this in different ways. They can participate in international meetings, workshops, projects, etc., publishing and explaining their ABS regulations and offering their support. Their long-term experience and reliable cooperation cast these provider countries in the role of very attractive collection sites. Users and providers are more likely to conclude or renew contracts with known partners than they are to look for new, unknown providers. Long-term partnerships are a specific investment, one that serves to reduce information gaps and transaction costs.

Recipient Countries

Since the adoption of the CBD, implementation has focused more on the establishment of ABS regulations in biodiversity-rich provider countries, addressing the behavior of agents in the provider countries. The measures described previously are examples of such provider measures. This situation has led to an imbalance regarding the efforts of provider and user countries to achieve the convention's objectives. By establishing the ABS concept and its requirements for PIC and MAT, the CBD determines user behavior in provider countries. However, users also have a responsibility to contribute to implementing the convention, especially when it comes to the third objective, fair and equitable benefit-sharing.

Some steps have been taken at the political level to integrate users into the process and assign more responsibility to them. The—voluntary—Bonn Guidelines concretize the idea of an international ABS regime and address both provider and user countries by proposing certain measures that should be implemented to reach the fundamental objectives of the CBD. These measures serve as a basis for the following evaluation. In addition, the WSSD action plan calls on governments to create an international regime in which users play a more important role.

The following sections analyze user measures with a view to their potential to address the critical factors and influence ABS effectiveness. They furthermore look into whether the instruments proposed are feasible and practicable with a view to implementation.

Documentation of the Flow of Genetic Resources: Certificates of Compliance[5]

Inappropriate assignment of IPRs (i.e., biopiracy) poses a problem for ABS governance. If genetic material is acquired outside of any ABS agreement, no benefits will be shared and no conservation incentives will be established. Many relevant cases have been reported. To avoid any misappropriation of genetic material, the ABS process needs to be monitored. It can be observed at different stages: the access phase (i.e., in the field or in ex situ collections), the import of genetic resources, the research and development phase, application for IPRs, and final product approval. Apart from the access phase, these activities usually take place in user countries and depend on the willingness of user countries to monitor the behavior and activities of users active there.

A traceability system for genetic resources can be used to monitor the appropriate use of the material. Certificates of compliance are seen as an instrument of traceability systems of this kind. Irrespective of their form, certificates of compliance can be used to monitor trade and the movement of resources at different checkpoints and discourage the unapproved and illegal use of genetic resources.

The certificate concept was originally developed for the use of patent application procedures to ensure compliance with the CBD and its ABS obligations (Tobin 1994). The original idea was that patent offices should require disclosure of the origin of genetic resources and associated TK as a condition for accepting applications for patents. It was suggested that the establishment of a standardized certificate of origin, which would serve as evidence of PIC, would relieve patent officers of the need to examine all documentation related to an ABS agreement to verify compliance with the CBD (Barber, Johnston, and Tobin 2003, 38–39).

The certificate concept has been under consideration in international negotiations for many years now. At COP 6, COP 7, and COP 8 the parties to the CBD decided to further examine an international certificate scheme regarding the concept's feasibility, operational functionality, and cost-effectiveness (CBD 2002, 2004, 2006). Rosendal (2006, 441) even interprets the discussion on certificates as a step toward a multilateral system.

Despite several preliminary investigations and discussions at international meetings, no clear understanding has emerged of how a certificate of origin system could operate in practice, or what should be the scope or nature of such a system. At COP 8, the parties generally agreed on the need to set up a group of technical experts that could examine options for the form, intent, practicality, feasibility, and costs of an international certificate of origin, source, or legal provenance (Earth Negotiations Bulletin 2006, 5). This group met in January 2007 in Lima and adopted some recommendations that have helped to move forward the development of a certificate system (International Centre for Trade and Sustainable Development 2007). The group formulated the following objectives for a certificate system: legal certainty, transparency, predictability, benefit-sharing facilitation, facilitation of legal access with minimal transaction costs and delay, technology transfer, prevention of misappropriation, minimization of bureaucracy, support for compliance with national law and MAT, enabling and facilitation of cooperation in the monitoring and enforcement of access and benefit-sharing arrangements, facilitation of the development of national access and benefit-sharing frameworks, and protection of TK.

The range of objectives is very broad. However, it is evident that two critical factors in particular, asymmetric information and administrative complexity, will be addressed by such an instrument designed to provide for information and facilitate processes. Existing procedures for access, collection, and export of resources are highly regulated and involve a plethora of approval processes and permit procedures. A certificate system would need to decrease administrative complexity and transaction costs. This requires capacity and political will in provider countries to streamline processes and overcome existing tensions among government departments for control over access issues.

Certificates also provide distinctive advantages from an economic point of view. They can alleviate the problem arising out of information asymmetries by serving as labels. The market for genetic resources is characterized by underconsumption due to information deficiencies regarding the quality of the material demanded. The quality of genetic resources as potential inputs for commercialization consists of different elements, including origin and biological traits, but also CBD compliance based on PIC and compliance with national ABS laws. Users are unable to discern whether genetic resources provided to them include these elements. They tend to estimate a value of which they are convinced they can be sure. This value is usually underestimated.

By disclosing origin, a certificate can supply further information about the material provided to users of genetic resources, including, for example, biological and geographical information. Providing the good with such information transforms genetic resources from simple commodities into differentiated higher-value products. By increasing their value, a certificate scheme would create incentives for the provision and conservation of genetic resources.

Certificates give providers of high-quality material the opportunity to signal the quality of the good to the user. By preventing adverse selection, this serves to reduce demand for low-quality genetic resources as well as to lower the output of such resources. In this case less material will be supplied that was not obtained in compliance with the CBD. On the one hand, it seems unnecessary to establish a market mechanism that aims to achieve a goal that should be already enforced by law. On the other hand, there is still a lot of material in the market that does not meet the CBD criteria. Many countries have not yet implemented the CBD's ABS provisions, mainly because of the existence of ex situ collections that collected material before 1992, or because there are some providers who offer illegally obtained material in violation of international and national law.

Often provider countries lack human and technological capacities to collect and transfer the quality data. It is therefore important to use capacity-building, training, knowledge, and technology transfer as means of enabling provider countries the ability to collect and transfer data in an appropriate format. This would benefit both providers and users.

A certificate scheme would have effects on the trade in genetic resources. If certificates of compliance are adopted as instruments of a mandatory certificate scheme, the supply of genetic resources will negatively affected by higher costs. The costs depend on existing frameworks and procedures and the extent to which they are in line with the introduction of a certificate scheme. However, if a certificate scheme helps to streamline ABS procedures in a country without raising costs, certificates could even have a positive effect. Certificates would serve to boost demand because certificates can reveal the real value of resources. Besides, during the process in which material is exchanged, they can reduce search and information costs. However, implementation and enforcement may lead to an immense increase in research and development costs.

Whether the system will be voluntary or mandatory is still an open question. The Lima Group sets out several options that range from a totally mandatory certificate system (provider must provide and users must request a certificate) to a system that leaves it to the discretion of providers and users to decide whether they want to provide or request a certificate. A mandatory system would provide the security that providers need to prevent any abuse of the material. However, the costs of implementation can be very high and need to be considered. Furthermore, the Lima Group concurs that the basic role of the certificate is to provide evidence of compliance with national access and benefit-sharing regimes. These certificates should thus be referred to as certificates of compliance with national law (CBD 2007b). In the past there were discussions over whether to use the terms "certificate of origin," "certificate of source," or "certificate of legal provenance" (compliance), depending what was expected of a certificate.

The CBD Secretariat commissioned a book on the monitoring and tracking of genetic resources. The book, an information document for the negotiations, was recently published (Garrity et al. 2009). It reviews recent developments in methods to identify genetic resources based on DNA sequences as well as possible ways to track and monitor genetic resources. It formulates several relevant recommendations:

- prompt definition of the minimum information contained in the documentation (e.g., PIC, MAT, origin)
- adoption of a well-developed persistent identifier (PID) system and deployment of lightweight applications using browser applications
- need for the system to consider biological and functional diversity
- development of strong policies to avoid data abuse
- testing via prototype tracking systems

The report is quite technical and excludes any recommendations on the political background.

What shape may a certificate system have in practice? Like a passport, a certificate can accompany genetic resources from the collection to the marketing phase and provide information on the material concerned (e.g., origin, compliance). It can be monitored and verified at different stages of access and use as well as across different jurisdictions outside the providing country (Ruiz, Fernandez, and Young 2003, 5). In keeping with the existing infrastructure, it would be possible to set up different checkpoints along the innovation line with a view to decreasing the costs resulting from the establishment of a certificate system. Some potential checkpoints would include customs, patent and product approval authorities, research funding organizations, and scientific journals. At these checkpoints a certificate can provide information on the origin and evidence that genetic resources have been obtained by legitimate means. In submitting articles to journals, authors would be required to submit a certificate in addition to information on the material used, which is already required. Research funding organizations could require this information during the funding period, once collection has gotten under way. Patent and product approval authorities could require submission of the certificate as part of the application process (see the following section). A registry at the national or international level would need to be set up to record transfers of genetic material.

A certificate system should cover all users and uses of genetic resources, including scientific research, to prevent loopholes. Certificates need to be reproducible to account for transformation and splitting up of material for multiple users and uses. The scheme needs to be flexible enough to adapt to the changing nature of resources as they move through various stages of research, development, and transformation, thereby modifying the circumstances under which the certificate was originally granted. This means that a certificate must be applicable to tangible and intangible material. However, it needs to be as comprehensive as possible to ensure that it provides security for providers (Dross and Wolff 2005, 136).

In discussing certificates, it is important to keep in mind the heterogeneity of users. The public and private sectors stand to benefit by having an appropriate instrument to differentiate the quality of material provided and to gain certainty of legal title concerning genetic resources. These benefits are much higher for the private sector, which uses genetic material for commercial purposes, because the private sector would actually be able to recover the costs it incurs in connection with the implementation and enforcement of a certificate scheme. Whereas public-sector users do not make profits by using the material, their function involves them in far more international transfers.

The survey on German users of genetic resources revealed that German users have a critical stance on the introduction of a certificate system. Even though the majority of users obtain their genetic material through intermediaries, legal uncertainty is reported to be a major problem. Implementation of this instrument would thus call for specific preparations; in particular it would be necessary to inform users and initiate stakeholder consultations (Holm-Mueller, Richerzhagen, and Taeuber 2005, 71–73). The same can be observed in Japan. A study on Japanese users sheds light on the utilization and documentation procedures in place there as well as on Japanese users' attitudes towards various certificate scenarios (i.e., subject matter, type, format, checkpoints, and registry) regarding practicality, feasibility, and costs. The publication indicates that certificates of compliance are judged critically by users from both the private and the public sector. Paper and electronic formats are probably the most common form of documentation already in place for material in use. To reduce costs, they should continue to be the preferred ones. All of the proposed checkpoints are judged positively, and an international registry is seen as preferable to a national registry (Richerzhagen 2005, 24ff.). In implementing a certificate system, it is essential to take into account existing infrastructure and attitudes. Only then will such a system be effective when it comes to practicality, feasibility, and costs.

Monitoring of Intellectual Property Rights Applications[6]

Monitoring of IPRs applications is one possible instrument to trace the use of genetic resources. At first this was the main instrument under discussion to prove origin (disclosure of origin) independently of other systems. However, recent discussions on an international regime have identified it as one possible checkpoint in a certificate scheme designed to provide evidence of compliance.

Disclosure already plays an important role in patent law. Only if an invention is fully disclosed can a patent be granted. Under the TRIPs agreement, applicants for a patent are required to disclose an invention in a way sufficiently clear and complete enough for it to be carried out by a person skilled in the art. This may require the applicant to indicate the best mode for carrying out the invention known to the inventor at the filing date or, where priority is claimed, at the priority date of the application (TRIPs 1994, Article 29.1).

A study on patents using biological source material reveals that in cases where plants are widespread and well known, like, for example, oat or lemon, origin is not specified in patent applications for plant extracts, but if the object of the patent is a rare or exotic species, the applicant usually provides information on its origin (World Intellectual Property Right Organization [WIPO] 2001). However, in most cases it is up to the user to reveal the origin. Today only a few national or regional regulations on IPRs, biotechnology, or biodiversity include some form of requirement or encouragement to disclose such information. The frameworks differ widely and range from mandatory requirements for disclosure of origin and legal access to disclosure requirements that encourage disclosure, but do not involve any legal consequence in cases of noncompliance (Baummueller and Vivas-Eugui 2004, 21). However, the Bonn Guidelines recommend that CBD parties implement disclosure requirements for patents based on the use of genetic resources (CBD 2002, VI–24; Gollin 2005).

In addition to the impact it has in connection with certificates, disclosure of origin may serve to compensate for the unequal distribution of property rights. By revealing the origin of their genetic resources on IPRs applications, providers do not become holders of such rights, but they are at least cited in the IPRs and therefore have a legal basis for demanding benefit-sharing.

A disclosure requirement within the patent system could serve to improve the examination of patent applications by making it easier to determine prior art, and it could also facilitate the determination of inventorship by patent offices or courts. In some cases, including, for example, endemic biological material, a disclosure requirement permits the execution of an invention (Correa 2003, 3). In view of the fact that the need to verify IPR applications constitutes an additional burden for patent offices, it is quite evident that other control systems and checkpoints are likewise important.

The debate on disclosure requirements has grown in intensity during the continuous review of the TRIPs agreement. The CBD has invited WIPO to prepare a technical handbook on methods used by the patent system for requiring disclosures relevant to genetic resources and TK, and to this end it has collected and analyzed positions and proposals from its member states. Many countries have made proposals on approaches to creating a control instrument of this kind. A group represented by Brazil and India, including Bolivia, Colombia, Cuba, Dominican Republic, Ecuador, Peru, Thailand and supported by the African group and some other developing countries, has stated its intention to amend the TRIPs accord. They propose that patent applicants should be required to disclose the country of origin of genetic resources and TK used in inventions, PIC, and benefit-sharing agreements. Switzerland has proposed an amendment to the rules of the WIPO's Patent Cooperation Treaty (PCT) under which domestic laws would require inventors to disclose the source of genetic resources and TK when they apply for patents. Failure to meet the requirement could hold up a patent approval, or if done with fraudulent intent, could lead to invalidation of a granted patent. The EU's position includes a proposal to examine a stipulation that would require all patent applicants to disclose the source or origin of genetic material. However, the legal consequences of not meeting this requirement lies outside the scope of patent law. The US has argued that the CBD's objectives on ABS can best be achieved through national legislation and contractual arrangements based on existing legislation; these might include commitments on disclosure of any commercial applications of genetic resources or TK (WTO 2007).

The legal nature and the aligned consequences of the disclosure are controversially discussed. A disclosure requirement may have the form of a formality in the patent procedure or even of a patentability criterion. However, because many members of the CBD are also members of the WTO, the legal implications of the TRIPs agreement need to be considered. Dedeurwaerdere and colleagues (2005, 5) state that a disclosure-of-origin requirement would only be compatible with the TRIPs agreement if:

- Disclosure of origin is only a formal requirement for patent application (and not a substantive criteria for patentability), which determines the eligibility of an invention.

- The disclosure obligation would apply only if the origin is known (hence the patentee would not be required to do any further research on origin).
- It would apply where the sanctioning mechanisms are outside the patent system.

Sanctions outside the patent system for noncompliance with disclosure requirements include criminal and civil sanctions. Placing sanctions outside the patent system would make it possible to impose penalties without having to engage in paralyzing research and development activities. In some cases sanctions could require a transfer of rights to a patent to an aggrieved party, in particular an indigenous or local community whose knowledge had been appropriated. Some developing countries, like the Andean community, have developed more rigorous requirements for disclosure, with sanctions established within the patent system.

Sarnoff and Correa (2006) recommend the establishment of an international system of mandatory disclosure-of-origin requirements that would be linked to TRIPs. According to their analysis, an international disclosure system would be consistent with international intellectual property treaties, and they argue that the system would provide sufficient benefits only if it were mandatory, because national disclosure systems are limited to national jurisdiction.

Certain problems have arisen in the preliminary stage of discussion on this instrument; these are closely related to certificates of compliance. A possible multiplicity of genetic resources makes it difficult to exactly characterize the country of origin. Some genetic resources can be found in more than one country or region, or may have acquired specific distinctive and genetic characteristics not found in the country where they were collected. Often genetic resources are not provided directly by the country of origin but by ex situ collections (e.g., gene banks, microbial collections, or botanical gardens). In these cases provider country and country of origin may not be the same.

To be effective, a disclosure requirement for genetic resources is in need of definitions and standardized procedures. To make the system feasible, it is necessary to develop clear regulations and sanctions bearing on the case of noncompliance. However, because many uses of genetic resources are non-IPRs related, any system needs to consider a range of regulatory and nonregulatory procedures for monitoring the use of genetic resources in product development and commercialization.

Certification Schemes for Institutions

Economic theory suggests certification as an instrument to address information asymmetry (Fritsch, Wein, and Ewers 2003, 297). Certification is some form of screening because the principal tries to get additional information to compensate her/his information deficiency. The critical factors indicate that providers lack information on user behavior, and this results in disproportionate and complicated regulations. Certification can serve as a signaling mechanism for users by providing evidence that they comply with the principles formulated in the CBD and the Bonn Guidelines. In addition, this could improve the user's reputation and improve the confidence of provider countries in their potential partners.

Certification systems verify practices of organizations on a voluntary basis. They may be self-implemented or implemented by a second party with an interest in an organization's practices. Alternatively, the operations of a given private or public organization could be assessed, by an independent third party, against a standard set of criteria. The use of certification by an independent third party has become the norm because of the importance of certifier credibility (Kanowski, Sinclair, and Freeman 1999, 14). Important aspects involved in the implementation of a certification system include creation of an independent standard-setting body, an agreed procedure for certification assessment, issuance of a written certificate that confirms compliance with the standards, and establishment of an appeals body for certification decisions (Barber, Johnston, and Tobin 2003, 23). Voluntary certification schemes are used widely and successfully, for example, under the International Organization for Standardization (ISO). The organization's work program ranges from standards for traditional activities, such as agriculture and construction, to mechanical engineering, medical devices, or even the newest developments in information technology. Alternative specialized schemes have been implemented for timber products extracted from sustainably managed forests, fisheries, organic food, and other environmental and social sectors (Barber, Johnston, and Tobin 2003, 23).

Corporate and Institutional Policies and Codes of Conduct

Corporate and institutional policies and codes of conduct are another signaling instrument that can serve users as a means to signal their will to comply with the CBD. In the past it has been observed that some users of genetic resources develop their own ABS policies, either individually or jointly, including whole sectors (ten Kate and A Laird 1999, 309). These users may operate in the private sector (e.g., companies) or in the public sector as nonprofit research institutions (e.g., botanical gardens). Corporate and institutional policies and codes of conduct developed in the framework of the Bonn Guidelines are among the measures that may prove useful in the development and implementation of ABS arrangements.

Corporate and institutional policies and codes of conduct are voluntary measures initiated by users or their representatives (A Laird and Wynberg 2002, 39). The interventions in the activities of a research institution or a company to which such measures lead are relatively small. Once such policies or codes of conduct have been developed and successfully implemented in an institution or company, they can be disseminated, with low transaction costs, in the entire sector concerned. They can provide sufficient flexibility to respond to the circumstances of specific research sectors and users of genetic resources if they are appropriately designed and adapted. Both users and providers stand to benefit from their established use. The use of corporate policies and codes of conduct boosts user transparency and with it the confidence of provider countries in their partners. The use of codes of conduct can facilitate access to genetic resources for members and reduce the need for other compliance procedures (Barber, Johnston, and Tobin 2003, 22). Control mechanisms of this kind, which apply to the early stages of research and development, can be established at costs lower than those that take effect in later phases. Corporate policies and codes of conduct have the potential to alleviate uncertainty and decrease the transaction costs for users and providers that may arise from the asymmetric distribution of information between them. According to a study, however, only a limited number of companies implement such policies or codes of conduct (Busch and Kern 2005, 86).

National Focal Points, Clearing House Mechanisms

National focal points as well as the Clearing House Mechanism (CHM) are institutions that have implications for asymmetric information and administrative complexity, once they have been established. The Bonn Guidelines assign major importance to provision of information in the ABS process for both providers and users. National focal points and the CHM are important for the collection, provision, and dissemination of information, and they play an essential role in raising awareness in user countries.

Under the Bonn Guidelines, each party of the CBD should designate one national focal point for ABS. The national focal point should provide users with information regarding the CBD and the Bonn Guidelines as well as regarding national ABS laws and regulations in provider countries. Applicants for access to genetic resources can in this way acquire information on procedures needed for PIC and MAT (including benefit-sharing) as well as on competent national authorities and relevant stakeholders (Bonn Guidelines 2001, IIA/13).

National focal points in user countries can support the exchange of information on and experiences with ABS issues. They can establish contacts to focal points and authorities in provider countries and facilitate the establishment of contacts among users. National focal points lower the threshold of entry for first-time users and give providers access to better information about potential benefits. Another important aspect is collaboration between national focal points with a view to decreasing costs and facilitating the exchange of information. The preliminary work done by focal points in user countries can serve to relieve the competent authorities in provider countries, which are often overburdened by complex ABS issues. More transparency and facilitated access to information in the market for genetic resources can alleviate the effects of the asymmetric distribution of information, including, e.g., complicated and restricted access. Provision of information can benefit both users and providers and decrease their transaction costs. Negotiations between users and providers can be considerably improved in this way.

Alongside the country-specific CHMs, the CBD has set up a CHM of its own. The first priority of this portal is to ensure universal access to the convention's official records, but also additional information such as case studies, national reports, etc. The idea is to increase public awareness of convention programs and issues. The Internet-based system supports and facilitates greater collaboration among countries through education and training projects, research cooperation, funding opportunities, access to and transfer of technology, and dissemination of information. Links are forged among experts as a means of facilitating joint work programs. The CHM can support scientific and technical cooperation by providing an information management and exchange system, and this in turn can support technology and knowledge transfer (SCBD 2005, 222ff.).

However, the CHM may also provide a good vehicle for user registration. The registry can improve the reputation of users because registration of a full-fledged ABS policy in compliance with the CBD would be seen as evidence of a good sense of corporate social responsibility (EU Commission 2003, 4). National focal points in user countries can assume some of the tasks of focal points in provider countries and relieve their burdens. This in turn would make it possible to address problems caused by administrative complexity. Additionally, the CHM can be used to boost the effectiveness of other user measures. Corporate policies and codes of conduct can be publicized through the CHM.

Projects and Standardized Contracts

By seeking to promote cooperation between users and providers and developing standardized MTA, governments of user countries can support the development and realization of projects. Project support and standardized model contracts decrease transaction costs arising from administrative complexity and decrease information deficiencies. They may furthermore serve to consolidate the bargaining position of provider countries. Government institutions monitor these projects and can ensure that users comply with the CBD. Providers will be more confident about their partners if ABS negotiations are conducted in the framework of such a project. By participating in such projects, users stand to gain reputation and constitute a positive example. The contracts developed can be made available for other users. The Bonn Guidelines already identify high transaction costs and legal uncertainty as major problems in ABS negotiations, and they see the development of standardized MTA and benefit-sharing arrangements for similar resources and similar uses as important instruments to address these problems (Bonn Guidelines 2001, IVD/42, b iv).

One interesting approach is the initiative International Cooperative Biodiversity Groups (ICBG), which was launched in 1992 by three agencies of the US government (National Institutes of Health [NIH], National Science Foundation, and US Agency for International Development). The program supports joint bioprospecting projects carried out by public and private US institutions and provider countries (Boisvert and Vivien 2005, 466). The projects are based on a certain design that includes, from the planning stage on, the active participation of host-country individuals and organizations as well as multidisciplinary research on diseases of both local and international significance, local training and infrastructure development in drug discovery and biodiversity management, biodiversity inventory and monitoring work, and equitable intellectual property and benefit-sharing arrangements (Rosenthal 1998, 3).

Technology Transfer

Technology transfer from user countries to provider countries is seen as a major element of the benefit-sharing process, and one necessary to set incentives at the local level to conserve and sustainably use biodiversity. Technology transfer is a nonmonetary benefit-sharing instrument, and it has the potential to bridge the gap emerging from the time lags between bioprospecting activities and the development of a marketable product. If provider countries are enabled to contribute to the research and development phase of a product, this will serve to strengthen their bargaining position and market power.

Technology transfer to different sectors, e.g., agriculture, fishery, or forestry, supports not only benefit-sharing but also the other two objectives of the CBD, conservation and sustainable use of biodiversity. Only if they are in possession of the relevant technologies will countries be able to reach these objectives.

A meeting organized by UNEP and Norway on technology transfer within the CBD identified a number of problems that need to be addressed in seeking to support the CBD objectives through technology transfer:

- social and economic conditions that hinder successful technology transfer and capacity-building
- inadequacy of information on available technologies
- uncertainty with respect to terms under which technology transfer could and should be undertaken
- lack of appropriate regulatory, financial, and institutional frameworks at the local, national, regional, and international levels

- the need to develop concrete targets and improved synergies between biodiversity and development policies and obligations and needs under other conventions, and between sectors at the national level, in order to achieve improved and better-targeted technology transfer and capacity-building

Technology transfer depends on an enabling environment. What this calls for is legal and political security, responsible institutions, and property rights that have been defined and assigned (UNEP 2003, 9).

A country's concrete initial situation will call for different forms of technology transfer. Simple technologies, for example, that improve agricultural and forestry techniques may help to alleviate both urgent environmental problems and poverty. Transfer of advanced technologies, e.g., biotechnology, which promotes more value-added research and development activities with genetic resources, enables provider countries to strengthen their position in the market by offering more developed and advanced products instead of raw genetic material. In addition, provision of processed material would make it easier to certify the resources accessed under a certificate scheme.

Implementation of Conflict Resolution, Arbitration, and Redress Mechanisms

The need to monitor deficits is a major problem that leads to asymmetric information and the consequences it entails. Adequate conflict resolution, arbitration, and redress mechanisms can mitigate this problem. For instance, if providers can be sure that they can enforce their rights, they will not react with overregulation. ABS agreements contain contract terms that can be violated by both providers and users. Providers are usually the first to meet the conditions of a contract by providing genetic material. They usually do not have the capacities to monitor whether the users of genetic resources actually meet their commitments. These difficulties may even increase once genetic resources have left the jurisdiction of the country of origin. If they are aware of this situation, provider countries often respond by establishing more restricted access regulations.

Control mechanisms such as monitoring of IPRs applications and assistance provided by third parties (i.e., access to information, information on patent applications, additional investigations of infringement, provision of visas, and legal aid) can help to identify infringements on the part of the users and provide important information to countries of origin whose laws have been violated. User country focal points could play a facilitator role by providing information, including information on their country's legal system (EU Commission 2003, 22). Conflict resolution, arbitration, and redress mechanisms can be developed and used with the support of these instruments.

Many user countries already have redress mechanisms in place for breaches of contract, and these enable providers to take legal action against misappropriation of genetic resources. Usually, every ABS contract defines the law applicable and the competent authority, both of which are part of the legal system of the provider or the user state. Despite such arrangements, problems may arise if one party decides to enforce its claims by legal action (EU Commission 2003, 21). If the law of the provider country is applicable and the competent authority is also situated there, it may prove difficult or impossible to prosecute a violation of national ABS law if the company in question has no assets in the provider country and is not willing or able to attend to court procedures. In that case provider countries are forced to rely on enforcement of court decisions in user countries. Whereas it is possible to enforce decisions handed down by a foreign court, whether or not a court decision is enforceable usually depends on a number of different factors (e.g., procedural fairness, reciprocity) and the decisions are made on a case-by-case basis. One way to avoid the difficulties that arise from enforcement of foreign court decisions is to have such cases adjudicated in user countries. In addition, it is important to consider the possibility of higher awards in cases involving tort actions (Barber, Johnston, and Tobin 2003, 36–37). However, this approach will probably fail for lack, in provider countries, of the financial and human capacity needed to enforce rights in a user country. A study on the real and transaction costs involved in the process of access to justice across jurisdictions estimates at US$250,000 the costs associated with bringing a claim for breach of an ABS agreement before an international arbitral tribunal, whereas the costs may vary between US$20,000 and US$100,000 for a claim settled before a court in the country in which the user is domiciled (e.g., US, France, Japan, Brazil; see Bernard 2008).

Another possibility that may be considered is recourse to the procedure provided by alternative systems, including, for example, arbitration, as mentioned earlier, or appointment of an independent ombudsman with the SCBD. This procedure would normally be faster and less costly, and it would not necessarily require legal representation or pose a risk of high costs if a lawsuit is lost. Probably the most important advantage is that both parties would need to consent to the procedure and agree to accept the result of arbitration (Barber, Johnston, and Tobin 2003, 36).

5 Implementation of ABS Regulations in Provider and User Countries

This chapter applies the analytical framework developed to assess ABS effectiveness to four case studies and seeks to determine which of the identified measures for addressing the critical factors have already been implemented and how successful they have been. This will make it possible to analyze the strengths and weaknesses of current ABS regimes in both provider countries and user countries. The chapter identifies the methods that have been implemented as well as future options for measures that can be put in place by countries in their capacity as providers and/or users of genetic resources; that is, the chapter explores the perspectives of ABS governance under an international regime. The main source of information for these case studies is qualitative interviews with relevant stakeholders in the respective countries.

The present book examines the effectiveness of global ABS governance using a multilevel approach. Whereas the previous chapters focused on the general global framework conditions, the attention of this chapter is focused on the national and regional levels, where implementation takes place. The findings and results are not limited to the case studies presented and discussed in this book. The analytical framework, which consists of the objectives and the critical factors, can be applied to a range of case studies on countries faced with the need to implement the ABS concept. Only with such an analytic framework is it possible to carry out a comparative analysis of different case studies. The case studies provide insightful experiences for other provider and user countries. Because the underlying questions of this book largely coincide with the questions with which international policy-makers are faced, the results may serve to support political discussions and negotiations as well as to propose options for further action.

The four case studies (the Philippines, Costa Rica, Ethiopia, and the EU), together with the analytical framework in Chapter 4, constitute the book's core. They provide empirical findings on the problem of biodiversity loss and the ABS concept, and they set the empirical ground to specify the critical factors, which are in turn based on both economic theory and empirical findings.

The regulations in place in Costa Rica and the Philippines have been taken as an example to provide insights into existing ABS regimes. Both countries were quite early to implement the ABS provisions of the CBD. Costa Rica developed the institutional infrastructure and concluded ABS agreements even before the CBD had been signed. A legal framework was adopted only in 1998. The Philippines was the first country to finalize and implement a legal ABS framework; it was revised early in 2005. These two countries can fall back on years of experience, which differ in some respects from the one country to the other. Costa Rica is regarded internationally as a model nation as regards ABS and environmental measures, whereas the Philippines has had major difficulties in implementing the CBD objectives. What follows will analyze the ways in which the critical factors derived from the theoretical framework are shaped in these countries and how their ABS regulations address these factors. Ethiopia has only recently adopted a set of ABS regulations. However, the Ethiopian government has a large measure of awareness regarding ABS. Ethiopia is an important actor especially at the international level. Whereas drafts of Ethiopia's ABS legislation have long been under discussion, it was only in early 2006 that the Ethiopian government finally adopted a set of regulations. Ethiopia may therefore stand in for many other biodiversity-rich countries that have signed the CBD but are faced with political and institutional difficulties in implementing its provisions.

In view of the fact that both the geographical locations of these countries and their approaches to implementing ABS differ extremely, the case studies selected appear very useful. Users are an indispensable part of an international ABS regime. However, there is little information available on user issues. The present study includes and considers them. The EU serves as an example of a user country community. The case study is mainly a desktop study, but one enriched with information gathered in workshops and conferences. Many EU member states have strong research and development capacities and distinct and diverse user sectors, including a wide range of different sectors, such as, for example, pharmaceuticals, agribusiness, and cosmetics. At the same time, the EU has been actively involved in negotiations in the CBD framework, and it has sought to support communication between users and providers. The last section of this chapter looks into whether the introduction of certain user or user country measures in the EU will suffice to meet the requirements derived from the identified critical factors.

THE PHILIPPINES

The Philippines is the first case study assembled by the author. The following sections will apply the analytic framework, which consists of the critical factors and potential measures. The first section will start out with a brief presentation of the case study methodology. The section that follows will then go on to introduce the case of the Philippines and the country's regulatory environment, including the legal and institutional setting. The main part of the analysis of the Philippines is concerned with applying the critical factors to the country-specific case. Taking into account the analytic framework as regards effectiveness (see Chapter 4), the section looks into what shape the critical factors have in the country and how they are being addressed. The analysis of the first case will end with a set of country-specific conclusions.

Case Study Methodology

One reason why the Philippines serves as a country case study is that efforts to implement ABS there have been ambivalent. On the one hand, the country has had years of experience in ABS implementation. On the other hand, implementation efforts there appear to be very ineffective. Since 1995, only a handful of bioprospecting agreements have been concluded. In order to address these implementation problems, the Philippines has revised its ABS regulations and recently adopted the second generation of ABS laws. That experience gives the country a considerable lead over other provider countries.

The case of the Philippines is assessed on the basis of the critical factors identified earlier. The question is whether the critical factors or their interdependency are sufficient to explain the evidently low effectiveness of the Philippine regime: low access rate, ongoing loss of biodiversity, and no benefit-sharing. The development of the new ABS regulation is considered here even though it was adopted only after the interviews had been conducted. The data are based on expert interviews conducted in the Philippines between March and May 2002. Semistructured interviews were used as a method for gathering and analyzing qualitative data (see Chapter 1). Different thematic areas in line with the critical factors identified were addressed throughout the interview process. The roughly thirty experts interviewed represent the spectrum of stakeholders, including individuals, communities, governments, universities, NGOs, scientific institutions, and industry that are involved in the ABS process or have expertise related to the ABS issue. Additionally, secondary literature, including books, journal articles, and reports, are used to complement the information gained from the interviews.

Introduction

The Philippines is one of the so-called "biodiversity hotspots." The country has regions with high levels of biodiversity and a remarkable number of endemic species. Nevertheless, these regions can also be described as areas experiencing major decline in habitats for these species (Myers et al. 2000). The extinction rates found in the Philippines are unparalleled in Southeast Asia.

The Philippines has an extraordinary diversity of ecosystems. Some 13,500 plant species can be found in Philippine forests. They represent 5 percent of the world's flora. Flowering plants are estimated to number between eight thousand and twelve thousand species in two hundred families and fifteen hundred genera; 20 percent is unknown whereas 27 to 75 percent is endemic (Protected Areas and Wildlife Bureau 1998, 2). Besides plant diversity, the country has a very high diversity of animals (i.e., vertebrates and invertebrates), freshwater ecosystems, costal and marine ecosystems, and agricultural plants. The spectrum of ecological niches or habitat types supports high species diversity. The number of species is estimated to be more than 53,577. High species endemism is observed among flowering plants, algae, lycopsids, ferns, amphibians, birds, and mammals.

Protected areas account for 7.8 percent of the Philippines' total land area (World Resources Institute 2003). Nevertheless, Philippine forest cover was reduced from more than 50 percent to less than 24 percent between 1948 and 1987 (Protected Areas and Wildlife Bureau 1998, 1–4). Today 19.4 percent of the land is covered by forests. According to FAO estimates, the annual deforestation rate is 1.4 percent (FAO 2003). Only about 5 percent of the country's coral reefs remain in excellent condition and about 80 percent of its mangrove areas have been lost. It has been estimated that about 50 percent of national parks are no longer biologically significant (Protected Areas and Wildlife Bureau 1998, 1–4).

The major threat to biodiversity in the Philippines is habitat destruction due to conversion of forest and grasslands for agricultural and urban use as well as due to overexploitation (i.e., overlogging) (Liebig et al. 2002, 31). Governmental organizations and NGOs reacted in the late 1980s, developing strategies to halt the loss of forests and biodiversity. Various environmental policies and biodiversity conservation programs have been formulated. In 1992 the National Integrated Protected Areas System (NIPAS) Law was adopted; it laid the groundwork for a comprehensive protected areas system (Benavidez 2004, 154). In their efforts to effectively implement such conservation measures, the Philippines is reliant on external support. The same goes for ABS regulations. The development and implementation of ABS laws have been supported by development agencies, including, e.g., the Gesellschaft für technische Zusammenarbeit (GTZ).[1] The Philippines developed and adopted an ABS legal framework shortly after the adoption of the CBD. Nevertheless, it appears that actual implementation has been unable to keep up with legislative input and thus has proven unable to effectively address the problem of biodiversity loss.

The establishment of the ASEAN (Association of Southeast Asian Nations) Regional Centre for Biodiversity Conservation (ARCBC) in the Philippines again indicates a strong commitment and an increasing willingness to actively address the problem of biodiversity loss. The center serves as an institutional linkage among ASEAN member countries and between ASEAN and EU partner organizations designed to enhance the capacity of ASEAN in promoting biodiversity conservation. Its aim is to support biodiversity conservation through improved cooperation in the Asian region by providing assistance for setting up a network of institutional links among ASEAN countries and between ASEAN and EU partner organizations. The center is to assist the ASEAN member countries in developing a framework for improving technical and institutional approaches through regional cooperation in managing biodiversity conservation (ARCBC 2006).

Regulatory Environment: Legal and Institutional Setting

In 1995 the Philippines government was the first to respond to the adoption of the CBD's ABS provisions, and it implemented them on the basis of Presidential Executive Order (EO) 247 (1995),[2] which was still a general framework. One year later Department Administrative Order (DAO) 96–20 (DAO 1996)[3] was elaborated as the order for implementing rules and regulations for EO 247. Before they were implemented, the collection of wildlife species was regulated by an administrative coordination and permit system that, carried out by the National Museum of the Philippines, was not in compliance with the CBD (Benavidez 2004, 154).

EO 247 is based on a constitutional provision that vests in the state the responsibility to preserve the environment and assigns to it ownership of wildlife, flora, and fauna. It covers the prospecting of biological and genetic material in the public domain, including natural growths on private lands. Consequently, the government now regulates ABS for biological resources found on Philippine territory. The aim of EO 247 is to regulate bioprospecting in compliance with the CBD. It should benefit the national interest and promote the development of local capability in science and technology to achieve technological self-reliance in selected areas (EO 247 1995, Section 1). Its scope is very comprehensive. It covers the prospecting of biological and genetic resources and their by-products and derivatives for scientific and commercial purposes. DAO 96–20 defines bioprospecting as research, collection, and utilization of biological and genetic resources for the purpose of using the knowledge derived there for scientific and commercial purposes (DAO 96–20 1996, 2.1 h).

The regulation system of EO 247 contains four basic elements:

- scheme of mandatory research agreements between the government and collectors
- setup of an Inter Agency Committee for Biological and Genetic Resources (IACBGR)
- regulation on obtaining PIC from local communities
- requirements to conform with environmental protection (La Vina, Caleda, and Baylon 1997)

Before bioprospecting activities are carried out, the Philippine government and the applicant have to negotiate an agreement based on MAT. An agreement of this kind can cover either scientific or commercial research. Contracts on scientific research, referred to as academic research agreements (ARA), are usually concluded with national research institutions (e.g., universities) for a period of five years, whereas contracts on commercial research, referred to as commercial research agreements (CRA), are concluded with national and international companies as well as with international scientific research institutions for a period of three years. In this case, the collection and use of the material is categorized as commercial even if a foreign research institution intends to collect the material only for scientific purposes. In order to enter into an agreement, a foreign applicant has to establish and financially support research cooperation with Philippine researchers. ARA provide more flexibility than CRA. For example, local researchers affiliated with an institution holding ARA are allowed to conduct research under the agreements. However, these researchers have to comply with the terms of the ARA, including, for example, the need to obtain PIC (EO 247 1995, Section 3).

PIC plays an important role in the Philippine ABS regulation as well as in the application process. Submission of a PIC certificate is a precondition for the conclusion of any agreement, and thus also for permission for access and collection. Depending on the distribution of property rights, the applicant is required to obtain a declaration of consent, from indigenous or local communities, private landowners, or—in the case of nature protection areas—from the Protected Area Management Board. The applicant therefore needs to inform these concerned groups about her/his intentions and the scope of the planned bioprospecting activities and to ask them for their consent (DAO 96–20 1996, Section 7).

Under EO 247, the IACBGR is responsible for the implementation and enforcement of the ABS regulations. The committee consists of representatives of the government departments concerned (environment, agriculture, science and technology, health, and foreign affairs), science communities, and NGOs and people's organizations. Supported by a technical secretariat, the IACBGR is responsible for the application process. In addition, it advises the government departments concerned with reference to the final signing of the contract and supervises compliance. Since 1996 the IACBGR has processed eight applications for CRA and seventeen for ARA. However, only one CRA and one ARA have been approved under EO 247 (Benavidez 2004, 157).

The commercial agreement was signed between the Marine Science Institute of the University of the Philippines and the University of Utah (US). The aim of the project, named "Anti-Cancer Agents from Unique Natural Products Sources," was the collection of funicates, sponges, and other invertebrate samples for biological assays to be screened for potential bioactive compounds. The application was submitted in February 1997 and the project was approved in June 1998. In the other cases applications have been withdrawn or are still pending. In 1998 an ARA was approved for the University of the Philippines on "Conservation-Related Studies as Part of Thesis Requirements." The commercial agreement has not thus far led to a marketable product, and the Philippine government as the contracting partner has not received any monetary compensation, apart from a low bioprospecting fee.

The approach adopted for EO 247 and its implementation has been widely criticized by national and international users of genetic resources. Many local scientists have criticized EO 247 for its very broad scope (Liebig et al. 2002, 38). The law regulates not only bioprospecting but also collecting and sampling. Any kind of collection, research, and utilization of biological resources, including research on conservation, is covered by it. As a consequence, access to biodiversity is impeded, as is any national and international research related to biodiversity. Local scientists who were interviewed stressed that foreign users of biodiversity complain about the time-consuming, nontransparent, bureaucratic, and costly application process. For this reason they opt for other countries.

In 2001, Republic Act No. 9147 Wildlife Resources Conservation and Protection Act (hereafter Wildlife Act) was adopted in response to problems associated with EO 247. The Wildlife Act is a general wildlife protection law with a focus on biodiversity conservation. Its aim is to conserve wildlife and habitats, enhance biodiversity, regulate collection of and trade in wildlife, implement international commitments, and support scientific research in the field of biodiversity. Its implementing rules and regulations were developed in 2004 on the basis of Joint DENR-DA-PCSD[4] Administrative Order No. 1.

Only two sections of the Wildlife Act (14: bioprospecting and 15: scientific researches) deal with ABS and bioprospecting. However, the act entails huge changes to existing procedures. It defines bioprospecting as research, collection, and utilization of biological and genetic resources for purposes of applying the knowledge derived solely for commercial purposes (Wildlife Act 2001, Section 5a). Any bioprospecting activity requires negotiations with MAT and the PIC of the persons or community concerned.

The DENR has jurisdiction over all terrestrial plant and animal species. The DA has jurisdiction over all declared critical aquatic habitats and all aquatic resources. In the province of Palawan, comprehensive jurisdiction is vested in the PCSD. If bioprospecting actually takes place, the chairperson of the PCSD, as authorized by the council, must be a cosignatory to the bioprospecting agreement (Wildlife Act 2001, Section 19).

As far as bioprospecting is concerned, the act addresses most of the concerns or criticisms leveled at EO 247 (Benavidez 2004, 165). It amends the provision on ARA set out under EO 247 in such a way as to ensure that a permit system in accordance with the Wildlife Act covers noncommercial research using biological resources. It explicitly delegates the power to make decisions on the approval of applications to the secretary of DENR or DA, who are supported by a technical committee of experts. Thus the IACBGR created under EO 247 is effectively dissolved. PIC and provisions on benefit-sharing as well as emphasis on the participation of local researchers in bioprospecting, research, and development activities are all that remain in terms of primary requirements for bioprospecting.

In early January 2005, the Guidelines for Bioprospecting Activities in the Philippines (hereafter Bioprospecting Guidelines) were approved to bridge the inconsistency between EO 247 and the Wildlife Act. The guidelines aim to streamline the procedure for access and to facilitate compliance with them by legitimate resource users, to provide guidelines for obtaining PIC as well as for negotiations, and to establish a cost-effective, efficient, transparent, and standardized system for monitoring compliance with the ABS provisions (Bioprospecting Guidelines 2004, Section 4).

The guidelines, jointly signed by DENR, DA, PCSD, and the National Commission on Indigenous Peoples (NCIP),[5] define a uniform procedure for evaluating and granting access to biological resources as well as for avoiding the potential problem of inconsistency in bioprospecting regulations for various components of biodiversity under the management jurisdiction of different government agencies (i.e., DENR, DA, and PCSD). The elements of the streamlining process include, for example, reduction of the bureaucratic procedure for review and approval of applications; reduction of the number of days required for review (from thirty to fifteen days), and definition of a definite timeline for approval of bioprospecting applications (within thirty days).

As regards benefit-sharing, under the Bioprospecting Guidelines a bioprospecting fee—minimum amount: US$3,000 for each bioprospecting undertaking—is paid to the national government and is passed on to the Wildlife Management Fund or Protected Area Fund. Local users not supported by foreign collaborators or investors are required to pay only 10 percent of this amount. Up-front payments are to go to the resource providers. An annual user's fee—US$1,000 per collection site—goes directly to resource providers. If a product is derived from the material collected, royalties are shared between the national government and the resource providers; and local governments are to have a share in the funds received by the national government, consistent with the provisions of the Local Government Code[6] (Bioprospecting Guidelines 2004, Section 14). These royalties amount to 2 percent of global gross sales of products (minimum); 25 percent go to the national government and 75 percent to resource providers.

The bilingual annex to the Bioprospecting Guidelines contains a number of helpful documents, including, for example, standard terms and conditions, MTA, PIC certificate, checklist of process and content indicators, compliance with proper procurement of PIC, and certificate of acceptance.

The instrumental penalties include, e.g., civil liability under contract law, criminal liability under the Wildlife Act, a blacklist published locally and internationally, and a report to the CBD secretariat on misappropriation.

The ASEAN Framework Agreement

Apart from the national framework, the Philippines is also integrated into a regional framework. ASEAN was established on August 8, 1967, in Bangkok by the five original member countries, namely, Indonesia, Malaysia, Philippines, Singapore, and Thailand. Today ten countries (Brunei Darussalam, Cambodia, Indonesia, Laos, Malaysia, Myanmar, Philippines, Singapore, Thailand, and Vietnam) are members. The association aims to accelerate economic growth, social progress, and cultural development in the Asian region and to promote regional peace and stability. ASEAN also deals with transnational issues concerning the environment, including, for instance, nature conservation and biodiversity.

In September 1997, at the eighth meeting of ASEAN, the Senior Officials on the Environment (ASOEN) requested that the ASEAN Working Group on Nature Conservation (AWGNC) develop a common protocol for member countries on access to genetic resources and IPRs. This process took quite some time and has not yet been finalized. In June 2000, during the tenth meeting of the AWGNC, the member countries were requested to provide comments on the draft of a framework agreement with a view to finalizing the draft by the eleventh meeting of the AWGNCB. Finally, at the fourteenth meeting of ASOEN, the draft framework agreement was reviewed and recommended for the consideration of the ministers at their Eighth Informal ASEAN Ministerial Meeting on the Environment (IAMME). In October 2004 some countries requested more time to review and to consult at the national level and to complete the national process for signature. At a 2006 meeting, the ASEAN member states were repeatedly asked to expedite the process of national consultation to clear the way for the framework agreement (Fuentes 2009).

The key provisions of the agreement are:

- The agreement's objectives broaden the CBD's provisions: the agreement aims to set minimum standards for regulating ABS, to strengthen national initiatives, to provide a forum for interregional cooperation, and to strengthen the voice of parties in related international agreements and negotiations.
- Transboundary genetic resources: if biological and genetic resources are indigenous to two or more parties, the parties are required to collectively discuss the terms and conditions of ABS and approaches to sharing the benefits.
- There is an obligation of the parties to take legislative, administrative, or policy measures to regulate ABS, to establish procedures for granting PIC (involving resource providers), and to disseminate information on access regulations, applications, etc.
- Establishment of a regional CHM: it should provide relevant information, subject to appropriate confidentiality provisions, as well as

terms and conditions that may be imposed by the party providing the information; it should also provide technical and legal support to the competent national authorities, and it should be used to establish a database for biological and genetic resources and the associated TK.

- There is an establishment of a common fund for biodiversity conservation, which is administered by the Secretariat but that is reliant on voluntary contributions (ASEAN Framework Agreement 2000).

Assigning Property Rights and Intellectual Property Rights

In the Philippines all lands in the public domain, waters, minerals, coal, petroleum, and other mineral oils, all forces of potential energy, fisheries, forests or timber, wildlife, flora and fauna, and other natural resources are owned by the state (Constitution of the Philippines 1987, Article XII). The state has the responsibility to preserve and protect the environment (Constitution of the Philippines 1987, Article II). The Wildlife Act assigns jurisdiction over these resources to DENR, DA, and PCSD. They support resource providers in negotiations. Although definition and assignment are clear, interviewees noted that there are competing rights holders. One example that was given is the island Palawan, which is governed by a special law on biodiversity. Palawan has its own Council for Sustainable Development that is responsible for environmental issues in the region, but the local government follows the national government because Palawan is a Philippine province. Another example may be seen in overlaps between ancestral domain and land rights and provincial access regulations.

It became clear in the course of the interviews that many commercial users have criticized the Philippine ABS negotiations because of the unrealistic expectations held by the provider side regarding the potential benefits. Nevertheless, it also became clear that most of the NGOs interviewed are convinced that commercial users are able to pay more than they offer to pay. Views on the expected benefits and the amount of compensation diverge. EO 247 and DAO 96–20 do not provide any benefits-related indicator for negotiations and leave the matter to the negotiators. The documents state only that all discoveries of commercial products and technology derived from the resources are to be made available to the Philippine government and that the benefits are to be shared equitably among the government, the Integrated Protected Areas Fund (IPAF), local communities, or individuals, if the resource concerned comes from private property (DAO 96–20 1996, Section 8). The new regulations define a framework for these negotiations, one with many improvements. Once a bioprospecting undertaking is concluded, the government (i.e., the implementing agency) receives a bioprospecting fee, whereas up-front payments accrue to the resource providers. Annual royalties (i.e., a minimum of 2 percent of total global gross sales) are shared between the national government (25 percent) and the resource providers (75 percent). Local governments should receive a share of the funds taken in by the national government, consistent with the provisions of the Local Government Code. As far as monetary benefits intended for the local community are concerned, measures must be taken to ensure that the funds received are used solely for biodiversity conservation or environmental protection, including alternative or supplemental livelihood opportunities for community members. Nonmonetary benefits may be agreed upon by the resource user and resource providers in addition to the minimum benefits provided.

In the Philippines, individuals at the local level do not hold property rights to biological material; all natural resources are owned by the state. However, the new regulation strengthens the role of resource providers by giving them an up-front payment and a 75 percent share of royalties. This regulation is very advanced and grants substantial compensation to resource providers.

Furthermore, even under the previous regulations, PIC was a very strong instrument in the Philippines, though also a very complex one. The final decision on access is left entirely to the communities concerned, and they are entitled to negotiate potential benefits. PIC is a controversial matter in the Philippines. Many of the stakeholders from NGOs interviewed for the present study stress that this principle needs to remain one of the core elements of the Philippine ABS regulation. Local researchers complained about the expense involved in meeting PIC obligations. For the only CRA concluded, Philippine researchers needed to obtain eight PICs, in advance, for the first year because they wanted to collect at different sites and that meant that many communities were affected. Language problems and lack of knowledge of local conditions would make it impossible for foreign users to engage in this activity. It is very difficult to identify the communities whose PIC is required. It is evident that there is a trade-off between the aim of strengthening the property rights at the local level and the risk of increasing user transaction costs. The new Bioprospecting Guidelines have retained the principle and stress the importance of increased resource holder participation.

Looking at the value chain from beginning to end, we find that IPRs also play an important role in the Philippines. The Philippines is a member of the WTO. The national law adopted to implement the minimum standards set by TRIPs is the Intellectual Property Code of the Philippines (IPC), Republic Act No. 8293. The criteria for product patentability are new, inventive, and applicable for industrial uses. This means that the Philippines allows users of genetic resources to acquire protected property rights, under the TRIPs agreement, on products derived from genetic resources. Plant varieties and animal breeds are excluded from patentability. In order to meet the TRIPS obligation to have a *sui generis* system in place in 2002, the country adopted the Philippine Plant Variety Protection (PVP) law, which is designed to provide protection for plant varieties. Under the UPOV Convention, the protection criteria are new, distinct, uniform, and stable (Benavidez 2004, 167).

As far as the case of cultured plants is concerned, Philippine law gives users the means they need to protect their breeds. In the interviews some NGO representatives criticized both the patenting of life forms (including microorganisms) and PVP. They reject patents on life forms for ethical and moral reasons, but also because they are convinced that the Philippines cannot benefit from such a system because the country is not sufficiently advanced in terms of research and development to make use of it. In adopting IPC and PVP, the Philippines has complied with WTO obligations. No disclosure of origin requirement is provided for, whereas the new Bioprospecting Guidelines stress origin requirements as a major control instrument. However, the guidelines are not based on an IPR system. For example, joint ownership of IPRs is not defined as an element of benefit-sharing.

Information Asymmetry

Information asymmetry can be identified as the strongest critical factor for this case. It is encountered at all levels identified. First, it occurs in the pre-contract phase because providers expect higher benefits than users are willing to pay. The interviews show that users in the Philippines complain that NGOs expect unrealistic benefits and have brought their influence to bear on ABS applications. However, it appears that the demand for higher benefits has not found its way into the negotiations. Whereas the CRA includes a royalty rate (5 percent) for commercialization, it does not extend to any other monetary benefits, and the interviews with the parties concerned document that benefit-sharing was not a serious problem in the negotiations. The expectations held by the two sides were not divergent. However, it is important to bear in mind that the Philippine Marine Science Institute is an equal partner of the University of Utah and has an interest of its own in the negotiations. It may be assumed that it was also in its interest to keep monetary benefits for the government and local communities as low as possible to realize the research project and benefit from it.

Post-contractual information asymmetries are a more substantial problem. In view of the post-contractual information deficiencies on the provider side, the application procedure has been designed in a very risk-averse manner. It is evident that in adopting EO 247 the Philippines has overregulated ABS and developed a quite inflexible and restrictive ABS regime, induced to do so by the negative experiences it has made in the limited capacity it has to control user behavior. One industry representative states in the interviews that everyone doing research in the Philippines is regarded as a "biopirate." The system, it was noted, is so restrictive that it discourages even local researchers from collecting biological material for scientific purposes. Instead of facilitating access to its genetic resources and developing effective strategies to prevent misappropriation, the Philippines has disrupted research of any kind—commercial and scientific—related to the collection of biological resources.

The new Bioprospecting Guidelines promise to address this problem. Instead of highly restrictive rules, the new guidelines establish compliance and monitoring instruments. The implementing agencies are responsible for most monitoring, although they may be supported by the Department of Foreign Affairs (DFA) (including embassies and missions) and the Department of Science and Technology (DOST), especially when it comes to monitoring inventions and any commercialization undertaken in foreign countries. These institutions are expected to be better suited to dealing with the need to prevent biological resources from entering countries without a bioprospecting contract, to control compliance with the disclosure requirement for country of origin in patent applications, and to enforce claims against collectors or commercializing entities. It is hoped that DFA and DOST will be able to establish and maintain contacts with users of biological material from the Philippines and to create trust between the partners. However, it is clear that these departments need capacity-building to be able to fulfill this function.

The main monitoring instrument is, however, that the bioprospecting guidelines continue to require cooperation between the user and a national partner. Foreign users are not permitted to engage in any bioprospecting activity unless a local collaborator has been engaged to participate. From a development policy perspective, this requirement is very positive, but it needs competent institutions to be successful. Other monitoring instruments include reporting requirements, including submission by the user of an annual progress report to the implementing agencies (e.g., on the status of the procurement of PIC, progress in collection of samples, benefit-sharing negotiations, progress on payment of benefits, or other contract provisions). The guidelines provide for several model certificates that the resource user is expected to use as proof of compliance and to submit to regional DENR, DA, or PCSD representatives. The certificates cover proper PIC procurement, delivery on benefit-sharing agreements (i.e., acceptance by resource providers of the monetary and/or nonmonetary benefits provided for in the agreement), and collection quotas. With a view to monitoring whether a benefit-sharing agreement may be considered fair and equitable, the Bioprospecting Guidelines provide a model of a checklist of process and content indicators. The checklist is available to contracting parties and other stakeholders. In addition, the Philippines seems to rely on the support of civil society, especially NGOs and people's organizations, and they are encouraged to support monitoring activities inside the country and abroad.

Less has been done to address the information deficiencies on the user side. Until the new regulation was adopted, users could not be sure that shared benefits would be invested in environmental protection and that they would receive exclusive and high-quality material. Under the new regulation, benefits are to be used for environmental protection, although, with a view to exclusivity, no concrete regulations have been formulated.

Because users are usually involved in collection activities, under the supervision of Philippine researchers, they have an influence on the quality of the material collected.

Accounting for Time Lags

Not many contracts have been negotiated. This outcome is a key weak point of the Philippine approach. The low number of contracts concluded reduces the chance of attaining benefits that constitute an incentive for conservation.

De facto only one CRA has been concluded thus far. The agreement stipulates that the University of Utah and the Marine Science Institute will share nonmonetary and monetary benefits. In the short term, the nonmonetary benefits are dominant. The Marine Science Institute has benefited in the short term through training, exchange, and technology transfer. In the long term, the Philippine government and resource providers stand to gain access to all product discoveries deriving from the material collected, and all of the technologies used should be made freely available. If a product is developed from collected material, the user is required to pay 5 percent of the net revenue to the DA. What share of these royalties will accrue to local communities is a matter that depends on decisions taken by the government. In all documents and publications referring to collected materials and their improvement, the provider must be acknowledged and the Philippines must be identified as the country of origin. If a third party obtains IPRs or commercializes a discovery or technology derived from the material, a separate agreement is needed between principal collector/co-collector and the third party to define the concrete sharing modalities for royalties and other monetary benefits or technology (Liebig et al. 2002, 47). No up-front payments have been made. The Philippine government receives only a small yearly bioprospecting fee of 10,000 Philippine pesos (PhP), about US$200. The local communities concerned benefit through education and training. It is not clear how they stand to benefit from monetary benefits because this is determined by the national government. Thus far, the Philippines has not received any monetary benefits arising out of this agreement. The cooperation between local and international collectors has created some nonmonetary benefits in terms of scientific education, but neither the resource providers nor the environment have benefited.

Compared with the regulations previously in place, the new guidelines deal in far greater detail with the issue of fair and equitable benefit-sharing. EO 247 and DAO 96–20 have left these terms open for negotiations between the responsible agency and the collector/co-collector. New contracts will have more detailed obligations, including annual up-front payments and royalties (2 percent of total global gross sales of the products concerned). Up-front payments in the form of annual use fees can serve, at least in small ways, to bridge the time lag and to set an incentive to conserve biodiversity.

Good Governance in Provider Countries

The general political situation in the Philippines is not bioprospecting-friendly. Poverty, economic stagnation, corruption, government incompetence, and conflicts with insurgents are destabilizing the political situation and undercutting the Philippines' attractiveness as a location for collection and research. The World Bank Governance Indicators show a clear picture. All indicators reflect deterioration between 1998 and 2005. For instance, only 17.5 percent of the 213 countries and territories covered rate worse than the Philippines on political stability.

Unlike many other countries, however, the Philippines does not lack access legislation. Owing to their pioneering status, EO 247 and DAO 96–20 have become quite popular at the international level. However, the frameworks have come in for heavy criticism by national and international users of genetic resources due to their restrictive, overregulated, and bureaucratic character. In the interviews, almost all stakeholders welcome the Philippine approach, but they also note that it is too ambitious and complain about the complex procedures involved in implementing it. The outcomes of this Philippine legislation already indicate vulnerability. Of fourteen CRA and twenty ARA applications,[7] only one CRA and one ARA have been approved. Some interested users have even withdrawn their applications.

Recently the Philippines implemented the second generation of ABS laws, and it is hoped that this set of regulations will provide for more efficiency, but also for more transparency. Responsibility has been transferred to the relevant ministries (DENR and DA) and the interagency committee has been eliminated. The committee's inability to process applications is seen as a major weak point in the Philippine system. It remains to be seen whether government institutions will be able to cope with the additional burden. Instead of being processed in the EO 247 framework, all pending ARA applications will now be handled through a free permit system established by the Wildlife Act. There is reason to believe that this will

Table 5.1   World Bank Governance Indicators, Philippines (1998, 2005)

Governance Indicator	1998	2005
Voice and accountability	58.9	47.8
Political stability/no violence	39.2	17.5
Government effectiveness	63.2	55.5
Regulatory quality	68.5	52.0
Rule of law	55.3	38.6
Control of corruption	50.5	37.4

Source: based on Kaufmann, Kraay, and Mastruzzi (2006).

facilitate biodiversity research and access to resources. Pending CRA will be processed under the new Bioprospecting Guidelines. Measures will be taken to ensure that the funds are used solely for biodiversity conservation or environmental protection, including alternative or supplemental livelihood opportunities for community members.

If the new regulation is to boost its reputation and finally convince users to bioprospect in the Philippines, the country will need work to improve governance, stabilize the political situation, and keep the promise set out in the new Bioprospecting Guidelines, to streamline and improve the application procedure.

Administrative Complexity

Administrative complexity was probably the main reason for the failure of EO 247. All interview partners confirmed that the application procedure, including the PIC provision, put inappropriate burdens on researchers and commercial users. The regulations were complex and restrictive, and the country lacked adequate human and financial resources to manage the challenge of implementing a system of this kind. Researchers from the Marine Science Institute stressed that it took seven months to complete a CRA. A number of problems emerged when they tried to renew it: the undefined relationship between the Wildlife Act and EO 247, no decision taken by the IACBGR because not all members were present when the application was set for discussion, and lack of communication between the IACBGR and the applicant. An industry representative also noted as a problem that often no quorum is given because members, all of them unpaid volunteers, are unable to attend. The members from industry are especially concerned. In another interview, a researcher from the Marine Science Institute noted that a second application for a CRA was submitted in 1998 and not processed. These researchers, in effect the only national researchers who engage in legally approved bioprospecting activities, state that the procedure is very time-consuming and that not many foreign partners are able and willing to accept this. The only reason why cooperation with the University of Utah works out is that the institution has been a partner for more than ten years and the Philippine applicant is a former colleague of the foreign partner.

The new regulation dissolves the IACBGR, but its powers and responsibilities are assigned to other agencies, depending on the location of collection or the type of resources concerned. There is no main contact point for users that could serve to facilitate communication. In view of the fact that the ministries concerned are already occupied with numerous tasks, the additional burden involved in processing ABS applications may overstrain their capacities, making an efficient procedure impossible. In the interviews, the IACBGR was mainly criticized for being made up of high-level government staff members who have many other responsibilities. The IACBGR's work is often not their top priority, and they may miss meetings or not fulfill their tasks. For example, in the case of the Marine Science Institute, the applicant received no comments from the IACBGR on a draft CRA, and the only reason why that procedure advanced was that instead of simply giving up, the applicant personally contacted several members of the IACBGR. Dissolution of the IACBGR alone is not enough to solve the problem of high administrative complexity. The matter now depends on how the agencies involved implement the new ABS provisions and whether they make additional financial and human resources available.

Under the guidelines, the implementing agencies should, if necessary, recommend qualified Philippine scientists to foreign users as research collaborators, but there are doubts as to whether the relevant government agencies are sufficiently familiar with the country's scientific infrastructure. An independent research institution would probably be better informed and more competent when it comes to these issues. If this intermediation proves inadequate, there will be every reason to expect users to have difficulties in meeting this initial condition.

Other factors that increase administrative complexity are the broad scope and time frames involved. The IACBGR was also responsible for regulating all biological resources, including ex situ collections, even though EO 247 and DAO 96–20 did not extend to them. However, their special nature calls for a specific system. The Wildlife Act has defined the scope of the ABS regulation. Under the guidelines, it applies for bioprospecting for any biological resource found in the Philippines, including wildlife, microorganisms, domesticated or propagated species, exotic species, and ex situ collections of biological resources sourced from the Philippines (Bioprospecting Guidelines 2004, Section 2). Nevertheless, the scope is still very broad and the resources concerned are still very diverse.

In addition, it took a period of at least five months to complete the application process, and even this was often not sufficient. EO 247 set a sixty-day requirement to obtain PIC once a research proposal had been submitted to a community. This requirement was removed from the Wildlife Act. However, because the present arrangement sets no time limits, incentives need to be set to accelerate the process. The overall process has also been streamlined, and now decisions on applications need to be made within fifteen working days after receipt of all application documents (Bioprospecting Guidelines 2004, Section 8).

Market Structure

It is not only the existing global market structure that has weakened the Philippines' position in the market. Ten years of efforts more to restrict than to facilitate access have undercut the country's reputation as a reliable partner. One interview partner from the industry side stated ironically that whereas EO 247 may be good for conferences and the Philippines may be first in Asia, there are no concrete results, no conservation, and no ABS.

It is difficult to assess the country's position in the market, because there is little empirical data available on ABS research and development. The Philippines has done little more than restrict research and development capacities. The scientists interviewed see the Philippines's advantage in marine instead of plant genetic resources, and they point out that many countries in Southeast Asia are likely to have the same resources. Before users gain more interest in starting bioprospecting activities in the Philippines, the country will have to prove that it is serious about changing its course and ensuring that user transaction costs will decrease significantly.

The Philippines is a member of ASEAN, and this integrates the country into a regional context. Even though the Philippine legislation is already the most advanced in the region, there is reason to expect that the country will benefit from the adoption of a projected regional framework agreement. Regional cooperation on transboundary movements and dissemination of information will strengthen the country's position. In addition, the Philippines is a member of the group of megadiverse countries. Coalitions of this kind can serve to strengthen the country's position.

Conclusions

The Philippines may serve as an example for a provider country that, whereas it has done pioneering work on developing ABS legislation, has still not managed to establish an effective regime. Only two ABS contracts have been concluded, and government, researchers, and resource holders have not received any major benefits, either monetary or nonmonetary. Forests and biodiversity are still on the decline in the Philippines, and this shows that the country still lacks other instruments needed to address the country's environmental problems.

The old EO 247 regulation was virtually unable to address the critical factors. This may explain why the regulation was unable to establish an effective ABS regime. Whereas new regulation tackles some of the important weak points, others remain. Most important, the regulation improves the property rights situation by granting resource providers substantial shares of up-front payments and royalties.

The new arrangement holds promise to streamline and improve the application process. Administrative complexity and high entry costs for users are two of the main remaining problems. However, these costs have declined somewhat compared with the initial situation, chiefly because the intersectoral committee has been abolished. At present a number of different ministries are responsible for processing ABS applications, a state of affairs that appears confusing for applicants. However, the time frames set will definitely serve to streamline the application process.

One recommendation would be to create concrete and realistic expectations for benefits in connection with negotiations. Up-front payments, which may help to bridge the time lag, are even more important, and these

Table 5.2 Overview of the Philippines and the Critical Factors

	Philippines
Property rights	State has property rights over biodiversity Local communities participate through PIC requirements, up-front payments, and royalties Government receives bioprospecting fee Plant varieties and animal breeds are excluded from patentability, but PVP Law as *sui generis* system
Asymmetric information	Pre-contractual: providers expect high benefits, but their demands have not become part of negotiations Post-contractual: substantial problems, addressed in part by new regulation (use of benefits, less overregulation due to better monitoring mechanism), but no guarantee of exclusivity and quality
Time lags	Only one commercial contract, but substantial nonmonetary benefits for Philippine research institute In future more weight on up-front payments
Good governance	General situation is not very positive New ABS law includes promising improvements
Administrative complexity	Costs have been very high Improved by abolishing ineffective inter-sectoral committee and adopting defined time frames Responsibility is still allocated to different agencies (DENR, DA, and PCSD) Academic research is excluded
Market structure	Ten years of overregulation have under-cut the country's market position ASEAN member/megadiverse countries

play a central role among the benefits referred to in the guidelines. The latter also do more to address information deficiencies. The former system used restrictive regulations to prevent misappropriation, whereas the new Bioprospecting Guidelines develop nonrestrictive instruments to monitor and solve problems arising out of information deficiencies. The political situation still remains largely unchanged, although legal certainty may improve if the new system is effectively enforced.

The new Philippine Bioprospecting Guidelines are a big step forward toward an effective ABS concept, but any legislative and institutional framework for an ABS regime will be only as good as the process through which it is implemented. The Philippines has to prove that it is willing to improve the situation, not only by developing this new regulation, but also by implementing it. If access is not facilitated and no ABS contracts are concluded, no benefits will be realized. All one can do at this point is speculate, and it remains to be seen whether the Philippines will be able to transform the legislative framework into actual practice.

COSTA RICA[8]

Costa Rica is the second case study compiled. The analysis follows the Philippine case. The analytic framework, developed on the basis of the critical factors and potential measures, is applied in a country-specific case in order to test and illustrate its applicability. The section will start out with a brief presentation of the case study methodology. This will be followed by a short introduction to the Costa Rican case and a look at the regulatory environment, including the legal and institutional setting. The main part of the analysis consists of an application of the critical factors to the country-specific case. Taking into account the established analytic framework regarding effectiveness (see Chapter 4), the section looks at how the critical factors are shaped and in what ways they are already being addressed in Costa Rica. The analysis of the second case study will end with a brief conclusion.

Case Study Methodology

The case of Costa Rica is assessed using the critical factors identified earlier. The underlying question is whether the specifications of these factors in the Costa Rican case can explain the country's apparent success and whether this success is related to effectiveness. Costa Rica's ABS approach is the world's most advanced, transparent, and experienced, but it is also still in the process of change and improvement. The analysis is based on expert interviews conducted in Costa Rica in November and December 2002. As a method, semistructured interviews were used to gather and analyze qualitative data. Throughout the interview process different thematic areas were addressed in keeping with the identified critical factors. More than twenty experts were interviewed who represent the range of stakeholders either involved in the ABS process or in possession of expertise related to the ABS issue, including individuals, communities, governments, universities, NGOs, scientific institutions, and industry involved. Stakeholders are defined here as persons who are affected by or have an influence on ABS regulations in Costa Rica. In addition, secondary literature (e.g., books, journal articles, and reports) was used to complement the information gained from the interviews.

Introduction

The tropical zones of the American continent contain more species than other tropical regions of the world, and many more species than the temperate and cold zones. Costa Rica covers 51.100 km² of the world's terrestrial surface, a figure that represents only 0.03 percent of global land area. Yet Costa Rica is considered one of the most diverse regions and has been identified as a biodiversity hotspot (Myers et al. 2000, 855). According to estimates, 4 percent of all living species are found there. During the 1970s and 1980s, a series of reports predicted that, based on the actual deforestation rate, Costa Rica's productive forests would vanish before the end of the century. The first step undertaken to conserve the country's rich biological heritage was the introduction of protection measures. Since 1970 the country has dedicated 25 percent of its national territory to conservation (Castro-Salazar and Arias-Murillo 1998, 5). The second response was the creation of the technical, institutional, and financial structure for a system of incentives and payments for environmental services. Costa Rica developed a diverse strategy to conserve forest areas and biodiversity with international and national support, and bioprospecting played an important part in this strategy. The country managed to address the ongoing decline of forests and biodiversity. Whereas in the 1980s Costa Rica had one of the world's highest deforestation rates, the deforestation rate has fallen dramatically since 1995. Before 1986, there was a net loss in annual forest cover. After 1986, a net gain in forest cover of 5.857 hectares per year was reported for the period from 1987 to 1997 (afforestation minus deforestation). In consequence, in 1997 Costa Rica had the same percentage of forest cover that it had twenty years before (Castro-Salazar and Arias-Murillo 1998, 15).

Regulatory Environment: Legal and Institutional Setting

The country's stable sociopolitical climate has been favorable for these developments. Costa Rica is one of the most stable and robust democracies in Latin America, with a long-standing commitment to economic growth and substantial progress on social indicators (Gámez et al. 1993, 54).

With the establishment of the Ministry of Natural Resources, Energy and Mines (MINAE) in 1986, Costa Rica's environmental issues became part of day-to-day policy. The ministry developed new administrative, financial, and institutional procedures. For instance, it used the new national System of Conserved Areas (SINAC) to take over and decentralize the administration of protected land, and it eliminated perverse incentives by adopting, e.g., the forest payment title, a subsidy designed to promote reforestation. It allowed landowners to make money twice: first by cutting and selling primary forest and second by reforesting the open areas (Miranda, Dieperink, and Glasbergen 2002, 5). Furthermore, it designed the National

Conservation Strategy for Sustainable Development in Costa Rica, and came up with new innovative financing mechanisms for conservation activities (Gámez et al. 1993, 55). In 1995 the ministry was renamed MINAE.[9]

Even before the adoption of the CBD in 1992, Costa Rica had concluded bioprospecting contracts with companies. The country adopted the comprehensive Law of Biodiversity in 1998 to implement the CBD, but many years before it had already established a quasi-ABS regime. In Costa Rica, the concept of ABS is embedded in a comprehensive environmental governance framework, one that appears to work well. The environmental situation has improved due to the expansion of protected areas, the removal of perverse incentives against conservation, and the implementation of conservation measures. Since the late 1990s, Costa Rica's biodiversity conservation policy has focused even more on the sustainable utilization of biodiversity as a means of promoting its conservation. In addition to bioprospecting, ecotourism and payment programs for environmental services have been established as instruments to internalize the costs of providing environmental services and, above all, biodiversity. Bioprospecting is thus part of a strategy, and it is embedded in a bundle of measures keyed to biodiversity conservation.

The main institution in Costa Rica dealing with bioprospecting issues is INBio.[10] INBio was created as a private but nonprofit institution to coordinate the various activities of universities, private organizations, and government and to become a national center of expertise in the field of biodiversity. The institute's mission is to raise awareness of the value of biodiversity and thereby promote biodiversity conservation and economic development in Costa Rica. INBio's various programs, including, e.g., biodiversity inventory, search for sustainable uses, accumulation of information, and dissemination of knowledge, complement one another and help to document the state of Costa Rica's biodiversity and to identify bioprospecting potentials. However, this is not only done by INBio. The institute is also networked with Costa Rican universities.

Except for some initial funding it was provided with, INBio is a self-supporting institution; it is entitled to receive grants and it enjoys tax-free status, although it remains responsible for its own funds and personnel. In 2001 the bioprospecting budget accounted for 11 percent of the institute's total budget, a figure that had fluctuated between 11 and 17 percent in previous years (Gámez 2003, 8). A cooperation agreement concluded between MINAE and INBio provides the legal framework for all of the institute's inventory and bioprospecting activities. Authorized through single research permits, INBio collects samples for its own inventory and bioprospecting divisions or for interested parties. Based on this agreement, INBio bioprospects only within the country's protected wild areas. Monetary benefits are shared with MINAE. The ministry receives, as an up-front payment, 10 percent of INBio's research budget and ex post 50 percent of any further royalties or milestone payments stemming from bioprospecting contracts. The benefits are used to finance the management and protection of conservation areas (MINAE 1994, Clausulas 12; Sittenfeld and Lovejoy 1999, 95).

It was only in 1998 that Costa Rica implemented the CBD, on the basis of Law on Biodiversity, No. 7788. Before that date, ABS was regulated in the framework of the Law on Wildlife Conservation and corresponding regulations. It is obvious that the experience gained with INBio, which attracted worldwide attention, had a decisive influence on the CBD. Nevertheless, with the Biodiversity Law Costa Rica adopted a new ABS approach by altering INBio's role. Some interview partners who were involved in drafting the Biodiversity Law stated that the drafting process was very fast and intensive. INBio was not to know about the new law before it was published for the first time because INBio was against the formulation of a new law. According to the interviews, the situation for INBio was better without a law like the Biodiversity Law. According to one interview partner, INBio perceives itself as the institution most competent in dealing with biodiversity issues. INBio has for this reason also prepared a draft of its own for a law, one developed mainly by scientists.

The Biodiversity Law introduces new procedures and institutions. Covering the use and management of biodiversity, associated knowledge, institutional authorities, and the basic requirements and procedure for ABS and IPRs, the new law provides the basic framework for access permits and bioprospecting contracts. It establishes the National Commission for the Management of Biodiversity (CONAGEBIO) as the institution responsible for ABS and defines its functions. CONAGEBIO is an intersectoral coordination body. It consists of ministers or representatives from the Ministry of Environment and Energy, Agriculture, Health and Foreign Trade, the Institute for Agricultural and Fishing, the Small Farmers Board, the Indigenous People Board, the National Council of Rectors, the Federation for the Conservation of the Environment, and the Union of Chambers of Commerce. The implementation process was delayed due to a challenge to the constitutionality of the extensive powers with which CONAGEBIO is vested. This is the reason why CONAGEBIO has only been operating since 2002. It has a permanent staff and its own budget. National law, and in particular the parts of it concerned with ABS, have been complemented by an ABS by-law (Rules on Access to Biodiversity 2003, Presidential Decree No. 31–514), which was published in December 2003 and defines CONAGEBIO's responsibilities. On the administrative level, CONAGEBIO is supported by a technical office, which has permanent staff.

The ABS procedure in Costa Rica can be broken down into four steps: (i) registry of applicants, (ii) conditions, (iii) approval process, and (iv) monitoring (see Figure 5.1).

Only CONAGEBIO and its technical office are authorized to grant access. PIC is obtained from other entities, e.g., conservation areas, indigenous territories, ex situ collections, and landowners. In cases in which

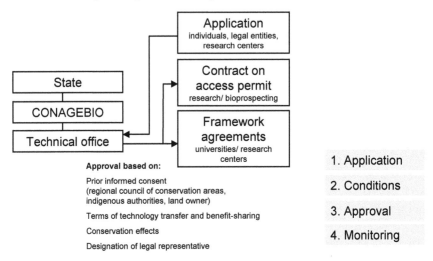

Figure 5.1   ABS procedure in Costa Rica.
Source: own presentation.

material is collected on private lands, authorization from state entities is also needed (Cabrera Medaglia 2004, 107). The permits can cover commercial and noncommercial bioprospecting permits. It is also possible to establish general framework agreements on collection permits with universities and other centers. Usually these are valid for three years and can be renewed. Permits contain a certificate of origin (Law of Biodiversity No. 7788 1998, Article 71). In general, the establishment of CONAGEBIO is seen as a very positive development because it includes all the relevant stakeholders and shifts authority to MINAE. Only one interviewee, from the university, believes that CONAGEBIO poses the same problems as IACBGR in the Philippine case.

Until the Biodiversity Law was adopted, INBio's activities were based on the Law on Wildlife Conservation and the MINAE–INBio agreement, which gave the institute much freedom and independence. The Biodiversity Law has changed this. INBio has since concluded more than twenty contracts with a number of life science companies, international research institutions, and universities (see Table 5.4). The agreements have some common criteria, as depicted in Table 5.3.

At the request of companies, the concrete terms of contracts, including, e.g., royalties, are not made public. This was criticized by some interviewees, who noted that concealing such information leads to nontransparency and mistrust.

One interesting example is a cooperation between INBio, the British Technology Group (BTG), and Ecos La Pacífica, the aim of which is to produce a nematicide for tropical crops. The nematicidal agent (DMDP) comes from a tree in the Costa Rican dry tropical forest. A product is expected

Table 5.3   Basic Criteria of Most of INBio's Bioprospecting Contracts

---

- Facilitate access to a limited amount of samples from natural resources for a limited period of time (exclusivity terms are limited)

- A significant part of the research is carried out locally and associated research costs are entirely covered by the industrial partner (defined as research budget)

- Up-front payments for conservation (a minimum of 10 percent of the research budget is transferred to MINAE for conservation purposes)

- Benefit-sharing mechanisms should be negotiated beforehand and should include, among other things:
  - Milestone payments for the discovery and development phases of a potential product, to be shared 50:50 with MINAE
  - A percentage of royalties on net sales of the final product (covering also derivatives from the original natural scaffold and/or any technology derived thereof), also to be shared 50:50 with MINAE
  - IPRs should include participation of INBio's scientists if applicable (joint patents and publications)

- Technology transfer and capacity-building for local scientists should be significant and should include state-of-the-art technologies

- The discovery and development of a product must make nondestructive uses of natural resources and be consistent with national legislation regarding access to and development of genetic resources

---

Source: adopted from Cabrera Medaglia (2002).

to enter the market some time in the future. BTG has paid a small amount of money to both INBio and Ecos for the licensing of a patent related to DMDP use (Cabrera Medaglia 2002, 20).

INBio's cooperation with international companies has served to support its scientific and technological capacity, a prerequisite for the realization of such projects. Funds from the Inter-American Development Bank have enabled small local enterprises using biological material as production to initiate low-cost projects for the local market that require relatively simple technologies and short development times. Unlike the projects carried out together with large international corporations, these small and simpler projects, none of which has been fully completed yet, are already considered to be successful initiatives, and likely to make contributions in terms of profit, employment, and agro-industrial developments with higher value added (Gámez 2003, 10).

If we take the number of contracts and their estimated share of royalties as an indicator for contracts with expectable benefits—the more contracts, the more research and the higher the possibility of discovering a substance for commercialization—the result turns out to be relatively satisfactory. In receiving an eventual royalty payment of 1 to 5 percent for one highly successful drug, Costa Rica could generate as much net national income during the life of the patent as a major crop (Sittenfeld and Gámez 1993, 75).

Table 5.4   Significant Commercial and Academic Agreements in Costa Rica, 1991–2004

Industry or academic partner	Application fields
Cornell University	Chemical prospecting
Merck & Co.	Human health and veterinary
British Technology Group	Agriculture
Ecos/La Pacifica	Agriculture
Cornell University and NIH	Human health
Bristol-Myers Squibb	Human health
Givaudan Roure	Fragrances and essences
University of Massachusetts	Insecticidal components
Diversa	Enzymes of industrial applications
Indena	Human health
Phytera Inc.	Human health
Strathclyde University	Human health
Eli Lilly	Human health and agriculture
Akkadix Corporation	Nematicidal proteins
Follajes Ticos	Ornamental applications
La Gavilana S.A.	Ecological control of pathogens of *Vanilla*
Laboratorios Lisan S.A.	Production of standardized phytophar-maceuticals
Bouganvillea S.A.	Production of standardized biopesticide
Agrobiot S.A.	Ornamental applications
Guelph University	Agriculture and conservation purposes
Florida Ice & Farm	Technical and scientific support
ChagasSpaceProgram	Chagas disease
SACRO	Ornamental applications
CIFLORPAN, Universidad de Panama	Extracts of plants
Harvard University	Extracts with potential activity from endophytic fungi

Source: adopted from Cabrera Medaglia (2002); INBio (2004).

Assignment of Property Rights and Intellectual Property Rights

Costa Rica has established property rights at all stakeholder levels, thus making it possible to earn rents from the commercialization of genetic resources and to institute conservation incentives. In the Costa Rican case efforts to assign rights and enable participation have addressed, in positive ways, the critical factor of property rights assignment. However, as in the Philippines, biodiversity is assigned to the state.

Costa Rica has implemented the principle of state sovereignty as follows. The Biodiversity Law applies to all components of biodiversity found under the state's sovereignty as well as to the processes and activities carried out under its jurisdiction or control (Law of Biodiversity No. 7788 1998, Article 3). The biochemical and genetic properties of components of biodiversity on Costa Rican territory are part of the public domain, but the state has the power to authorize their exploration, research, bioprospecting, and use (Law of Biodiversity No. 7788 1998, Article 6). This has served to create a second property rights regime in addition to private property rights for tangible biological material, which may be held by landowners (i.e., individuals, communities, state). This second regime for the genetic and biochemical information contained in resources is held by the public domain and carried out by the state or the commission (CONAGEBIO).

But even though the state has control over biodiversity under the Biodiversity Law, an important part of the benefits flow back to the National System of Conservation Areas (apart from other benefits, at least 10 percent of the research budget, 50 percent of later bonuses), indigenous communities, or to private owners, depending on the property rights on the land concerned. Conservation incentives are set by establishing a benefit-sharing scheme that permits those economic agents who decide on the use of biological resources to participate in the benefits.

Thus far bioprospecting has been undertaken only in conservation areas on state property where property rights are clearly defined and assigned. However, in the interviews representatives of indigenous people state that they do not feel that the rights of indigenous people are well represented. The majority of protected areas in Costa Rica, especially the areas where bioprospecting takes place, are scarcely inhabited. However, twelve of the twenty-four indigenous territories in Costa Rica are protected areas. In these cases PIC has been granted by the state, without participation of indigenous people.

In the interviews it became clear that it was mainly the government and INBio that benefited from such bioprospecting activities. MINAE has channeled the benefits directly to conservation areas. The way in which the benefits arising out of INBio's contracts are distributed is transparent. Between 1991 and 2000 MINAE received a total amount of US$512,148 owing to the 10 percent research budget rule. US$790,649 was directly received by the conservation areas (Cabrera Medaglia 2002, 25). According to one interview partner, MINAE invested the money entirely in conservation activities: the Island of Coco, which is absolutely uninhabited. Compared to revenues gained through selected agricultural and forest products and tourism, this contribution is small. The foreign exchange generated by timber in the same period (1991–2000) was US$2,613,000; the corresponding figure for bananas was US$57,051,000; for coffee US$32,659,000; and for tourism, one of the country's most important economic activities, US$71,986,000 (Gámez 2003, 3).

Table 5.5 Contribution to Biodiversity Conservation in Costa Rica as well as to Universities

	1991–1993	1994	1995	1996	1997	1998	1999	2000	Total
MINAE (10%)	110,040	43,400	66,670	51,092	95,196	24,160	38,793	82,797	512,148
Conservation areas	86,102	203,135	153,555	192,035	126,243	29,579	0	0	790,649
Public universities	460,409	126,006	46,962	31,265	34,694	14,186	7,123	4,083	724,728
Other groups in INBio	228,161	92,830	118,292	172,591	129,008	0	0	0	740,882
Total	884,712	465,371	385,479	446,983	385,141	67,925	45,916	86,880	2,768,407

Source: adopted from Cabrera Medaglia (2004, 111).
Estimated amounts since 1991.

As a WTO member, Costa Rica is obliged to implement IPRs protection in line with the TRIPs agreement. Patent, Drawings, and Utility Model Law No. 6867 was reformed by Law No. 7979 in 2000 to make it compatible with TRIPs. It covers microorganisms, biological processes, genes, and genetic sequences, as long as patentability requirements are met. A draft on plant breeders' rights has been formulated in accordance with UPOV 1991 (Cabrera Medaglia 2004, 116).

Its very wide scope enables the Biodiversity Law to do justice to Costa Rica's TRIPs obligations in the area of biodiversity. Apart from issues directly connected with biodiversity conservation, it addresses IPRs issues very explicitly, especially in terms of scope of application. Before they grant any kind of IPRs for biodiversity components, the National Seed Office and the Registers of Intellectual and Industrial Property are required to consult the technical office of CONAGEBIO and provide certificates of origin and PIC in order to monitor exceptions of patentability (i.e., DNA sequences, plants and animals, not genetically modified microorganisms, etc.). The technical office can prevent the registration of a patent or another IPR (Law of Biodiversity No. 7788 1998, Article 80). With the exception of the Andean Community's IPRs law (Andean Community Decision 486 2000, Article 26h), there are no other international or national IPRs laws that require such a certificate. This means that the control and prevention mechanism applies only to Costa Rica, and not to important locations like the EU or the US.

Under the terms of the contracts used, Costa Rica and INBio, as providers, are usually not involved in a patent because they are not regarded as inventors of the final product. If INBio contributes to the invention, a joint patent is possible, but thus far this has not been the case. The contributions provided by the country and the biodiversity institute are considered and acknowledged only through PIC and benefit-sharing.

ABS has become more or less accepted in Costa Rica, and it is regarded as the outcome of implementation of international obligations. Nevertheless, there are environmental, farming, and indigenous groups that object to the concept. The main reason why indigenous and farming groups are concerned is that they do not regard the rights of indigenous people and farmers as well represented. Environmental groups, which reject patents on life, consider INBio a "legal biopirate" or one "international company" selling Costa Rica's biodiversity to other international companies. INBio is strongly supported by the government. This was underlined by many interviewees. The former minister of the environment (2002–2006) was previously INBio's lawyer, and this is a clear indication of the strong relationship between INBio and the government. However, most civil society groups are seeking not to prevent bioprospecting but to increase their influence and realize their ideas by participating in CONAGEBIO or by attending negotiations in the capacity of observers and consultants, as they did, for example, in the debates on the draft bylaw for ABS.

The bylaw guarantees the participation of the local level by establishing clear rules on access applications and benefit-sharing. Because bioprospecting has taken place only on state property, no experience has been made with negotiations and benefit-sharing with private landowners. However, if this should happen in the future, ABS is unlikely to pose problems.

Information Asymmetry

Pre-contractual problems with asymmetric information do not appear to have emerged. INBio has gained considerable experience, and it now takes a realistic approach to negotiations. According to INBio, MINAE has never participated in negotiations because of its lack of capacity and interest. INBio has therefore negotiated contracts on its own, with MINAE signing them later.

Costa Rica has recognized and addressed post-contractual problems on both sides. The country has sought to protect itself against misappropriation. Interested parties do not collect bioprospecting material themselves; they receive it directly from INBio or a small number of other intermediaries (e.g., the Organization of Tropical Studies). The fact that INBio is in charge of processing nearly all bioprospecting activities makes it easier to control the uses to which Costa Rica's resources are put. According to INBio's staff, bioprospecting contracts are concluded for a certain amount of samples from specified areas. INBio keeps an identical sample in its inventory and delivers coded material to the user. If contractual partners are interested in receiving more of the material collected, they have to return to INBio. In this way, INBio keeps important information on collected material and controls its export. As already indicated, the Biodiversity Law also regulates the patenting process for bioproducts in Costa Rica. The provision of a PIC certificate amounts to an obligation within the patent application process. That is, the legal origin of the biological material used for a patent is guaranteed. However, this does not prevent patenting of material obtained illegally outside Costa Rica. The only asset Costa Rica has in this respect is the interest of companies in continuing to cooperate with INBio.

On the user side, Costa Rica has undertaken measures to address the problem of asymmetric information regarding the use of the benefits and exclusivity. Utilization of the benefits has been quite transparent so far. MINAE and INBio have made public the amounts of benefits they have received and disclosed the ways in which they have used them. This was the procedure under the old system. Even though the new approach is far more complex and many other stakeholders are involved, it can be expected to be more transparent. INBio guarantees users temporary exclusivity that varies between six months to two years. However, at present INBio does not offer any guarantee regarding the quality of the material it provides. Users are not involved in the collection process and have to trust that INBio will provide the material it promises. Nevertheless, this lack of information has not reduced companies' interest in collaborating with INBio. In working successfully and reliably in this field for more than ten years, INBio has gained experience and developed procedures, pioneering and resulting in lasting partnerships with industry and research institutions. Signaling reliability has helped INBio to stand out from the other providers and to overcome the problem arising out of the asymmetric distribution of information.

Accounting for Time Lags

Time lags can be addressed through adequate payment schemes. The bioprospecting contracts that INBio has negotiated include royalty payments and later milestone payments. However, apart from minor up-front payments, Costa Rica or INBio have not received any payments so far. In the years 1991 to 2000, the total contributions of bioprospecting activities to biodiversity conservation and education added up to US$2,768,407 (see Table 5.5). For a ten-year period, the monetary contributions due to direct payments, payments for specific samples, and coverage of research budgets have been relatively small. Due to this long and uncertain period of development, no product has yet reached the market and no royalties have been paid. However, there are some products under development, especially related to herbal applications (see Table 5.6; Cabrera Medaglia 2002, 19).

Table 5.6 Outputs Generated since 1992 as a Result of the ABS Agreements with INBio

Project	Initiated	Output
Merck & Co.	1992	Twenty-seven patents
BTG/ECOS	1992	DMDP on its way to commercialization
NCI	1999	Secondary screening for anticancer compounds
Givaudan Roure	1995	-
INDENA	1996	Two compounds with significant antibacterial activity
Diversa	1998	Two potential products at initial stages/publication under way
Phytera Inc.	1998	-
Eli Lilly & Co.	1999	-
Akkadix	1999	Fifty-two bacterial strains with nematicidal activity
CR-USA	1999	One compound with significant antimalarial activity
LISAN	2000	Two phytopharmaceuticals in the process

Source: adopted from Cabrera Medaglia (2002).

Consequently, a substantial part of benefits, in the form of future royalties and milestone payments, is still being waited for. Around 50 percent of the total revenues from bioprospecting activities have gone directly to conservation areas; research groups within INBio and national public universities have received the rest. Thus far nonmonetary benefits have dominated the ABS process, playing a major role for sustainable development. Costa Rica and INBio have benefited in different ways. Transfer of important technology has improved the infrastructure of INBio and public universities and enabled the institute to conduct research and develop products of its own, or at least more highly processed, value-added samples. The material collected, and financed by bioprospecting partners, has expanded the biodiversity inventory. Scientists and technicians have been able to build scientific capacity in terms of state-of-the-art technologies, joint research, and acknowledgments in publications. INBio and Costa Rica benefit through development of negotiation expertise and spillover effects on other economic activities like ecotourism and improvement of local legislation with a view to conservation issues (Cabrera Medaglia 2002, 26).

In monetary terms, time lags remain a problem, even though milestone payments are anticipated. These payments are relatively small. The main benefits accruing without delay to the country, and to INBio and the government in particular, are nonmonetary in nature, especially benefits that have positive effects on research capacity. This fact is acceptable for Costa Rica as management of biodiversity is the hand of the state, the dominant landowner of collection sites, and INBio is the only institution involved. In the future this picture may change as more actors become involved. This indicates that even in the case of relative success payments would rarely prove able to influence the decisions of local agents because only nonmonetary benefits are received during the time lag.

Good Governance in Provider Countries

Good governance is one factor that explains the high number of bioprospecting contracts concluded with Costa Rica. Costa Rica offers a stable democratic political system. One interviewee called it a comparative advantage that is not related to biodiversity. Costa Rica does far better than the Philippines on the World Bank Governance Indicators. For instance, 70.3 percent of the 213 countries and territories included rank lower than Costa Rica on political stability. However, all indicators showed a downward trend in the 1998–2005 ranking, although the country still has a very high ranking.

Aside from political stability, encountered relatively infrequently in biodiversity-rich countries, it is the country's clear-cut legislation and activities associated with INBio that appear to be highly valued by companies. INBio is quite independent, flexible, and reliable. It is only bound by its agreement with MINAE. This situation will change because MINAE's position will be stronger in the future. However, the comprehensive Biodiversity Law and

Table 5.7   World Bank Governance Indicators, Costa Rica (1998, 2005)

Governance Indicator	1998	2005
Voice and accountability	87.0	76.3
Political stability/no violence	84.0	70.3
Government effectiveness	72.7	64.1
Regulatory quality	80.8	68.8
Rule of law	76.0	65.7
Control of corruption	76.0	66.5

Source: based on Kaufmann, Kraay, and Mastruzzi (2006).

the bylaw developed for ABS will even further strengthen the legal framework for ABS. Other intermediaries have also been active in Costa Rica, although their activities are not regulated. In particular, their work is framed by the new regulations. Some interview partners stress that companies can find various resources in many neighboring countries where resources are cheaper and there are no rules in place on ABS. However, they prefer to come to Costa Rica because the country has a system of national parks and an adequate documentation system, and the country provides security.

According to INBio, there is a relatively high level of interest on the part of international companies and research institutions in bioprospecting in Costa Rica (together with INBio). Costa Rica and INBio have concluded many more contracts than other countries. The situation of legal certainty in the country is a guarantee that the Costa Rican partner will meet its contractual commitments. INBio's application procedure is quite transparent. INBio is not the only intermediary in Costa Rica that bioprospects and assists interested companies and researchers. Private persons as well as other organizations seek to work in the field, but not on the same scale as INBio. These intermediaries have no agreement with MINAE, and that means that they carry out their activities in a gray area. The number of contracts concluded with such intermediaries is not significant; an observation that supports the argument that lack of legal certainty deters companies from undertaking bioprospecting activities.

It remains to be seen whether CONAGEBIO will be able to offer the same level of security as INBio. One interviewee from the industry side has doubts and states that CONAGEBIO will be unable to provide the same services, and in particular the confidentiality, that users have valued so highly.

ADMINISTRATIVE COMPLEXITY

INBio was founded with international support and with the objective to support the country's responsibilities in biodiversity inventory, the search for sustainable uses, accumulation of information, and dissemination of knowledge. The biodiversity institute is the national center of expertise for bioprospecting. This means brief time frames in the negotiation of contracts, and it thus serves to lower transaction costs for companies. According to INBio's staff, it is possible to conclude a bioprospecting contract with INBio within one year; in other countries the process takes much longer. Experiences seem to prove that a specialized—possibly private (be it profit or nonprofit) organization is in a better position to fulfill this function in a more efficient manner than government institutions, especially when it comes to the process of applying for access. INBio even has a business development officer responsible for cooperation with bioprospecting partners. Users can thus find a competent contact person at the institute. The Biodiversity Institute is not part of the complex government administration, and it operates as a consultant. INBio's nonprofit status prevents it from abusing its preeminent position in relation to bioprospecting. In setting up an independent institution with expertise in crucial fields, one embedded in a stable political system, Costa Rica has succeeded in gaining a leading position in bioprospecting.

There are varying assessments concerning the changes in processing expected to result from the creation of CONAGEBIO as the new government national focal point for biodiversity policy and management. In the interviews, the demand side appears to be very content with the existing regulations. Although the Biodiversity Law is referred to by some experts as the most ambitious and elaborate national law of its kind, bioprospectors and intermediaries assume that the new regulation will make the process of application more complicated and that Costa Rica's competitive advantage in the bioprospecting market will vanish. One Costa Rican researcher who is involved in bioprospecting complained that Costa Rica tends to follows the Philippines. Under the new bylaw, INBio can still work as an intermediary, but CONAGEBIO is authorized to participate in and supervise negotiations with bioprospectors and to approve MAT and PIC. The composition of CONAGEBIO, which represents the major stakeholders concerned, may lead to longer negotiation and decision-making processes due to differences in opinion. Besides, one interviewee notes that its members are also very busy and may at times not attend meetings, just as in the Philippine case. The transaction costs for both the provider and the user side are expected to increase, and this is bound to undermine the efficiency of ABS. Even though the interview partners support the new system, they underline that the process will be a more complex one.

It would appear that the Costa Rican structure, with only one independent agency, is one of its assets. The resulting short decision processes were especially interesting for the demand side. The new processes will presumably be more time-consuming, taking, as they must, account of the interests of stakeholders that were formerly not part of the process. However, Costa Rica will benefit even if this increased participation of stakeholders raises transaction costs. This participation will also be a requirement even if bioprospecting takes place not only on state property but on private and community property as well.

Market Structure

In principle, Costa Rica's bargaining position is relatively weak due to the oligopsonistic nature of competition. Despite the ongoing loss of biodiversity, the total supply of diverse genetic material is still sufficient to satisfy demand. It is still possible to obtain samples, even though the total number of species is decreasing. In many countries access is not regulated and can be had free of cost. The degree of competition among buyers is therefore far lower than on the supplier side. The diverse biological resources found in the Mesoamerican biological corridor, from Mexico to Colombia, tend to be similar, and an interested company has no trouble substituting one country for another. In fact, INBio and Costa Rica have succeeded in attracting many interested parties, more than any other country in the Mesoamerican biological corridor, even though unregulated access was available in competing countries. This success can be attributed to the scientific capacity of INBio, the National System of Conserved Areas, and other institutions (e.g., the Organization of Tropical Studies), and this in turn is the result of years of research conducted by international biodiversity scientists in the country as well as of the transfer of technology, knowledge, and human capacity. Because transaction costs are much lower in Costa Rica than in other countries, users are highly interested in bioprospecting in Costa Rica, and this has substantially improved INBio's bargaining position.

Since 2002 a group of megadiverse countries has been established, with Costa Rica as one of its members. A coalition of this kind may be expected to strengthen the market position of supplier countries if the group is treated as such. However, the bargaining position of provider countries is still weakened by the existence of ex situ collections. The Biodiversity Law applies for Costa Rica, and bioprospecting samples, in situ or ex situ, can be obtained on the basis of an access permit. Nevertheless, access to ex situ collections in other countries and access to pre-CBD, stored material is not regulated internationally and companies still fall back on these collections. Their selection is limited, though, and expectations of finding promising genetic material in these collections is not as high as they would be for samples obtained from in situ sites or ex situ collections created after the adoption of the CBD. Hence, industry continues to have a great interest in bioprospecting contracts (Wynberg and A Laird 2005).

Conclusions

Costa Rica is one example for a relatively successful ABS strategy. The number of contracts with companies in the life science industry is high, and considerable nonmonetary benefits accrue to Costa Rica. However, thus far the benefits have been only scientific, academic, and industrial in nature; conservation benefits have played a very small role. The popularity the country enjoys in connection with the bioprospecting contracts it signs affects other economic activities, including nature-oriented tourism. INBio has developed into an outstanding research institution with high scientific and technological capacity in Central America. The national university also benefits from the institution's work. Successful partnerships with local enterprises that have developed in the agro-industrial sector in connection with Costa Rica's bioprospecting program have created jobs and benefited the local level by developing new products for the local market.

Table 5.8   Overview on Costa Rica and the Critical Factors

	Costa Rica
Property rights	Tangible material is subject to private property rights; intangible material is subject to state property rights At present, bioprospecting only on state property IPRs application process requires certificate of origin
Asymmetric information	No pre-contractual problems Post-contractual problems on both sides have been recognized and addressed: users cannot collect themselves; exclusivity and quality are guaranteed; benefits flow to protection areas
Time lags	Bioprospecting contracts include rules for milestone payments and royalties Apart from minor up-front payments, no payments have been received by Costa Rica or INBio so far (many patents, products expected soon)
Good governance	Stable democratic and political system favors bioprospecting INBio, ABS framework, and experience provide security
Administrative complexity	INBio is a very efficient non-state institution Complexity will increase when the intersectoral committee takes up its work
Market structure	High reputation and low transaction costs improve market position Member of the group of megadiverse countries

The ecological data on Costa Rica also show positive development. The monetary benefits are modest, though. This is one important indicator for the fact that the ecological progress in Costa Rica is not only, and perhaps not even mainly, due to the commercialization of biodiversity associated with bioprospecting. In Costa Rica, ABS is only one part of a comprehensive strategy. Nevertheless, there are good reasons to take Costa Rica as a model country for designing ABS procedures. The country handles many of the critical factors analyzed here in an outstanding way. With the establishment of one single authority in the bioprospecting process, Costa Rica has lowered transaction costs (in contract preparation and enforcement) for interested companies, thus greatly improving its bargaining position. The bioprospecting procedure alleviates the country's informational deficiencies on the use of biological material, and thus at the same time its enforcement costs.

INBio, sharing joint responsibility with the government as the agents responsible for the management of biodiversity in the country, is also in charge of the bioprospecting process. In this respect, incentives have been set correctly.

It must be noted, though, that this has taken place in a very favorable environment. Good governance and political stability have helped INBio in important ways to win its good reputation in bioprospecting. Costa Rica is a small and not too densely populated country. Property rights over biological resources are defined and assigned. This has all helped in designing an efficient institutional setting. Nevertheless, there are problems not yet solved. Payments come late, and they tend to be uncertain. The efficient decision process involved operates without much influence from other stakeholders. Thus far INBio has not managed to gain acceptance among stakeholders, who have not yet participated formally in the bargaining process. However, as an NGO and non-state organization, INBio should be in a position to integrate all stakeholders' views.

In conclusion, it appears that the establishment of an intermediate organization like INBio that provides technical and scientific capacity and assists partners in bioprospecting activities may enable countries to greatly enhance their chances to participate in the benefits of bioprospecting. This may contribute to changing attitudes towards the sustainable use of natural resources, and thus have a positive impact on the ecological situation. It should not be hoped, though, that ABS alone—with the uncertain payments promised in connection with it—can stop deforestation processes. A comprehensive strategy is the minimum requirement to make any progress in this field.

ETHIOPIA[11]

Ethiopia was chosen as the third case study. Ethiopia is a very special case because the country is a very strong actor at the international level, whereas

it falls behind many other countries when it comes to national implementation and the empirical data it provides is quite limited. The analysis presented in this case study follows the other two case studies. The analytic
framework developed, which is based on the critical factors and potential
measures, is viewed in the country-specific case in order to test and illustrate its applicability. We will start out by briefly presenting the case study
methodology. This will be followed by short introduction to the Ethiopian case and a discussion of the regulatory environment, including the
legal and institutional setting. The focus of the introduction is wild coffee
genetic resources, the reason being that the author participated in a project
dealing with the specific case of wild coffee genetic resources in Ethiopia. Genetic wild coffee resources are a very interesting example because
whereas wild coffee is a crop, its characteristics are similar to the wild plant
genetic resources used in pharmaceutical research. This case study is therefore seen as be very useful for the present analysis.

The main part of the analysis consists of an application of the critical
factors to the country-specific case. Taking into account the established analytic framework regarding effectiveness (see Chapter 4), the sections looks
at how the critical factors are shaped and how they are being addressed in
Ethiopia. Because Ethiopia has only recently adopted a set of regulations,
lack of data sets limits to the analysis. However, we have come up with some
very interesting results; they are summarized in the "Conclusions" section.

Case Study Methodology

The expert interviews in Ethiopia were carried out in cooperation with the
Center for Development Research in the framework of the project "Conservation and Use of Wild Populations of *Coffea arabica* in the Montane
Rainforests of Ethiopia." This explains why the focus of this case study is
on the use of coffee genetic resources. Other crop genetic resources are also
highly relevant and under threat in Ethiopia. However, coffee serves as an
interesting example because it is a product of high commercial value. This
case study looks into the regulatory framework for all genetic resources in
Ethiopia; however, it focuses in particular on coffee. Whereas the emphasis
of the other two case studies is on wild plant genetic resources, wild coffee
is an example of crop genetic resources that are not domesticated but are
available in the wild.

Like Costa Rica and the Philippines, Ethiopia is a country with a high
level of biodiversity, and it suffers from a major loss of the forests that
harbor this diversity. Compared to the other case studies, Ethiopia's high
diversity consists in particular of crop genetic diversity. When the case
study was in progress (October 2003), Ethiopia had not put any ABS system in place, although it was heavily involved in the international negotiations in the CBD framework. The declaration "A Proclamation to Provide
Access to Genetic Resources and Community Knowledge and Community

Rights" (Proclamation No. 482/2006) was adopted in February 2006, and its implementation is in progress. The relevant provisions and implications of this legal document are factored into the analysis. However, as far as genetic resources are concerned, Ethiopia is at present an open-access country. A considerable amount of biological material stemming originally from Ethiopia has been used for research, development, and commercialization abroad, but few benefits have been shared with the country.

Some time ago, Ethiopia started to develop a legislative framework to address these problems, and it has finally adopted a document that implements the CBD's ABS provisions. The Ethiopian case is, therefore, excellently suited for a closer look. The case of Ethiopia is also assessed on the basis of the critical factors identified earlier, and this includes an analysis of how these factors or their interdependence will affect the current situation and efforts to implement the national ABS regime in Ethiopia. Even though Ethiopia has only recently implemented its ABS regulations, and thus no experiences with the implementation of ABS are available, the analysis of the critical factors can still be used. Based on the experiences gained in the past as well as on an analysis of the proclamation indicating the course Ethiopia has chosen to implement the ABS concept, it is possible to highlight the problems involved and to draw valuable conclusions.

The data are based on expert interviews conducted in Ethiopia in October 2003. Semistructured interviews were used as a method for gathering and analyzing qualitative data. Various thematic areas in line with the identified critical factors were addressed throughout the interview process. Because ABS has not yet played any role in Ethiopia, it was possible to identify only a limited number of experts. About fifteen experts were interviewed. They represent the variety of stakeholders involved in the ABS process or persons in possession of expertise related to the ABS issue (see list in the Appendix). Additionally, secondary literature (e.g., books, journal articles, and reports) is used to complement the information gained from the interviews.

Introduction

Thanks to its geographical characteristics, including range of altitudes, rainfall patterns, and soil variability, Ethiopia is in possession of substantial biodiversity and natural resources as well as many endemic species. The country's complex topography and environmental heterogeneity offer suitable environments for a wide range of life forms. The vegetation types found in Ethiopia are highly diverse and range from Afro-alpine to desert vegetation. It has a large number of plant species: over seven thousand species, of which about 12 percent are probably endemic (Institute of Biodiversity Conservation and Research [IBCR] 2007). Only a limited number of studies have been conducted to assess Ethiopia's diversity and to estimate its economic value.

Ethiopia is one of the world's major Vavilovian centers of origin and crop diversity. Famous examples include coffee and teff, the major stable food of Ethiopians. For instance, wild coffee varieties derived from wild populations of *Coffea arabica* with a large potential future value still exist in Ethiopia's montane forests. These forests are situated in the south and southwestern parts of the country (Kumilachew 2001, 115–122). These genetic resources not only have potential OV, they also have DUV. Wherever accessible, coffee is harvested directly from these naturally regenerating and unmanaged wild coffee trees. This forest coffee system contributes about 6 percent to Ethiopia's total coffee output (Demel Teketay 1999). Furthermore, there are wild coffee trees in inaccessible forest areas that are not utilized at all.

Besides this in situ existence of coffee genetic resources, there are landraces of coffee in the other coffee-farming systems of Ethiopia, the semi-forest and the home garden coffee system (Tadesse Woldemariam and Demel Teketay 2001, 131–141). In addition to in situ and on-farm management, coffee genetic resources have been collected and conserved ex situ in field gene banks in Ethiopia as well as in various other countries (FAO 1998). The users of wild coffee are breeders. Coffee breeding at the national level is found mainly in countries other than Ethiopia (e.g., Columbia, Kenya) as well as at international research institutes (e.g., Agricultural Research for Developing Countries [CIRAD]). It is interesting to note that although worldwide coffee processing and marketing is mainly in the hands of the private sector, breeding research is done mainly in the public sector (Richerzhagen and Virchow 2007, 69). In view of the fact that this unique situation of a country of origin where genetic resources still exist in situ, on-farm, as well as in ex situ conservation facilities, it is important to note that this situation is threatened and—without determined commitment right now—the country's valuable coffee genetic resources may be lost both in situ and on-farm within one or two decades.

This threat of extinction for plant genetic resources is due to the fact that Ethiopia's remaining natural montane rain forests, the habitat of wild plants, are under constant pressure bound up with land use conflicts in forests and on forest fringes. One hundred years ago, natural forest covered more than 40 percent of the country's highland area. Today the figure has decreased to less than 3 percent (Gebre Markos Selassie and Deribe Gurmu 2001). Ethiopia's forests are threatened by demand for forest products on the one hand and by conversion of forest areas into agricultural or settlement land on the other. The former is determined by demand for fuelwood (95 percent of overall demand for forest products), construction timbers (4 percent), and industrial timber (1 percent). The underlying force is population growth and the related increase in energy demand and construction activities. With demand outstripping supply, one of the critical results is uncontrolled wood harvesting. The gap between supply and demand is widening significantly to the disadvantage of the remaining forest, due to a lack of major reforestation programs (Berhanu Mengesha and Million Bekele 2001, 97–114). It appears that this gap will continue to grow if little heed continues to be paid to the need for investment in forestry.

Conversion into agricultural or settlement land is the second major reason for the plight of Ethiopia's rain forests, one that threatens to wipe out wild populations of plants and their genetic resources. Rapid rates of clearing to open up new agricultural and settlement land are driven in part by the need for compensation for land lost through degradation, but above all by the need to accommodate the rapidly increasing population and its need for new agricultural land. The concentration of population in the Ethiopian highlands poses a threat to the remaining forest areas. Seventy percent of Ethiopia's population lives in the highlands, which occupy only 40 percent of the country's total area (Gebre Markos Selassie and Deribe Gurmu 2001). Besides internal population growth, migration to forest areas is generated by various external pressures, including, for instance, poverty, lack of employment opportunities, and droughts on the northern highlands leading to government-planned resettlement schemes in the southwestern rain forests (Tadesse Woldemariam et al. 2001, 237–248; Yonas 2001; Reusing 1998; Alemneh Dejene 1990). These resettlement schemes are, however, not a sustainable answer to the famines experienced in the northern part of Ethiopia, and it is already clear that migration will continue, further endangering the survival of both rain forests and wild plant genetic resources in the montane rain forests of Ethiopia (Yonas 2001). Aside from this intersectoral aspect of migration, another reason for the deforestation process is the present movement of people within forests due to unsustainable shifting cultivation or pressures to move exerted by forestry staff or settlement policies.

In addition, the country's rain forest areas are attracting the interest of investors due to their high ecological potential for growing coffee and tea. Hence, forest areas are in the process of being either thinned out or cleared for coffee, tea, or rubber tree plantations, and this has a negative impact on the habitats of wild genetic resources (Kumilachew 2001, 115–122).

According to Demel Teketay (2002), deforestation of the montane rain forest continues at a pace of up to 200,000 hectares per year. At present, only 2.3 million hectares of montane rain forest are left, and which 0.7 million hectares of this area is slightly disturbed and 1.6 million hectares highly disturbed by human activities. Based on the deforestation rate reported for the 1990s, there is reason to expect that Ethiopia's whole montane rain forest, including all of its wild plant genetic resources, will have disappeared in less than fifteen years. Today about 5 percent of Ethiopia's territory is officially protected, but even these areas suffer from poaching and illegal logging.

The minor efforts undertaken by the government to allocate needed financial resources to forestry conservation are an indication of the government's marginal commitment to forest and wild coffee conservation.

Between 1992 and 1999 only 0.1 percent of all investment projects in Ethiopia were related to forestry, and just 0.04 percent of all financial resources were allocated to forest conservation and development (Berhanu Mengesha and Million Bekele 2001, 97–114).

With US$160 gross national income (GNI) per capita in 2005, Ethiopia is one of the world's poorest countries (GNI: Philippines US$1,300 and Costa Rica US$4,590 in 2005) (World Bank 2006a, 2006b, 2006c). In 2004 Ethiopia ranked 170th among 177 countries on the UNDP Human Development Index (HDI). Of the population, 80.7 percent live on less than US$2 a day, and 42 percent of the population is undernourished (UNDP 2004, 142). In the past thirty years, Ethiopia has suffered from wars, food shortages, political instability, and famine, all of which has aggravated the situation extremely. This situation has also led to high pressure on Ethiopia's environment.

To sum up, Ethiopia's montane rain forests are declining at an alarming rate, and together with forests, wild genetic resources, and especially the endemic wild populations of *Coffea arabica*, are at risk of extinction. What Tewolde exclaimed sixteen years ago: "Arabica coffee has the bizarre distinction of being commercially one of the most important and, at the same time, in terms of genetic conservation, is one of the most neglected crops in the world" still holds true for all of Ethiopia's genetic resources with commercial potential (Egziabher Tewolde Berhan Gebre 1990, 65–72).

Regulatory Environment: Legal and Institutional Setting

The Institute of Biodiversity Conservation (IBC) is the leading agency for biodiversity management and ABS issues in Ethiopia. The IBC's proclamation of establishment authorizes IBC to grant permission for the collection of biological resources (Proclamation No. 120/1998). Until 2005 IBC was the IBCR and its mandate also covered research. Whereas this mandate was abolished, conservation-based research is still an issue.

Other organizations involved in biodiversity issues include the Environmental Protection Authority (EPA) and the Ethiopian Wildlife Conservation Organization (EWCO). EPA represents Ethiopia at international conferences and develops the legal frameworks for environmental protection. EWCO is responsible for the implementation of CITES (Yifru 2003, 108).

Ethiopia is a member of the CBD, but the country has not developed and implemented legislation to specifically implement the convention. In 1998 the country adopted a nonbinding National Policy on Biodiversity Conservation. For a long time the only law that broadly addressed access to and use of biological resources was the Forest Conservation, Development and Utilization Proclamation of 1994. This law generally aims to ensure the participation of local communities in forest conservation activities and benefits arising out of the utilization of forests (Yifru 2003, 112). At the international level, Ethiopia was heavily involved in the development of an African Model Law on ABS. The Ethiopian Institute for Sustainable Development (ISD) and EPA prepared the draft for the law that was later adopted. Even though Ethiopia was involved in the development of the African Model Law, it has only recently implemented a set of ABS regulations.

In 1998, a national committee led by the IBC and EPA started to develop a draft proclamation on access to genetic resources. The draft has been discussed in various workshops and among stakeholders. The involvement of local communities has been very limited. The draft proclamation was finally adopted as a proclamation in February 2006. In the interviews an EPA representative explained the delay with reference to the urgency of other problems and advantages of a defensive position. The civil war (1998–2000) stopped Ethiopia's development process and generated problems that required considerable resources. Developing an ABS regime fell back among the country's priorities. Another reason is that Ethiopia has no patent system that can be applied to life forms. Because patented genetic resources that originate from Ethiopia can still be used in Ethiopia, ignoring foreign patents, the problem was not considered very urgent. According to the EPA, Ethiopia decided to concentrate its resources to fight at the international level, for example, by developing the model law and by standing up for its position in the international negotiations.

The objective of Proclamation No. 482/2006 of 2006, "Access to Genetic Resources and Community Knowledge, and Community Rights," is "to ensure that the country and its communities obtain a fair and equitable share from the benefits arising out of the use of genetic resources so as to promote the conservation and sustainable utilization of the country's biodiversity resources" (Article 3). Many parts of the law follow the ABS sections of the African Model Law, and the law addresses genetic resources collected in situ and ex situ in Ethiopia. It applies neither to the customary use and exchange of genetic resources by and among Ethiopian communities nor to trade in biological resources used for direct consumption (Proclamation No. 482/2006, Article 4).

According to IBC staff, until the proclamation was adopted the IBC used MTA in accordance with the FAO Code of Conduct to transfer material for public and postgraduate research. Addis Ababa University has also developed guidelines and standard MTA to transfer material for research purposes.

It was mentioned in an interview with a staff member of the National Herbarium that two important ABS contracts have been concluded in the past. The first is on teff. Teff is a crop indigenous to Ethiopia and at the same time the country's major staple food. A Dutch company improves teff varieties, grows them, and produces gluten-free flour, an ingredient used in gluten-free diets and sports foods. The company has agreed, in a memorandum of understanding with the Ethiopian Institute for Agricultural Research (EIAR, formerly Ethiopian Agricultural Research Organization [EARO]), on benefit-sharing that offers Ethiopia joint ownership for teff varieties developed by the company (Feyissa 2006, 9). Ethiopia will receive as compensation €10 for every hectare of teff sewn outside of Ethiopia. The company has also agreed to deposit 5 percent of net profits in a fund that it will use to support Ethiopian farmers, for instance, by promoting a commercial approach to teff cultivation. The company will deposit €20,000 annually in that fund until it starts to make a profit on teff. Ethiopia now wants to revise these agreements because they were concluded before the proclamation came into force. A committee has been appointed in Ethiopia to look into this issue. Negotiations with the Ethiopian government on how to share the profits are progressing slowly, but the company is proceeding with its applications for IPRs to grow its teff crop as well as for production of all products containing teff or teff flour. The company has been criticized by several NGOs regarding these applications. It won the Captain Hook Award for biopiracy in 2004, an award given by an NGO to companies, individuals, or institutes that it considers to be biopirates (Coalition Against Biopiracy 2007).

Apart from the teff agreement, one other ABS agreement was signed in 2006. The Ethiopian government and Vernique Biotech, a British-based start-up company, agreed on a contract to commercialize vernonia oil. Vernonia is a—once nearly extinct—weed that grows in eastern Ethiopia. Its seeds yield oil that may provide a living source for epoxy compounds. These compounds are currently produced entirely from petrochemicals. At present epoxy sales amount to US$15 billion per year, and this means that there is a huge market for its potential substitute. In exchange for access, the company agreed to pay a mix of license fees, royalties, and a share of profits to the Ethiopian government over the next ten years. Because vernonia grows only close to the equator, Vernique decided to cultivate it in Ethiopia. Cultivation started in 2004 with 200 hectares, but the company intends to expand the area to thousands of hectares. Many local farmers will thus be paid to cultivate vernonia in an area that is reportedly not well suited for crop production (Cookson 2006).

Ethiopia and the African Model Law

Many African countries regard the CBD and TRIPs as agreements that run counter to their understanding of property rights. They argue that the CBD acknowledges the sovereign rights of states over their biological resources, whereas TRIPs confers monopoly rights on the basis of IPRs without acknowledging technologies, innovations, and practices of local communities and their collective ownership of common goods (Ekpere 2000, 1). In their opinion, TRIPs cannot protect and reward valuable indigenous knowledge. Nevertheless, many African countries are members of the WTO and therefore obliged to implement the TRIPs agreement. In order to fill the gap and to provide these countries with a *sui generis* system for protection of plant varieties, a chapter on breeders' rights was included in the model law. It was hoped that such a model law would be able to reconcile the conflicting approaches arising out of the CBD and TRIPs and assist African countries in their efforts to implement the CBD (Zerbe 2003, 13). Furthermore, the African countries intended to widen the scope of the model law to include agricultural development, indigenous knowledge systems, conservation and sustainable use of biological resources, community rights, equitable sharing of the benefits, and national sovereignty consistent with the provisions of the CBD (Zerbe 2003, 16).

The African Model Legislation on the Protection of the Rights of Local Communities, Farmers, Breeders and the Regulation of Access to Biological Resource was approved at the conference of the Organization of African Unity (OAU)[12] in Lusaka, Zambia, in July 2001. A draft of the model law had been developed by the Ethiopian EPA, the Third World Network, and the ISD in Ethiopia. It was discussed and finally adopted as a draft model law in Addis Ababa in 1998. In the same year the sixty-eighth Ordinary Session of the Council of Ministers of the OAU recommended that governments of member states should adopt the draft model legislation. Until 2001, the law was further developed and redrafted, and it was supposed from then on to assist Union members in formulating their own national legislation.

The objectives of the model law reflect its broad scope. Against the background of food security, it aims at conservation, evaluation, and sustainable use of biological resources, including agricultural genetic resources, knowledge, and technology. The model law applies not only to in situ genetic resources but also to ex situ collections and derivatives from biological resources. It acknowledges and aims to protect the rights of local communities over their biological resources, knowledge, and technology. Its main features include a system of access to resources and knowledge, promotion of a mechanism for fair and equitable benefit-sharing, and the acknowledgment and protection of communities', farmers' and plant breeders' rights as explained in the following:

- System of access to biological resources: the system is in line with the CBD, including PIC, MAT, and benefit-sharing. Patents on life forms and biological processes are not recognized.
- Community rights: the model law defines community rights as rights that entitle communities to sovereign rights over their resources, innovations, practices, knowledge and technologies, and benefits arising out of their use.
- Farmers' rights: the model law recognizes farmers' contributions to the conservation, development, and sustainable use of genetic resources and regards the recognition of farmers' rights as a necessary incentive to continue these achievements. In the model law farmers' rights are defined as the rights to participate in benefit-sharing, to save, use, exchange, and sell farm-saved seed, and to use protected varieties to

develop farmers' varieties and save, use, multiply, and process these newly developed varieties.

- Breeders' rights: the model law recognizes breeders' efforts toward and investments in the development of new varieties of plants. Plant breeders' rights include exclusive right to sell or license material of a newly developed variety if the variety is clearly distinguishable, stable, and homogenous. Despite its recognition of these rights, the model law emphasizes the rights of farmers to save, exchange, and use seed material in order to produce seeds for a second sowing.

Although ambitions were high, efforts to overcome the initial problems have failed due to implementation problems. Thus far the model law has not been widely adopted across Africa. Due to financial, institutional, and political problems, only a few countries have taken steps to establish legal frameworks for its implementation (Zerbe 2003, 22). It appears that the model law will not be implemented unless capacities are available and certain frameworks have already been established. The model law has been criticized by WIPO and UPOV mainly for its rejection of patents on life forms and biological processes and its provisions on farmers' and breeders' rights (Egziabher Tewolde Berhan Gebre 2002).

Assigning Property Rights and Intellectual Property Rights

Under the Ethiopian Constitution, land belongs to the state and citizens have only use rights to it (Constitution of Ethiopia 1994, Article 40.3). Tenure is insecure. The absence of integrated land use policies and regulations contributes significantly to the loss of forest resources and biodiversity as well as to the expansion of agriculture into forests. The government regularly redistributes land. Without secure forestland tenure, farmers have no incentive to make any long-term investments in forestry (Melesse Damtie 2001). Without legal instruments, it is difficult to prosecute alleged offenders and impose adequate penalties. The interviews made it clear that the government of Ethiopia does not intend to legalize private property rights to land in the near future. Nor are analogous private IPRs to biological resources accepted. Ethiopia is not a member of the WTO. Whereas it has observer status and is seeking membership, at present the country is not bound by the TRIPs agreement. The interviews at EPA made it clear that some people involved in ABS policy-making strongly object to patents on life forms and consider CBD and TRIPs contradictory. In fact, Ethiopia has even played a major role in uniting Africa to come up with a position against patents on life forms (Yifru 2003, 116). At present Ethiopia excludes all life forms (i.e., plants, animals, and microorganisms) from patentability. However, if Ethiopia becomes a member of the WTO the country will have to alter this view.

The ABS regulations in Ethiopia give consideration to national characteristics and the African Model Law. Under the proclamation, ownership of genetic resources is vested in the state and the peoples of Ethiopia (Proclamation No. 482/2006, Article 5.1). However, the state has the authority to decide on the use of Ethiopian genetic resources. PIC has to be granted by the competent national authority, which is IBC. In keeping with the African Model Law, the Ethiopian proclamation recognizes and protects community rights. Local communities have the right to use and exchange genetic resources and share in the benefits, but their PIC is not required if their genetic resources are subject to an ABS agreement. Rights over the knowledge of communities are protected more strongly (Proclamation No. 482/2006, Article 6–10).

The proclamation stipulates that the benefits should be shared between the state and communities. Communities should receive 50 percent of the benefits in the form of money, which should be used to the common advantage of the local communities concerned (Proclamation No. 482/2006, Article 9). However, the government is responsible for distribution. Communities will be dependent on the mechanism developed by the government. Such a mechanism is still missing. Due to the absence of a land use policy, not much can be expected. In some the interviews doubts were expressed as to whether Ethiopia's government will be able to realize this aim.

Information Asymmetry

In Ethiopia there are no observable pre-contractual problems arising from information deficiencies regarding expected benefits. Post-contractual problems on the provider side are much more relevant. The proclamation seeks to address these problems. However, the document in no way addresses information problems on the user side regarding exclusivity, use of shared benefits, and quality. Many interview partners stress that Ethiopia has very little capacity to monitor the flow of genetic material with Ethiopian origin. Thus far Ethiopia, supported by international NGOs, has used the power of public relations to disclose cases of inappropriate behavior. Many interviewees underlined that Ethiopia depends on the support of user countries, including, for example, Germany. Nevertheless, as long as Ethiopia has not implemented the CBD provision on ABS, no such activities are illegal, even if they are not compatible with the CBD.

Ethiopia now intends to monitor ABS activities in the country by creating joint research projects and encouraging the participation of Ethiopians in collection and research. Besides, the proclamation calls on local communities and regional bodies to monitor the use of genetic resources (Proclamation No. 482/2006, Article 28). NGOs representatives in particular note that public awareness is quite low and that it will take time to integrate local communities into the process.

Applications of foreigners for access to genetic resources are accepted only if they include a supporting document from the competent authority that has been issued with regard to the CBD in their home countries (e.g., the environment ministry in Germany) and if they agree to be accompanied by personnel from IBC to another designated institution. However, users of genetic resources can do even more than merely comply with these obligations. Establishing research or even development units in the country will certainly facilitate monitoring and build trust between Ethiopia and users. Users are urged to provide regular progress reports on their work and deposit samples of their material with IBC (Proclamation No. 482/2006, Article 17).

Furthermore, it was underlined in the interviews that export controls designed to monitor the flow of genetic material leaving Ethiopia play an important role. The proclamation also emphasizes this. Customs officers, quarantine control institutions, and mail service institutions are required to inspect material taken out of Ethiopia and to ask for an export permit (Proclamation No. 482/2006, Article 30/31/32). At present it appears that Ethiopia lacks the human resources to check exports in general. According to the interviewees, training for customs officers will present a big challenge.

The penalties that can be imposed on collectors for unapproved use of genetic resources are relatively high. Depending on the circumstances and the type of genetic material concerned, any person engaged in access activities without securing an access permit from the competent authority can be punished with prison (between three months and twelve years) or a fine (between US$600 and US$6,000; Proclamation No. 482/2006, Article 35).

National research is exempt from ABS regulations. IBC can grant researchers access permits, and these are not issued on the basis of the access procedure. Here Ethiopia has addressed an issue that is hotly debated at the international level, and this simplified access for national researchers.

Ethiopia rejects the patenting of life forms and hopes to be able to prevent the misappropriation of genetic material originating in Ethiopia. User measures such as disclosure of origin in patent applications are not applicable in this case. Ethiopia is expected in the long term to become a member of the WTO. In this case, the Ethiopian government will have to review its position due to its noncompliance with the TRIPs agreement.

Accounting for Time Lags

Ethiopia has very little experience with ABS at the national level, and time lags have not played a major role because, until recently, no ABS agreement had been concluded and no payment schemes that could adequately address the time lag had been developed. In the interviews it was often stressed that the main reason why Ethiopia has already lost much of its genetic resources is that it has been an open-access country. However, this will change in the future. The first ABS agreement on teff, concluded before the proclamation was adopted, already indicated such change. The company pays a fee of €10 to Ethiopia for every hectare of teff sewn outside of Ethiopia. Besides, there is a 5 percent royalty rate, a figure at the upper end of supposed "world market rates" (1 to 5 percent), which flows into a fund. Furthermore, the company makes an up-front payment in the form of a deposit of €20,000. Nevertheless, it is not clear how the local level will benefit. Even if community rights are recognized and monetary benefits are shared, there are doubts whether this mechanism will set incentives for conservation at the local level and bridge the time lag.

However, Ethiopia focuses strongly on nonmonetary benefits. Nonmonetary benefits are benefits that emerge independently of the up-front payments. The interviews with IBC made it clear that Ethiopia wants research on genetic resources collected in Ethiopia to be done in Ethiopia, and in a manner that facilitates the participation of relevant agents in the country, including, e.g., local organizations and academic institutions designated by IBC. Only in the case that this is not possible is it permissible to conduct such research activities abroad. Ethiopia's research infrastructure is quite poor. Unlike Costa Rica, Ethiopia lacks the scientific capacities that result from long-term research by international scientists and transfer of technology, knowledge, and human capacity. It is likely that only a limited number of companies and researchers will find initial conditions and incentives sufficient to induce them to invest in research and development in Ethiopia. Unfortunately, IBC attaches less importance to research (with the exception of conservation-based research) than it does to policy and conservation activities.

Good Governance in Provider Countries

The general political situation in Ethiopia may be described as relatively unstable. In the past ten years Ethiopia has undertaken many efforts to advance democratization and decentralization. However, these processes were slowed down by the border war with Eritrea from 1998 to 2000. It was only in May 2005 that democratic reforms led to heavy participation in elections. However, the results were contested and civil unrest ensued (Lemma Teigist 2006). The World Bank's Government Indicators 1996–2005 confirm this finding.

Table 5.9 World Bank Governance Indicators, Ethiopia (1998, 2005)

Governance Indicator	1998	2005
Voice and accountability	28.0	19.3
Political stability/no violence	18.9	8.0
Government effectiveness	51.7	15.8
Regulatory quality	36.0	13.9
Rule of law	53.8	28.0
Control of corruption	53.9	25.1

Source: based on Kaufmann, Kraay, and Mastruzzi (2006).

The indicator for political stability amounts to 8 percent, i.e., only 8 percent of the other 213 countries and territories in the world rank lower than Ethiopia, whereas 92 percent rank higher.

The unstable political situation is reflected in Ethiopia's environmental policy. One thing that can be observed is a lack of political will to protect and develop forests. According to Berhanu and Million (2001), Ethiopia has in place neither a federal government policy on forest conservation nor any clear forest policy in general. It can also be stated that the Ethiopian government has shown gross negligence in the protection and development of forest resources (Melesse Damtie 2001). The government of Ethiopia admits that it is unable to effectively conserve and develop forest resources in the country. On the contrary, communities, NGOs, the private sector, and professional associations are called upon by the government to become actively involved in the conservation of Ethiopia's forests (Mengistu Hulluka 2001). Even worse, the government encourages "investors" to open up land for food production, tea and coffee plantations, and logging, without conducting an environmental impact assessment beforehand (Yonas 2001).

Even though Ethiopia was strongly involved in the development of the African Model Law, the country has not been able to develop and implement its own biodiversity legislation and policies. Only just recently were the ABS regulations implemented. However, responsibility for access, but not for benefit-sharing, was assigned to IBC. Benefit-sharing has remained an unclear issue. The legislation that has served until now to define IBC's responsibilities and work has not implemented the obligations of the CBD sufficiently and efficiently. This lack of regulations indicates that governance in Ethiopia is too weak to be able attract users of genetic resources. Moreover, the existence of a number of different responsible institutions appears confusing. In the teff case, it was EIAR (formerly EARO) that negotiated the memorandum of understanding.

Administrative Complexity

Due to a lack of empirical data, it is difficult to estimate the level of administrative complexity. However, in the teff case the users regard the negotiations as an unnecessarily time-consuming process. Too many institutions are still involved in the ABS process. By defining one competent authority, for example, IBC, as the agency responsible for all ABS activities in Ethiopia, the country could decrease administrative complexity, which appears to be a problem in many countries when it comes to implementing ABS regulations. It is important to ensure that responsibilities are not split up among different institutions. In ways comparable to INBio, IBC can lower transaction costs for companies if it manages to reduce bureaucracy. A focus on biodiversity activities and a separation of them from governmental procedure can lead to short time frames for negotiations on contracts, and this in turn can help Ethiopia become an interesting source of genetic resources for users. The interviews made it clear that most interview partners think it is impossible to establish an intersectoral committee of the kind in place in Costa Rica. However, many issues are not addressed by the proclamation. For example, both the application procedure and the procedure for obtaining PIC remain unclear.

Market Structure

Ethiopia's initial bargaining position has been very weak due to the country's market structure and general political and institutional environment, but also for lack of a clear-cut legislation able to boost user interest. Thus far only a few agreements have been concluded with the private sector for commercial purposes. Many more scientific research agreements have been concluded. However, Ethiopia and IBC have the potential to improve the situation. Once other critical factors have been addressed, Ethiopia will be able to strengthen its position in the market. Nevertheless, the first condition would be to effectively implement the newly formulated ABS legislation. In many interviews, especially with staff from IBC, it was mentioned that Ethiopia is a weak country when it comes to negotiations, but also as far as monitoring is concerned. In addition, Ethiopia has no private sector (e.g., breeding institutions and seed enterprises) that uses genetic resources. This also weakens the country's position (Feyissa 2006, 13).

Progress on implementation of the African Model Law in many African countries, as well as stronger cooperation between these countries, can boost Ethiopia's bargaining position. Ethiopia also plays a strong role in the international negotiation process, coming out in favor of the implementation of an international regime. However, things look different at the national level. Once it has adopted clear-cut legislation, Ethiopia will be able to use its strength at the international level to improve its position.

As in the other case studies, there are no rules on access to ex situ collections in other countries and access to material stored before the CBD was adopted, and companies are still able to fall back on these collections. A lot of material with Ethiopian origin will already have left the country before any legislation is finally put in place. This was underlined by many interviews. In this case, Ethiopia is dependent on regulations at the international level that address the problem.

Conclusions

It is obvious that Ethiopian forest and genetic resources need to be preserved. Therefore, strategies have to be implemented to reach this goal. Ultimately, implementation of the ABS regulations could work out and contribute to conserving these resources if the critical factors are addressed and specific institutional arrangements are in place to ensure that the necessary tasks are carried out. Even though the proclamation has been adopted, there are still no detailed rules, e.g., on how benefit-sharing is to be implemented. The absence of implementing measures is problematic and may be the main reason why it is likely to be difficult to enforce provisions of the legislation. Nevertheless, the guidelines pave the way for a better approach than the one that has been in use until now. The guidelines cover many important issues and integrate experience made in other countries, including, for example, regulations on national research. Based on these guidelines, IBC has the potential to evolve into an adequate ABS institution if it receives support for capacity development. With such an institution in place, the conditions would be given to establish ABS as a conservation concept in Ethiopia. This will require time and sufficient financial resources and capacity development.

The most critical factor in the Ethiopian system is property rights. For lack of adequate property rights and appropriate land use policies, it is unlikely that an ABS regime will be able to address the problem and effectively contribute to the conservation of biodiversity in Ethiopia. The other critical factors are also hardly addressed. Even though they are given

Table 5.10 Overview on Ethiopia and the Critical Factors

	Ethiopia
Property rights	No private property rights system, but communities strengthened Benefits to be shared between government and communities (50:50), but no distribution mechanisms No IPRs on biological resources
Asymmetric information	Post-contractual problems, but none before contracts signed ABS regulations address only post-contractual problems on the provider side (e.g., export, joint research, documents from competent authorities in user countries)
Time lags	Country focuses strongly on nonmonetary benefits Participation in research and development
Good governance	Generally unstable situation Just recently the country has adopted ABS regulations, despite its efforts concerning the African Model Law
Administrative complexity	IBC is an excellent institution, one suited to be responsible for ABS Too many institutions involved
Market structure	No experience: weak market position African Model provides opportunities to strengthen African countries as a coalition

consideration in the proclamation, it is evident that the country lacks the capacity to effectively implement the provisions. Ethiopia needs support from other African countries, but also from industrialized countries, to set up an efficient system. To guarantee legal security, responsibilities need to be clearly defined, and the number of institutions involved needs to be reduced. Both the new proclamation and concentration of responsibility with IBC are steps in the right direction. IBC has the potential to work together with interested companies as a reliable partner. The institute is the center of biodiversity activities in Ethiopia, and it has the experience and capacities needed to increase user interest in bioprospecting in Ethiopia. With the proclamation on ABS, Ethiopia has gained a good instrument that can strengthen the role of IBC, but it needs to take more measures to move the country ahead with regard to ABS and biodiversity conservation. The institute needs political and financial support to meet its tasks and to fully implement the proclamation.

ABS needs to be integrated within a broader conservation program that receives political support. Policy and institutional deficiencies are holding back these developments. The national government of Ethiopia is embarking on a decentralization of political power. The responsibility to establish, manage, and utilize forests and most protected areas has devolved to regional governments, which struggle with insufficient technical and management capacities in seeking to carry out their new responsibilities (Leykun Abunie 2000). The decentralization process was carried out at so fast a pace that the regions were not at all prepared for their new tasks, and mainly without adequate financial and human resources.

EU AND GERMANY

The EU, with a special focus on Germany, serves as an example for a group of user countries. The analysis of the EU and Germany complements the analysis of the three other case studies. Whereas the other case studies are concerned with provider countries, the analysis of the EU focuses on the user side, which has been neglected so far. However, in an international regime the user dimension is the second pillar alongside the provider dimension. The analysis follows up on the investigations presented in the three previous case studies. The analytic framework, developed on the basis of the critical factors and potential measures, is applied in the EU context, with a special focus on Germany, in order to test and illustrate its applicability. This section starts out with a presentation of the case study methodology. This is followed by a short introduction to the role played by the EU and Germany. The main part of the analysis is devoted to the application of the critical factors to the EU case. Taking into account the analytic framework worked out for effectiveness (see Chapter 4), a look is taken at how the critical factors are shaped and how they are being addressed in the EU and through the EU's regulatory framework. The analysis of the EU case study ends with a short conclusion.

Case Study Methodology

In discussing ABS issues and using the terms *user* and *provider countries*, the main criteria used for differentiation are the amount of biodiversity in the country and the existence and development of biotechnological, pharmaceutical, and agricultural industries. Due to the unequal distribution of resources and research and development capacities in the world, biodiversity-rich developing countries are classified as provider countries, whereas most of the industrialized countries are termed user countries. However, neither the distinction nor the generalization holds in all cases. For example, Australia is an important provider of genetic resources, whereas Brazil has a highly developed biotechnology and agro-industry sector (Barber, Johnston, and Tobin 2003, 18). User countries are characterized as countries that have high demand for genetic resources and the capacity to use them for research, development, and commercialization, regardless of whether or not they also provide biodiversity. Users are those agents that import or use genetic resources for commercial or scientific purposes. User countries reflect the competent legal and political authorities under whose jurisdiction the users of genetic resources act and operate (Barber, Johnston, and Tobin 2003, 18). User measures are understood as a package of legal, administrative, and policy measures designed to promote compliance by users of genetic resources and TK by establishing obligations regarding PIC, MAT, and benefit-sharing. These measures can be applied by either the private or public sector and may be mandatory or voluntary (CBD 2002, 17).

With a view to the analysis in Chapter 4, the following sections look into different user or user country measures and their implementation in the EU on the basis of a review of the literature as well as an activities review. The sections analyze whether the introduction of these measures may suffice to meet the requirements derived from the identified critical factors. As already indicated, there is a wide range of user measures that promise to support the objectives of the CBD and that can be applied in both the private and the public sectors. The introduction of such measures requires different degrees of intervention in the existing situation on the part of the governments of user and provider countries as well as on the part of the providers and users themselves. In the following, selected user measures are evaluated with regard to their feasibility, efficiency, interrelationships, and their potential to address the critical factors.

On the one side, the measures considered are corporate and institutional policies and codes of conduct, the initiation of voluntary certification schemes, most of them applied in the private sector, as well as the establishment of a CHM. On the other side, the measures to which consideration is given are national focal points, the monitoring of IPRs applications, certificates of compliance, and the implementation of conflict resolution, arbitration, and redress mechanisms that are applied exclusively in the public sector. The list of user measures considered here is not exhaustive, but does contain user measures that are under heated discussion in the international arena and that, in the author's view, promise most success when it comes to implementation and targeting.

Introduction

The EU is an important community of user countries of genetic resources for research and product development, and it possesses substantial commercial research and development capacity. The European life sciences industry constitutes an important sector of the European economy (EU Commission 2003, 6). In 1993 the Community became a member of the CBD, and it is committed to the implementation of its provisions, including ABS. Responding to requests from developing countries, the EU supported, at COP 4 of the CBD (in Bratislava, 1998), the launching of a negotiation process on the question of ABS to explore options for access to genetic resources and benefit-sharing on MAT. This process led to the adoption of the Bonn Guidelines on ABS, a set of detailed, voluntary provisions conceived to help implement the ABS provisions of the CBD (EU Commission 2003, 7). Some member states, including, for example, Belgium and Germany, have been active in addressing provider countries' concerns and requests by financing ABS governance research projects and establishing and supporting the introduction of user measures.

Users in the EU assign different preferences to certain user measures. The German user survey revealed that German users generally support user measures that are currently under discussion at the international level, including, e.g., government support for ABS projects, certification systems, certificates of compliance, disclosure of country of origin, codes of conduct, internationally standardized ABS contracts, and central information offices (focal points). German users see instruments in the form of services that have less impact on their activities as more useful than measures that regulate the way they handle genetic resources. They see the most useful instrument in a central information point in Germany that actively provides information about access possibilities and conditions in provider countries and assists them in approaching the latter (Holm-Mueller, Richerzhagen, and Taeuber 2005, 50–53).

Property Rrights and Intellectual Property Rights

Disclosure of origin has been identified as a strong instrument to balance the distribution of property rights between user and provider country. In some countries, both user and provider countries, the concept has already been implemented in the form of a stand-alone disclosure requirement. This means that noncompliance has no effect on patentability or patent enforceability. Besides, the consequences of noncompliance are beyond the ambit of patent law. Denmark and Norway have followed this approach. Noncompliance with disclosure requirements does not affect the handling or the validity of a patent. Belgium has recently introduced a formal requirement for disclosure of geographical origin. Theoretically, failure to comply with this requirement could result in the patent application not being processed. However, the Belgian patent office does not check compliance, as it is not a monitoring authority, and so this case is unlikely to occur. Wrongful disclosure would not affect the validity of patents already granted, although it could result in a fine. Switzerland has proposed similar legislation. Under its draft legislation, nondisclosure would lead to rejection of a patent application and wrongful disclosure would be an offence prosecuted *ex officio*, the applicant being liable to a fine. The provider countries have stronger regulations. In the Andean Community, Brazil's, Costa Rica's, and India's failure to disclose geographical origin and/or PIC will result in rejection of a patent application or its subsequent nullification (Chatham House 2006, 2–3).

EC Directive 98/44/EC on the legal protection of biotechnological inventions gives specific consideration to ABS. The directive encourages patent applications to include information on the geographical origin of biological material, but it is nonbinding and voluntary in nature (Directive 98/44/EC 1998, Recital 27). This provision supports compliance with national legislation in the source country of biological material and with contractual arrangements governing the acquisition and use of that material. It is without prejudice to the processing of patent applications or the validity of rights arising from granted patents (Straus 2001, 161).

Furthermore, European patent law already contains a regulation whose aim is disclosure of the origin of genetic resources, not as an instrument to monitor compliance with the CBD but rather as an instrument to enable the reproduction of an invention. EC Directive 98/44/EC states that where an invention involves the use of or concerns biological material that is not available to the public and that cannot be described in a patent application in such a manner as to enable the invention to be reproduced by a person skilled in the art, the description must be considered inadequate for the purpose of patent law, unless the application as filed contains such relevant information as is available to the applicant on the characteristics of the biological material deposited (Directive 98/44/EC 1998, Article 13(1)b). In this case, disclosure of origin serves only the purpose of enabling others to reproduce an invention, and it would be applied in only a small number of cases (EU Commission 2003, 17).

Information Asymmetries

Post-contractual information asymmetries due to a lack of monitoring capacity on the provider side can be addressed by certain user measures, some of which have been developed and implemented by the EU. These are corporate and institutional policies and codes of conduct, voluntary certification schemes, national focal points and the CHM, and promotion of cooperation and the use of standardized contracts.

Corporate and Institutional Policies and Codes of Conduct

In the EU there are some stakeholder initiatives geared to developing and implementing policies and codes of conduct that comply with the CBD and national ABS legislation in provider countries. Scientific research institutions and networks of ex situ collections in the EU have developed institutional policies and codes of conduct on ABS to facilitate the acquisition and exchange of genetic resources in accordance with applicable national and international law. Important initiatives have been undertaken by European botanical gardens, microbial culture collections, and germplasm collections (EU Commission 2003, 10).

The "Principles on Access to Genetic Resources and Benefit-Sharing for Participating Institutions," developed under the auspices of the Royal Botanic Gardens, Kew, and involving twenty-eight botanical gardens from twenty-one countries, is an important example, as is the International Plant Exchange Network (IPEN). IPEN is an exchange system for botanical gardens under the CBD; it was developed by the Verband Botanischer Garten (an association of botanical gardens in German-speaking countries) on behalf of the German Federal Ministry of Environment, Nature Conservation, and Nuclear Safety. Botanical gardens that wish to join the network must sign and abide by a code of conduct that sets out gardens' responsibilities for acquisition, maintenance, and supply of living plant material and associated benefit-sharing. The botanical gardens themselves are in charge of monitoring the accession, conservation, and dissemination of genetic resources. The objective of this initiative is to promote the conservation and sustainable use of biodiversity, to comprehensibly document living plant material in order to secure the rights of the countries of origin in accordance with the CBD, and to strengthen mutual trust with the countries of origin with the aim of ensuring that access to genetic resources and their use remain possible in the future (Holm-Mueller, Richerzhagen, and Taeuber 2005, 24).

The project Micro-Organisms Sustainable Use and Access Regulation International Code of Conduct (MOSAICC), which is financed by the EU and has been developed by the Belgian Co-Ordinated Collections of Micro-Organisms (BCCM) conjointly with sixteen international organizations, is another example. MOSAICC is a code of conduct developed to facilitate access to microbial resources and to help partners in developing practical agreements when transferring microbial resources. MOSAICC provides a system based on identification of the in situ origin of microbial resources via PIC and the monitored transfer of resources as well as on

MTA defined by provider and user. It is already frequently used by institutions using microbial resources (BCCM 2007). Furthermore, a group of researchers has used microbial resources as a test case to explore the problematic nature of data sharing. Their work focuses on the transformation of the innovation chain, i.e., the role of bioinformatics and IPRs for knowledge generation, data access, and data sharing. The project results are integrated into the process of building a European biological resources platform (Dawyndt, Dedeurwaerdere, and Swings 2006; Dedeurwaerdere 2006; Hess and Ostrom 2006).

Furthermore, some European pharmaceutical and biotechnology companies have developed corporate policies on ABS. Other smaller sectors, including horticulture and botanical medicines, do not appear to have developed comprehensive corporate or sector-based policies on ABS (EC 2002, 34).

Voluntary Certification Schemes

Measures designed to help bioprospecting companies build a reputation would be the simplest way to establish confidence between partners and overcome the problem of asymmetric information. On the user side, some large pharmaceutical companies (e.g., Merck) have already improved their image by concluding ABS agreements in compliance with the CBD. But even though the market for genetic resources is dominated by a small number of companies, there are still a large number of small biotech firms in the market and there is a growing tendency for large, established pharmaceutical, agricultural, and other life science companies to cooperate with these smaller, start-up biotechnology research companies (Hill 1999). These small start-up research companies are new in the market and lack the time they would need to gain a reputation. Participation in a certification system can improve the user's reputation and provide a basis for provider countries to feel more confident about their potential partners.

The EC Eco-Management and Audit Scheme (EMAS) offers an interesting example that should be considered for the development of voluntary certification schemes for organizations complying with the CBD, the Bonn Guidelines, and national ABS regulations. Nevertheless, it has not so far received much attention in relation to the CBD and an integration of the approach has not been discussed seriously. EMAS is a voluntary scheme for organizations; it was established to evaluate and improve the environmental performance of organizations and to provide relevant information to the public and other interested parties. It is open to any organization in both the public and private sectors in the EU (Regulation [EC] No 761/2001, Article 1/3, 1). Participation in EMAS requires that an environmental review be carried out to look into all environmental aspects of an organization's activities, products, and services; an effective environmental management system be established; an environmental audit be carried out; and an environmental statement be submitted (Regulation [EC] No 761/2001, Article 3, 2). The direct and indirect environmental aspects that need to be considered include emissions into the air, the use of natural resources and raw materials, and effects on biodiversity (Regulation [EC] No 761/2001, Annex VI). The European Commission has developed guidance on identification of the environmental impacts and assessment of their significance that can be used by companies and research institutions to identify significant direct and indirect impacts of their activities on the conservation and sustainable use of genetic resources (EU Commission 2001a).

Application of EMAS in the ABS process would appear to be appropriate. The principles formulated in the CBD and in the Bonn Guidelines could be incorporated into organizations' environmental policies and environmental management systems established under EMAS and would then be reflected in their environmental statements. Independent environmental verifiers accredited under EMAS would check the reliability, credibility, and correctness of the data and information contained in the environmental statement. EMAS is based on an international standard, ISO 14001, for its basic management system, and it even goes beyond the standard in relation to public transparency, credibility, and environmental performance (EU Commission 2003, 23). EMAS can be used to support the establishment of an international certification system for genetic resources. A modified EMAS could also be implemented in other user countries.

National Focal Points and the CHM

National focal points in user countries, in addition to CHMs, serve to increase transparency and trust, especially in cases where information deficiencies may compromise the relationships between provider and users.

The EC-CHM is an important portal and database for biodiversity issues. However, it is not widely known and not frequently used by users. In September 2005 the EC launched the EC ABS Portal (EC 2007). It provides information on European policy and legislative measures related to ABS as well as links to Web pages of international organizations that are active in this field. The Bonn Guidelines are available in different European languages. As a network platform, it provides details of contact points in all the member states of the EU and links to information on ABS in the member states. The portal is a tool well suited to significantly improve Europe's information policy. However, utilization of a portal of this kind requires stakeholders to be prepared to provide information documents. At present the portal is not widely used.

Most member states of the EU have designated national CBD and/or ABS focal points. The EC-CHM provides access to some—albeit incomplete—information on policies, legislation, funding opportunities, databases, sources of expertise, etc., of EC institutions. It publicizes links to other European institutions and organizations (i.e., governmental, private, and NGOs) that provide useful information. It also links to Web sites of global organizations such as the CBD Secretariat's Web site and the CHMs of EU member states (e.g., Belgium, France, Germany). National CHMs play a very important role in informing users on biodiversity-related issues and ABS in their own language. Recently Germany launched a new ABS portal in addition to its CHM (Bundesamt für Naturschutz 2007). The portal provides essential information on ABS for German citizens and especially users.

Promotion of Cooperation and Standardized Contracts

Governments of user countries can support the development and execution of projects aiming at the promotion of cooperation between users and providers and the development of standardized MTA. Government institutions monitor these projects and can ensure that users comply with the CBD. Providers will be more confident about their partners if the ABS negotiations take place in the framework of such a project and facilitate access. By participating in such projects, users can gain reputation and set a positive example (Holm-Mueller, Richerzhagen, and Taeuber 2005, 25).

The German Federal Ministry for Education and Research (BMBF) financed a project known as "Process-oriented development of a model for equitable benefit-sharing for the use of biological resources in the Amazon Lowlands of Ecuador" (ProBenefit). The main participants in the project were German institutions (Institute of Biodiversity, University of Göttingen), the Association of German Engineers, and a German company, one of the leading manufacturers of phytomedicines worldwide. The objectives of ProBenefit were to develop a model agreement on equitable benefit-sharing in Ecuador's Amazon region, to explore the potential for using medicinal plants, and to develop possibilities for sustainable use of those plants. ProBenefit started in June 2003 and continued until 2007. In the end, the project did not succeed and no ABS agreements were concluded due to disagreement on how the consultation process was to be conducted (ProBenefit 2007).

Accounting for Time Lags

Technology transfer is the most relevant nonmonetary benefit. It can serve to address the time lags between bioprospecting activities and the development of a marketable product.

The EU has the potential and the possibilities to transfer technology to provider countries. However, no data are available to draw conclusions about actual implementation. The EU has no policy measure in place to specifically address technology transfer and ABS. Technology transfer is supported through general rules of competition, partnership agreements, and framework programs for research and development. Technology transfer in the EU is very diverse and carried out at the member state level. In Germany several hundred institutions in different sectors (government-based international cooperation sector, science sector, governmental sector, private sector, and nongovernmental sector) are active in dealing with aspects of biodiversity technology transfer (Paulsch et al. 2004, 4). In the EU there is no legislative and policy measures in place that specifically address research and technology transfer under the CBD. The EU Declaration ratifying the Biodiversity Convention highlights technology transfer and access to biotechnology in accordance with CBD Article 16 and in compliance with IPRs (EC 2002, 8).

Decision No 1982/2006/EC of the European Parliament and the Council of December 18, 2006, concerning the Seventh Framework Programme of the European Community for research, technological development, and demonstration activities establishes rules with regard to international scientific cooperation, technology and knowledge transfer, and human resources. It stresses the importance of the need to consider developing countries' interests (EU Parliament and Council 2006). These proposed rules do not, however, incorporate provisions on ABS in the context of the CBD.

The partnership agreement between the members of the African, Caribbean and Pacific (ACP) states and the EC and its member states (Cotonou Agreement 2000) could also serve to enable technology transfer under ABS partnerships between EU institutions and countries that provide genetic resources. A compendium on cooperation strategies is part of the agreement; it provides strategies and guidelines for scientific, technical, and research cooperation. The compendium's section on scientific, technological, and research cooperation in particular stresses the importance of strategies with regard to the implementation of research and development projects and programs established by the ACP countries; the establishment and promotion of activities aimed at the consolidation of appropriate indigenous technology; the acquisition and adaptation of relevant foreign technology; and the promotion of scientific and technological cooperation between ACP states themselves, between ACP countries and other developing countries, and between ACP countries and the EC and its member states (EU Commission 2001b, 35–36). Additionally, the compendium states that the aim of ACP/EC collaboration is to continue to stimulate partnerships between all sectors of society, both users and generators of knowledge. It stresses that cooperation should support the efforts of the ACP countries to create and develop technology and research (EU Commission 2001b, 36).

Good Governance in Provider Countries

Thus far good governance has been discussed only in the provider countries. User countries can use their development and foreign policies to support measures aiming at stabilizing general political stability, but also to support the development and implementation of biodiversity and ABS laws. Nevertheless, it is difficult or even impossible for the EU to ensure that the regulations are actually enforced. The influence of the EU and its possibilities to contribute positively to this critical factor are therefore very limited.

Administrative Complexity

The EU has no means to directly influence problems related to administrative complexity, except through support provided in connection with development cooperation. However, national focal points and CHMs have a positive effect on the administrative complexity of provider countries. By implementing certain user measures, the EU can assume some responsibility in the process and lessen the burden of provider countries. For example, the national focal points of an EU member state could inform potential users about the ABS regulations in provider countries. In addition, they could issue some kind of document to the user that she/he in turn can use as a proof of registration as required under the Ethiopian Proclamation. National focal points and CHMs in user countries can also support the exchange of information on and experience with ABS issues. They can also establish contacts to national focal points and authorities in provider countries and in this way facilitate the establishment of contacts among the users. By informing users—who are often insufficiently informed regarding ABS—about their obligations, the national focal points provide relief for provider countries.

The German user survey revealed that German users of genetic resources are poorly informed about the international legal framework concerning access to and use of genetic resources and generally not familiar with the terms of the CBD. Many users, regardless of the size of their company or institution, are not familiar with the convention and the meaning of the terms "access and benefit-sharing," "national focal point/national competent authority," and "clearing house mechanism." More than half of the users who are familiar with the CBD consider themselves not sufficiently informed. This lack of knowledge and information is distributed unevenly among sectors. Public institutions (i.e., ex situ collections, universities, and other research institutions) are more familiar with the terms and feel better informed than private institutions and companies. The main channels through which users obtain information are secondary sources: the Internet, associations, and scientific journals. National authorities in Germany or in the countries of origin are of minor significance as sources of information (Holm-Mueller, Richerzhagen, and Taeuber 2005, 59).

Market Structure

Transfer of technology from the EU to provider countries, which has already been discussed in this chapter, will certainly serve to boost their position in the market, both compared with other providers and vis-à-vis users. Technological improvement enables provider countries to use their country's biodiversity for research and development or even for commercialization. If it is possible to establish and technically equip research facilities in provider countries, they will be able to offer more processed and higher-value genetic material in the market instead of raw genetic material. Positive effects on economic development can be expected from this. Furthermore, technology transfer related to biodiversity conservation and environmental protection has a positive influence on the environmental situation in the provider country.

Conclusions

The EU is taken as an example for an important community of user countries of genetic resources in research and product development. The life sciences industry constitutes an important sector of the European economy and has considerable demand for genetic resources.

User measures can take effect even where provider influence and capacities are very limited. Such measures can benefit users and providers, and they have the potential to advance the international governance of ABS. On the policy level, some European user measures have already been implemented or are in the process of discussion and design. They can serve as an example for the introduction of user measures in other user countries, even though they are still in the development stage. The EU's user measures address the factors that have been defined here as critical for an effective international ABS regime geared to conservation, access, and benefit-sharing. Scientific research institutions and networks of ex situ collections in the EU have developed institutional policies and codes of conduct on ABS to facilitate the acquisition and exchange of genetic resources. These measures increase user transparency and facilitate user acquisition activities. There is probably less need for other compliance procedures. By transferring important technologies, the EU member states can bridge the time lags between provision and compensation and strengthen the bargaining position of provider countries. Voluntary certification schemes like EMAS and monitoring of the use of genetic resources in research and development and IPRs applications can help to verify the transparency of the ABS process and compliance with the CBD obligations. Furthermore, they serve to eliminate information deficiencies on the part of providers and users. Creation of national focal points is important as an official contact point for applicants as well as for information dissemination. The same goes for the CHM. Moreover, the CHM supports scientific and technical cooperation by making an information management and exchange system available. Conflict resolution and redress can be achieved using the traditional systems already in place.

Table 5.11   Overview on the EU and the Critical Factors

	EU—Germany
Property rights	Encouragement: disclosure of origin in order to comply with the CBD, but also to enable reproduction of an invention
Asymmetric information	Few examples of corporate and institutional policies and codes of conduct (e.g., botanical gardens, microbial collections)
	Use of voluntary certification schemes not sufficient
	National focal points and the European CHM
	Promotion of cooperation and standardized contracts (e.g., ProBenefit)
Time lags	Technology transfer is carried out, but is not sufficient to solve problem
Good governance	Support only through development cooperation
Administrative complexity	National focal points can provide relief for provider countries by informing and preparing users
Market structure	Technology transfer can enable provider countries to offer higher value-added products (enhanced market position)

The EU's activities regarding disclosure of origin may be seen as very limited because they rely on a unilateral and voluntary system. What would be preferable here is a multilateral system with a stand-alone disclosure requirement in patent applications. Under such a system, providers of genetic resources who have granted access to their resources would have the opportunity to observe the utilization and commercialization, outside of their territory, of the genetic material they have provided. However, such a multilateral system, associated with the TRIPs Agreement, the PCT, or the Patent Law Treaty (PLT), seems unlikely to be established because of the difficulty of negotiations in the WTO or WIPO framework. Policymakers should therefore support the development of a binding disclosure requirement for patent applications in the EU—possibly as a formal condition for patentability. This could improve the situation and pave the way for a multilateral solution.

Looking at the EU as an example, it has to be kept in mind that in international negotiations on ABS the EU has always been a CBD party supportive of the CBD's ABS provisions in response to developing country requests. The EU's activities regarding the establishment of user measures are therefore not surprising. However, the EU case allows us to draw some important conclusions that can be applied to other user countries. The analysis of user measures shows that many actual and potential measures do not require the development of new national or international laws and regulations or new and complex institutions. This plays an important role for their feasibility. Rather, it can be concluded that user measures can best be implemented by adjusting and modifying existing systems in the areas of voluntary certification, monitoring of IPRs, and certificates of compliance. The implementation of user measures in user countries should provide effective and feasible measures regarding the CBD's ABS objectives, measures that do not hinder the use of and trade in genetic resources. These measures, therefore, need to be designed in such a way as to avoid the creation of time-consuming and bureaucratic regimes associated with high transaction costs.

Even if user countries outside of the EU do not have the same institutional and legislative environment as EU member states, they should give consideration to European measures and experiences in designing and implementing user measures within their own territory. User measures play a significant role in an international ABS regime in support of compliance with the obligations and responsibilities arising out of the ratification of the CBD. Only in this case will it be possible to realize any fair and equitable benefit-sharing.

6   Conclusions

Since 1992 ABS has been promoted as a promising concept to halt the ongoing loss of biodiversity. However, success has thus far proven elusive. Biodiversity is still declining. ABS has been implemented in about forty countries; however, only a few successful cases have been reported. Researchers and industries that rely on wild genetic resources complain that access has been restricted, and provider countries complain that no shared benefits have been channeled to the countries that hold resources and that their genetic material is still used without their approval. It is therefore legitimate to ask how the ABS regime needs to be designed to reach effectiveness.

To answer this question, this book establishes an analytic framework to measure the effectiveness of the ABS concept at the national and regional levels. Effectiveness is defined as the capability of the ABS regime to (i) set incentives for the sustainable use and conservation of biodiversity, (ii) facilitate access to plant genetic material, and (iii) enhance a fair and equitable benefit-sharing, which also implies prevention of any misappropriation and unapproved use of genetic resources. Six critical factors determine the level of effectiveness and realization of these objectives. These are property rights, asymmetric information, time lags, good governance, administrative complexity, and market structure.

User and provider countries have different options to develop and implement measures that have the potential to address the critical factors and thus to improve ABS governance and contribute to building an international regime. The measures can be distinguished by the party mainly responsible for their implementation. User measures are implemented by users and provider measures by providers, but most measures depend on the commitment of both sides or are interlinked. The respective provider measures are assignment of property rights, compensation schemes, institutional capacity-building, coalitions, screening, and signaling. The respective user measures are monitoring of IPRs applications, documentation of gene flow, certification schemes, corporate and institutional policies, national focal points and CHMs, projects and model contracts, technology transfer, and conflict resolution. The following section discusses the main results of the book regarding the relationship between the critical factors and the provider and user measures.

ABS AND THE CRITICAL FACTORS

The ABS concept still suffers from the high expectations providers and environmentalists placed in it when it was developed and integrated into the CBD. In the early 1990s, genetic resources were considered as green gold that had high economic value due to their genetic potential. It was hoped that if a share of the benefits arising out of the utilization of genetic resources flowed back to provider countries, it would facilitate access to genetic resources and set incentives for conservation and make destructive activities less economically interesting. However, it can be observed, even without the deeper insights provided by the case studies, that these expectations have not materialized. Not many contracts have been concluded since 1992, and the contracts concluded have not generated sufficient incentives to stop the ongoing loss of biodiversity. This is the point of departure of this book. The question is whether ABS is a silver bullet that can effectively contribute to keeping its promises, which are: (i) facilitated access to genetic resources, (ii) conservation of biodiversity, and (iii) fair and equitable benefit-sharing. The latter implies prevention of the misappropriation and unapproved use of genetic resources. Only if the three elements are affected positively by the critical factors can the approach be seen as effective.

In general, it can be concluded that, despite generally disappointing experiences made with it, ABS is a useful concept that can contribute to reaching the three goals. The CBD and ABS have improved the situation. Before, biodiversity was considered common heritage and treated as an open-access resource. The tangible resource and its intangible components have suffered from exploitation. The ABS concept in the CBD can accomplish two important things. First, it assigns responsibility for action to the provider countries. Under the principle of state sovereignty, provider countries are not only responsible, they are also autonomous when it comes to decision-making. Second, it internalizes part of the TEV of biodiversity: the commercial value of genetic resources and their contribution to research and development. Other values are not considered. Users of genetic resources are obliged to share the benefits they gain from their use. It is therefore clear that ABS alone will never be sufficient to provide an incentive for biodiversity conservation. It needs to be embedded in a comprehensive strategy that internalizes values other than the commercial. Moreover, ABS does not take effect only in one dimension. Besides its impact on access, conservation, and benefit-sharing, ABS can have large-scale impacts on the economic and social situation in provider countries. It has the potential to alleviate poverty and support economic development. For example, if ABS attracts foreign direct investment, drives the establishment of new industries, and supports the improvement of research potential, it can assist countries in reaching their development goals. Therefore, ABS needs to be seen in a much broader sense of sustainable development and cannot be reduced to environmental objectives alone. For example, Costa Rica is a case that shows that ABS has supported a country's will and capability to establish and advance a research institution.

The CBD and the ABS concept have raised awareness about biodiversity and provided environmentalists and policy-makers with economic arguments to conserve biological diversity. As shown by the Stern report, which caused quite a stir, economic arguments are perceived much better than any others by decision-makers and the population.

Bearing in mind the limitations set to internalization, theory suggests that the approach is still very promising within this defined scope. Whereas reality shows different results, the reasons for this divergence have not been analyzed in the relevant literature. This book provides a new analytical framework to measure effectiveness on the basis of six determinants (property rights, asymmetric information, time lags, political and legal security, administrative complexity, and market structure). The ABS concept itself is very ambitious, and there is a long way from theory to practice. The analysis shows that due to the interlinkages between the determinants and the possible instruments and measures, providers and users need to address the configuration of the critical factors. The ABS concept is very complex. There is no "perfect" or "optimal" specification of the critical factors. However, it is possible to formulate some rules of performance for the critical factors. The crucial matter is always how and to what extent specific critical factors and measures undertaken are able to take effect together. It is therefore necessary to consider both sides. Even if one critical factor indicates poor performance for a country when the right provider or user measures are in place, the result may nevertheless be satisfactory. However, based on the analysis, we can make some precise statements regarding the specification of the critical factors.

Property rights, including IPRs, and especially their strength and distribution among providers and users, are the most relevant critical factor in the ABS concept. Property rights impact all three elements of ABS effectiveness: conservation, access, and benefit-sharing. If property rights are not assigned, resource holders are unable to grant access, and there is no benefit-sharing. Property rights enable property owners to market their resources. Only if the agents responsible for conserving biodiversity have adequate property rights over biological resources can they grant access to them, and only then are they in a position to receive the benefits that, at the next stage, establish incentives for biodiversity conservation. If the property rights situation in a country is not sufficient, a national trust fund can be used to ensure that fair and equitable benefit-sharing takes place.

IPRs take effect at the other end of the value chain, providing users with strong rights after a product has been developed. A proper balance in the distribution of property rights and IPRs is essential. Property rights or IPRs must in place at those levels that are most effective at maintaining an asset and investing in it, and adequate compensation payments must be made in real time to make other, destructive uses less profitable. The granting of IPRs needs to ensure that such rights are granted only if material has been obtained legally. Disclosure of the origin of genetic resources when users apply for a patent on them is an appropriate instrument. Certificates of compliance issued by provider countries can be used as relevant documents to prove that material has been obtained legally.

Asymmetric information is the second important critical factor. In the form of pre-contractual and post-contractual problems, it impacts the access and benefit-sharing objective. Information deficiencies are reciprocal. They occur on both the user side and the provider side. Providers lack information regarding the benefits genetic resources are expected to deliver and how the material will actually be used once it is in the user's hands. Providers are unable to estimate the value of the expected benefits, and they in some cases ask for unrealistic benefits. As a consequence, not many contracts are concluded. What are needed to address this problem are more economic studies on the commercial value of genetic resources and publication of more contracts. Model contracts and projects as well as economic assessments can serve to put negotiations on a solid basis.

Providers are unable to observe the use to which the material they provide is put. Concerned about unapproved uses, provider countries tend to overregulate and stop trading in genetic resources. To confirm their eligibility, users can signal their willingness to comply. In addition, providers can screen users on the basis of specifically designed contracts.

Users lack information regarding exclusivity, quality, and the utilization of the benefits they receive, and they tend to react by substituting one country for another if deficiencies are really pronounced. Users can also screen providers to ensure the provision of better quality. This is especially relevant in cases where intermediaries play a growing role. All scenarios can lead to a situation in which no access and benefit-sharing takes place. Adequate conflict resolution mechanisms serve to set the stage for trust-building among users and providers because providers can have recourse to them if they feel their rights have been compromised.

Time lags strongly impact the conservation objective. If the time frames between the collection and the flow of benefits are too large, no incentives for conservation are set. Adequate compensation schemes or fund-based solutions can be used to address these problems. Up-front payments need to be included. However, many companies, especially small ones, are not able to make payments in advance. Here a fund solution would be adequate. Users of genetic resources would have to make some advance payments into a fund, and from then on all payments would be channeled through a biodiversity trust fund managed by independent stakeholder representatives. This group would even decide on how benefits are distributed among providers. In this case, payments would be decoupled from the assignment of national property rights. In the form of asymmetric information, the next two critical factors assume major relevance from a transaction cost perspective.

Good governance plays an important role for the transaction costs that arise in the access phase of ABS. The overall transaction environment is important, especially if users collect material themselves. Costa Rica is a good example for a developing country that provides a high level of legal and political security. Another important factor is whether the provider country has already put clear ABS regulations in place. Otherwise, users are likely to react with country substitution. A solution is needed for cases where countries are not able to develop an ABS regulation. The international regime should take measures to close these legal loopholes. Efforts to strengthen institutions and political systems as well as to support the formulation of laws serve to facilitate the development of good governance.

Administrative complexity is another aspect of governance, one that mainly impacts the access phase. It can heavily increase user transaction costs. Competent, multifunctional institutions are required in provider countries to design and allocate rights, manage conservation areas, coordinate activities, negotiate ABS contracts, control compliance, and sanction misappropriation regarding the use of genetic resources. The case studies have shown that one agency specialized in dealing with ABS can leverage the process. Many developing countries lack such institutions. Efforts to strengthen institutions in provider countries and to streamline ABS policies and procedures are therefore very important. Introduction of documentation systems, including, e.g., certificates of compliance, can support such processes.

Market structure also impacts the benefit-sharing objective of ABS. To reach a fair and equitable benefit-sharing, negotiations on ABS also need to be fair and conducted by equal partners. Due to their market conditions, provider countries tend to be in a weaker position. However, even though the industry argues that genetic resources have become less important, recent data indicate that, for example, users in Germany expect to continue to use genetic resources or even expand their use. However, ex situ collections that provide material collected before the CBD was adopted is one alternative for users, and one that weakens the bargaining position of providers. Coalitions, like the group of megadiverse countries, are one option to strengthen the position of providers in the market. The same applies for the use of model contracts and model projects on ABS.

It is evident that the provider measures analyzed are able to address the critical factors. Most of them are highly target-oriented and address only one critical factor. Four of the six measures (assignment of property rights, coalitions, screening, and signaling) have only a one-dimensional impact,

Table 6.1 Critical Factors and Provider Measures

	Assignment of property rights	Compensation schemes	Institutional capacity-building	Coalitions	Screening/ Signaling
Property rights	strong effect	weak effect			
Asymmetric information		weak effect			strong effect
Time lags		strong effect			
Good governance			strong effect		
Admin. complexity			strong effect		
Market structure				strong effect	

■ strong effect ▨ weak effect ☐ no effect

Table 6.2 Critical Factors and User Measures

	Monitoring IPR applications	Documentation gene flow	Certification schemes/ institutional policies/	Focal points / CHM	Projects/ model contracts	Technology transfer	Conflict resolution
Property rights	strong effect						
Asymmetric information	weak effect	strong effect	strong effect	strong effect	strong effect		strong effect
Time lags						strong effect	
Good governance				strong effect			
Admin. complexity	weak effect	strong effect			strong effect		
Market structure					weak effect		

■ strong effect ▨ weak effect ☐ no effect

and one other measure (compensation schemes) has a strong impact on one critical factor (time lags) but weaker effects on property rights and asymmetric information. Institutional capacity-building affects both good governance and administrative complexity. A variety of provider measures will be called for if a variety of different critical factors pose problems for ABS effectiveness.

Users have at their disposal a comprehensive set of measures that have the potential to address all critical factors. However, as in the case of the provider measures, the individual instruments are able to address only one or two critical factors. The measure "projects and model contracts" is the only one with promise to function as a broader instrument because it impacts up to four critical factors.

The user measures have been analyzed with a view to their potential to address the critical factors. Nevertheless, other criteria have to be looked at to determine whether they are feasible and practicable. In international discussions, the feasibility of user measures is persistently questioned by users. The analysis shows that all of the measures investigated are feasible. Some have already been implemented and applied, including, for example, the coalition of the group of megadiverse countries on the provider side or the various CHMs on the user side. Some measures are still under discussion or in development, including certificates of compliance. However, the analysis makes clear that most of these instruments are not fully effective yet. They need to be adjusted to be applied and used in better and broader ways. Measures based on voluntary initiatives and agreements, e.g., institutional policies, projects and model contracts, and certification systems, are easier and take less time to implement. Measures that require changes in the legal system (e.g., disclosure of origin) are subject to long and taxing political and legislative processes. However, because the deadline for the international regime is 2010, the climate is favorable to clearing the way for some mandatory measures, possibly for a certificates of compliance system.

CASE STUDIES

The three provider country case studies have proved to be excellent examples of how developing countries deal with the challenge of implementing an international concept that aims to protect a formerly open-access resource. From many points of view, the case studies differ considerably, and they indicate the range of aspects that need to be looked at in analyzing the effectiveness of ABS. Costa Rica and the Philippines are pioneers in implementing the ABS concept. However, they have taken different approaches. The Philippines had already developed a regulation in 1995, but since then only one commercial agreement has been concluded. Costa Rica, on the other hand, had negotiated and concluded many contracts on bioprospecting even before the CBD was in place. Comprehensive legislative frameworks were adopted there only in 1998 and at the end of 2003. However, this has not prevented the country from establishing a research institute, namely INBio, which has successfully conducted more than twenty research projects on bioprospecting. Ethiopia is a latecomer when it comes to the development and implementation of ABS laws as well as to concluding contracts. Only in 2006 did Ethiopia adopt its ABS proclamation. However, Ethiopia has concluded only a few bioprospecting contracts, and it is now on the way to applying the ABS concept. In environmental terms, Costa Rica has been able to improve the situation and slow down deforestation. The situation in the Philippines and Ethiopia is less promising. Nevertheless, this positive development cannot be traced back only to the implementation of ABS. Inclusion of ABS in a comprehensive environmental and forest protection strategy and diversification of the instruments used to protect forests and internalize environmental costs are better explanations of this success.

Based on the case studies, this book analyzes the strengths and weaknesses of current ABS regimes in provider countries and user countries with a view to the critical factors. On the one hand, the book analyzes, in the three provider countries, the configuration of the critical factors in a country-specific context, looking into whether they have already been addressed or whether there are still gaps. On the other hand, the book identifies potential user measures in the group of user countries and analyzes them with regard to their feasibility, efficiency, and potential to address the critical factors.

There are differences between the **property rights** systems in place in the three provider countries. Ethiopia's approach in particular is very different from those pursued by Costa Rica and the Philippines. In the latter two cases, the state holds the property rights as well as authority over biodiversity as assigned by the CBD. In the Philippines these rights apply to all forms of biodiversity, whereas in Costa Rica only intangible material is state property, and tangible material is subject to private property rights. However, the role of the private level is acknowledged in the Philippines, and local communities are able to participate on the basis of strong PIC requirements that are already in use because the government recognizes the right of private landed property. Under the regime in place, the government receives the bioprospecting fee, whereas resource holders receive the up-front payments and a considerable share of royalties. In Costa Rica private landowners and communities can also participate on the basis of PIC. However, thus far bioprospecting has taken place only on state property, and only the government and INBio, as intermediaries, have received benefits. The experiences made in Costa Rica have therefore been ambiguous and only partial useful. In Ethiopia, biodiversity—but also land—is state property. Communities have the right to control access and to participate through PIC and benefit-sharing.

IPRs are a strong counterpart to property rights over wild genetic resources, and they are treated differently in the three countries. Ethiopia is not a member of the WTO and thus does not need to comply with TRIPs. All biological resources are exempted from patentability. Both the Philippines and Costa Rica are members of the WTO and comply with TRIPs. In the Philippines plant varieties and animal breeds are also excluded from patentability, but the country has adopted a PVP law as *sui generis* arrangement, and it serves to strengthen the hand of users of genetic resources. In Costa Rica the hand of providers is strengthened in that IPRs application processes require the submission of a certificate of origin.

The possibilities open to user countries to influence the critical factor of property rights are limited because national property rights systems are fully under the control of nation-states. User countries can make a positive contribution only by adopting user measures that address IPRs, e.g., disclosure of origin in patent applications. Most IPRs are granted in user countries because the majority of products are sold there. One example is the EC directive on the legal protection of biotechnological inventions, which specifically encourages patent applications to include information on the geographical origin of biological material. However, the directive is nonbinding and voluntary in nature.

The Philippines is faced with both pre-contractual and post-contractual problems due to **asymmetric information**. Pre-contractual problems arise in connection with the benefits providers expect to receive. Philippine providers expect high benefits. These unreasonable expectations have paralyzed negotiations. Post-contractual problems arise on the user side regarding the use of benefits, exclusivity, and quality. The problem is partly addressed by the new ABS regulation. The use of benefits is clearly defined, and better monitoring mechanisms have led to less overregulation. However, there are no guarantees for users regarding the exclusivity and quality of material provided. In Costa Rica pre-contractual problems do not occur, although post-contractual problems on both sides have been recognized and addressed. Users are not allowed to collect biological material themselves, but they are guaranteed exclusivity and quality. The benefits received flow into protection areas. In Ethiopia all of the post-contractual problems mentioned occur, and the ABS regulations in place address only post-contractual problems on the provider side, using measures like increased export monitoring, joint research, and the need to submit a document from the competent authority in user countries.

In order to address the problem of asymmetric information, user countries can signal that they are willing to comply with the CBD and screen providers, especially intermediaries. Only a small number of examples of corporate and institutional policies and codes of conduct are known from the EU. It is mainly botanical gardens and microbial collections that adopt such policies. Most EU member states have established national focal points and CHMs to increase transparency and inform providers and users on existing procedures and activities. However, in most cases their work is not sufficient. Measures like promotion of cooperation and standardized contracts, as, e.g., in the case of the ProBenefit project, are useful examples of how user countries can contribute to mitigating information deficiencies in the market.

All three provider countries have difficulties with the **time lags** between collection of genetic resources and marketing of a product, and they focus more on nonmonetary benefits and diversified compensation schemes to address this problem. Only one commercial contract has been concluded in the Philippines. However, this contract has provided substantial nonmonetary benefits for a Philippine research institute. In the future, the country will place more weight on up-front payments. In Costa Rica all bioprospecting contracts include rules on milestone payments and royalties. However, apart from nonmonetary benefits and minor up-front payments, Costa Rica and INBio have received no payments so far. Even so, many patents have come out of the INBio–Merck agreement. Ethiopia strongly focuses on nonmonetary benefits, e.g., participation in research and development. Monetary benefits play a subordinate role. Here it becomes clear that in Ethiopia ABS is considered an instrument that serves more to strengthen local research capacities than to set incentives for conservation. User countries in the EU can address the problem by providing monetary contributions for a fund that allows for payments independently of whether or not a product is commercialized. Another option available to bridge the gap and enable providers to offer higher value-added genetic resources is increased technology transfer.

In Ethiopia and the Philippines **governance** is much weaker than in Costa Rica because the general political situations there are not very positive, especially regarding stability. However, in the Philippines it is hoped that the situation will improve slightly due to the revised ABS regulations. Ethiopia has only recently adopted ABS regulations, despite the efforts the country has undertaken regarding the African Model Law. In Costa Rica the picture is different. The country has a stable democratic and political system that favors bioprospecting. In addition, INBio, the ABS framework, and the country's experience signal security and attract users, even though the country's ABS regulation was adopted at a late date. The influence that user countries have on the governance of provider countries is limited. User countries can use development cooperation to support efforts to strengthen institutions, actors, and political processes.

Administrative complexity plays a significant role in the Philippines and is less important in Costa Rica and Ethiopia. In the Philippines, access and negotiation costs have been very high for users and have hampered the conclusion of ABS contracts. Especially the existence of the ineffective intersectoral committee and the long and costly application process have proven to be a problem. Eliminating the ineffective committee, establishing time frames, and the exclusion of academic research will serve to improve the situation there. The committee is to be replaced by government agencies. However, responsibility is still assigned to different agencies, and this makes coordination difficult. In Costa Rica INBio has been the leading agency for bioprospecting, including the application process. INBio, a nongovernmental institution, has worked very efficiently. Due to regulatory changes, and the new intersectoral committee, which is very similar to the one dissolved in the Philippines, administrative complexity is bound to increase. Ethiopia has mandated IBC, a government research institute, to oversee and manage bioprospecting. Previously, many institutions were involved in bioprospecting. Because IBC's work, like INBio's, concentrates on biodiversity, the organization appears very well suited to handle bioprospecting. It is also excluded from political processes. The institute is thus expected to be able to work efficiently.

User countries, including the EU, can mitigate the burden of provider countries by informing—e.g., German—users on the conditions and regulations in place in provider countries. National focal points can serve to inform and prepare users and provide relief for provider countries.

In general, provider countries have a weak position due to their **market structure**. This goes as well for the three provider countries in the case studies. Additionally, ten years of overregulation have even further undercut the market position of the Philippines. However, the country is a member of ASEAN. Membership in such a regional coalition can serve to strengthen its position. Besides, the country is, like Costa Rica, also a member of the group of megadiverse countries. In contrast to the Philippines, Costa Rica has been able to improve its market position. The country and INBio have gained a high reputation by proving to be reliable partners for bioprospecting and for causing low transaction costs for users. Ethiopia's weak position has changed only slightly since the ABS law has been implemented. Due to the small number of cooperation projects concluded there, Ethiopia has not had a chance to increase its reputation and attractiveness by providing reliability and good services. The African Model provides Ethiopia and other African countries opportunities to strengthen the African countries as a coalition. The EU can support provider countries through technology transfer. This can enable provider countries to offer higher value-added products and increase their market position.

RECOMMENDATIONS

What can we learn from this analysis? What feasible measures should be undertaken by the international community and policy-makers to improve the concept and make it work? The analysis of the effectiveness and the perspectives of the ABS concept allow us to derive recommendations on how to improve the ABS concept.

Policy-makers need to initiate studies, analyze the critical factors in their countries, and derive specific measures designed to address them in adequate ways. The analytical framework developed in this book can be used to support these investigations, and it can be applied to other countries faced with the need to implement the ABS concept. All these countries, both users and providers, need to look into their own regulatory and institutional frameworks and assess the shape of the critical factors: property rights, asymmetric information, time lags, good governance, administrative complexity, and market structure. This information is needed as input to advance the international negotiations, but also to streamline the concept at the national/local level. Only if the critical factors are borne in mind will an effective implementation be possible.

However, although they need to be tested in in-depth research, it is evident that the findings and results derived here are not limited to the case studies presented. They have general and global dimensions across the countries concerned. ABS can only work in an international context. Users and providers have already wasted too much time on disputes instead of efforts to cooperate and create an effective ABS framework. Only together can providers and users implement the concept and address the critical factors. This is the reason why it is necessary to have a comprehensive international regime. The negotiations on an international regime need to be strengthened and brought to a successful conclusion. However, the regime needs to be formulated in such a way as to ensure that it addresses the critical factors.

Not all of the measures analyzed in this book and found to be suited to address the critical factors are negotiable at the international level because providers or users are not in agreement on them. The measures under discussion in the international forums are mainly user measures, but there is no reason not to also include provider measures as a means to ensure that the international regime is more balanced and users have a greater incentive to agree to some user measures. Another important factor is the interplay between user and provider measures. Only an international regime can lay the foundation for an effective interplay. The international regime needs to provide the framework as well as an array of different options. Because users and providers, as well as ABS activities, are highly heterogeneous, an international regime needs to be flexible. There is reason to expect that very few mandatory measures will be included in the regime due to the unwillingness of user country governments to accept commitments. To be effective, the regime does not need to build on mandatory measures. The analysis shows that a range of measures are necessary to address the critical factors. These particular measures thus need to be implemented jointly with the international regime on a voluntary basis. This would provide the flexibility needed.

Some possible approaches have been introduced and explicitly analyzed in this book. They indicate a point of departure. Whereas some of them are already in place, they do not function well. For provider countries, it is important to assign property rights. Property rights are the heart of the overall concept and a guarantee for participation. Institutions have to be strengthened and good governance has to be maintained or developed to create a good ABS environment and signal this fact to users. Capacity development is very important. Jointly with national governments, the international community should support capacity-development activities. If providers can build research capacity and increase vertical integration, their position in the market will be stronger, as will their participation in economic benefits. By providing valued-added products based on genetic resources, ABS can deliver on some of its promises. Provider countries need to strengthen their position in the market and make coalitions work. As presently constituted, the group of megadiverse countries appears to be too heterogeneous and indecisive. When ABS contracts are concluded, providers need to make sure that payment schemes are in place that will lead to a perceptibly fair and equitable benefit-sharing. A biodiversity trust fund would be an appropriate instrument to remove this burden from providers and to overcome the time lag. The analysis presented in this book strongly supports the establishment of a fund of this kind that would allow providers to benefit directly from the use of their genetic resources and set a strong incentive for conservation.

On the user hand, there is reason to expect that certificates of compliance, in conjunction with disclosure of origin, will be the only mandatory measure in an international regime. This is the only measure under serious discussion at the international level. The results of this analysis fully support this political development. However, it has to be kept in mind that these measures alone will be unable to solve problems related to ABS. Other voluntary user measures are very important and need to be implemented and improved. There are many measures available to address asymmetric information and build trust among the parties. One possibility is a certification scheme to certify "good" users. However, if it proves too costly to establish such a complex system, corporate and institutional policies need to be implemented by user institutions and user countries need to establish or improve their national focal points and CHMs. These have a very important role to play. Some of them are already in place, but they are too passive and do not assume the responsibility they should. Besides, insufficient use is made of individual and sectoral approaches such as projects and model contracts. They need to be applied broadly. Often the public sector is more active than the private sector.

In the international debate the question is often raised whether the bilateral ABS concept is adequate to reach the goals of conservation, access, and benefit-sharing, and some voices are calling for a multilateral system like the ITPGRFA. Compared to the bilateral system, a multilateral system would lead to far lower transaction costs in the form of search and information costs, bargaining costs, and enforcement and monitoring costs. However, in this case the shared benefits will be lower and not directly linked to the genetic resources of a given country.

Even though this argument has been put forward, no serious study has been written to analyze the options of a multilateral regime under the CBD.

In the negotiations there are doubts as to whether the states involved (both provider and user countries) will agree to move from bilateral to multilateral benefit-sharing. Provider countries fear losses of sovereignty, and user countries worry about even more complicated access. One thing that is definite is that more research is needed to analyze this issue.

Whereas ABS provides an instrument that can serve to monetize the commercial value of genetic resources, an effective implementation of the concept is difficult due to the complexity of the problem and the involvement of numerous actors. ABS alone cannot stop the ongoing loss of biodiversity. Therefore, the international community needs to agree on and advance other approaches designed to protect biodiversity.

Notes

NOTES TO CHAPTER 1

1 In this book biodiversity includes agrobiodiversity in the form of wild plant material and wild plant genetic resources (e.g., wild coffee), which are of major interest for research and development (ten Kate and A Laird 1999, 44–45).

NOTES TO CHAPTER 2

1. Thomas Lovejoy coined the term *biological diversity* in 1980. The term *biodiversity* was used at the American Forum on Biological Diversity organized by the National Research Council (NRC) and it first appeared in print in 1988, when entomologist E.O. Wilson used it in the title of the forum's proceedings (Dybas 2006, 792).
2. IUCN considers this number to be a gross underestimate because the Red List has assessed less than 3 percent of the world's 1.9 million described species.
3. Roundup Ready corn is designed for tolerance to the Monsanto broad-spectrum herbicide Roundup. It allows farmers to drench both their crops and cropland with the herbicide so as to be able to kill nearby weeds without killing the crops. The company can use economies of scope by using this specific trait for multiple crops (e.g., soybeans, canola, and cotton), and it offers a bundled package of products, one tied to the other.
4. The UK book was published as Latorre (2005); the German book appeared as Holm-Mueller, Richerzhagen, Taeuber (2005); and a summary of the major findings appeared in Richerzhagen, Holm-Mueller, Taeuber (2006).
5. In the past, incidents where genetic resources were illegally obtained have had a negative impact on both the image associated with the use of such material and on the image of the users themselves.
6. The UN List is prepared jointly by the IUCN World Commission on Protected Areas (IUCN-WCPA) and UNEP-World Conservation Monitoring Center (WCMC).
7. CBD (1992, Article 8j): "Subject to its national legislation, respect, preserve and maintain knowledge, innovations and practices of indigenous and local communities embodying traditional lifestyles relevant for the conservation and sustainable use of biological diversity and promote their wider application with the approval and involvement of the holders of such knowledge, innovations and practices and encourage the equitable sharing of the benefits arising from the utilization of such knowledge, innovations and practices."

NOTES TO CHAPTER 4

1. The problem of quality-related information deficiencies is analyzed in more detail in Richerzhagen (2005) and (2007).
2. *Voice and accountability* is the extent to which a country's citizens are able to participate in selecting their government, as well as freedom of expression, freedom of association, and free media; *political stability and absence of violence* are perceptions of the likelihood that the government will be destabilized or overthrown by unconstitutional or violent means, including political violence and terrorism; *government effectiveness* describes the quality of public services, the quality of the civil service, and the degree of its independence from political pressures, the quality of policy formulation and implementation, and the credibility of the government's commitment to such policies; *regulatory quality* is the ability of the government to formulate and implement sound policies and regulations that permit and promote private-sector development; *rule of law is* the extent to which agents have confidence in and abide by the rules of society, and in particular the quality of contract enforcement, the police, and the courts, as well as the likelihood of crime and violence; *control of corruption* is the extent to which public power is exercised for private gain, including both petty and grand forms of corruption, as well as "capture" of the state by elites and private interests (Kaufmann, Kraay, and Mastruzzi 2006, 4).
3. $Q, Q_g > 0, Q_z > 0, Q_{gg} < 0, Q_{zz} < 0, Q_{gz} > 0,$ and $Q_{zg} > 0.$
4. $\Phi_g > 0, \Phi_z > 0, \Phi_{gg} < 0, \Phi_{zz} < 0, \Phi_{gz} > 0, \Phi_{zg} > 0.$
5. The main ideas in this section are based on Richerzhagen (2005, 2007) and Dedeurwaerdere and colleagues (2005).
6. Many ideas in this section are based on Dedeurwaerdere and colleagues (2005).

NOTES TO CHAPTER 5

1. The GTZ has supported several projects that aim at advancing the implementation of the CBD, for example, (http://www.gtz.de/en/themen/umwelt-infrastruktur/19336.htm).
2. EO 247: Prescribing Guidelines and Establishing a Regulatory Framework for the Prospecting of Biological and Genetic Resources, their By-Products and Derivatives, for Scientific and Commercial Purposes, and for Other Purposes.
3. DAO 96–20: Implementing Rules and Regulations on the Prospecting of Biological and Genetic Resources.
4. Department of Environment and Natural Resources (DENR), Department of Agriculture (DA), Palawan Council for Sustainable Development (PCSD)
5. The NCIP was added as cosignatory to the joint administrative order to ensure that the bioprospecting regulations apply to ancestral domains covered by the Indigenous Peoples Rights Act of 1997.
6. The Local Government Code of 1991 establishes a system of provincial, city, municipal, and barangay governments in the Philippines. It is the governing law on local governments.
7. Six CRA applications and three ARA applications were exempt from the provisions of EO 247.
8. The case of Costa Rica has already been analyzed by the author. The results have been published in Richerzhagen and Holm-Mueller (2005). This section is based on that article.

9. Since 2006 the ministry has been named Ministry of the Environment, Energy and Telecommunications (MINAET).
10. INBio was visited in connection with the present publication, and interviews were conducted with a business development person and INBio's lawyer. INBio is the most important intermediary (others are marginalized) and plays a preeminent role. This is why the analysis focuses on INBio.
11. The main ideas and findings regarding the conservation of montane forests in Ethiopia are based on Richerzhagen and Virchow (2007).
12. The OAU is an antecedent organization to the African Union (AU). It was established in 2001 and consists of fifty-three African states.

References

A Laird, Sarah, and Estherine E. Lisinge. 2002. Protected area research policies: Developing a basis for equity and accountability. In *Biodiversity and Traditional Knowledge, Equitable Partnerships in Practice*, edited by S. A Laird. London: Earthscan Publications.

A Laird, Sarah, and K. ten Kate. 2002. Biodiversity prospecting: The commercial use of genetic resources and the best practice in benefit-sharing. In *Biodiversity and Traditional Knowledge, Equitable Partnerships in Practice*, edited by S. A Laird. London: Earthscan Publications.

A Laird, Sarah, and Rachel Wynberg. 2002. Institutional policies for biodiversity research. In *Biodiversity and Traditional Knowledge. Equitable Partnerships in Practice*, edited by S. A Laird. London: Earthscan Publications.

Action Group on Erosion, Technology and Concentration. 2005. *Global Seed Industry Concentration—2005*. ETC Group 2005 (accessed 04/14/2007). Available from: http://www.etcgroup.org/upload/publication/48/01/seedmasterfin2005.pdf.

Adams, William M., Ros Aveling, Dan Brockington, Barney Dickson, Jo Elliott, Jon Hutton, Dilys Roe, Bhaskar Vira, and William Wolmer. 2004. Biodiversity conservation and the eradication of poverty. *Science* 11/2004 (306): 1146–1149.

Alchian, Armen A. 2007. *Property Rights*. Liberty Fund, Inc. (accessed 04/21/2007). Available from: http://www.econlib.org/LIBRARY/Enc/PropertyRights.html.

Alemneh Dejene. 1990. *Environment, Famine and Politics in Ethiopia: A View from the Village*. Boulder, CO, and London: Lynne Rienner Publishers.

Anuradha, R.V. 2001. IPRs: Implications for biodiversity and local and indigenous communities. *Review of European Community & International Environmental Law* 10 (1): 27–36.

Artuso, Anthony. 2002. Bioprospecting, benefit sharing, and biotechnological capacity building. *World Development* 30 (8): 1355–1368.

ASEAN Regional Centre for Biodiversity Conservation. 2006. *Asean Regional Centre for Biodiversity Conservation 2006* (accessed 12/28/2006). Available from: http://www.arcbc.org.ph/.

Baillie, J.E.M., C. Hilton-Taylor, and S.N. Stuart, eds. 2004. *IUCN Red List of Threatened Species. A Global Species Assessment*. Gland and Cambridge: IUCN.

Balmford, Andrew, Aaron Bruner, Philip Cooper, Robert Costanza, Stephen Farber, Rhys E. Green, Martin Jenkins, Paul Jefferiss, Valma Jessamy, Joah Madden, Kat Munro, Norman Myers, Shahid Naeem, Jouni Paavola, Matthew Rayment, Sergio Rosendo, Joan Roughgarden, Kate Trumper, and R. Kerry Turner. 2002. Economic reasons for conserving wild nature. *Science* 297 (5583): 950–953.

Barber, Charles Victor, Sam Johnston, and Brendan Tobin. 2003. *User Measures Options for Developing Measures in User Countries to Implement the Access and Benefit–Sharing Provisions of the Convention on Biological Diversity. 2nd ed. Vol. 11/2003, UNU-IAS Reports*. Tokyo: United Nations University.

Barbier, E.B. 2000. How to allocate biodiversity internationally? In *The Economics of International Environmental Problems*, edited by H. Siebert. Kiel: Institut fuer Weltwirtschaft, Universitaet Kiel.

Barrett, C.B., and T.L. Lybbert. 2000. Is bioprospecting a viable strategy for conserving tropical ecosystems? *Ecological Economics* 34 (3): 293–300.

Barzel, Yoram. 1997. *Economic Analysis of Property Rights*. 2nd ed. Cambridge: Cambridge University Press.

Baumgaertner, Stefan. 2002. Biodiversity as insurance—the case of agricultural crop variety. Paper presented at *2nd World Congress of Environmental and Resource Economists*, Monterey, June 24–27.

Baummueller, Heike, and David Vivas-Eugui. 2004. Towards effective disclosure of origin—the role of the international ABS regime. *ICTSD Analysis* 4:21–22.

Baumol, William J., and Alan S. Blinder. 1994. *Economics: Principles and Policy*. 6th ed. Orlando: Dryden Press.

Belgian Co-Ordinated Collections of Micro-Organisms. 2007. *BCCM—MOSA-ICC Micro-Organisms Sustainable Use and Access Regulation International Code of Conduct 2007* (accessed 04/10/2007). Available from: http://bccm.bel-spo.be/projects/mosaicc/.

Benavidez, Paz. 2004. Philippines: Evolving access and benefit-sharing regulations. In *Accessing Biodiversity and Sharing the Benefits: Lessons from Implementing the Convention on Biological Diversity*, edited by S. Carrizosa, S.B. Brush, B.D. Wright, and P.E. McGuire. Gland and Cambridge: IUCN.

Berhanu, Mengesha, and Million Bekele. 2001. Investment on forestry development in Ethiopia: Opportunities and constraints. In *Biological Society of Ethiopia: Imperative Problems Associated with Forestry in Ethiopia. Proceedings of a Workshop*. Addis Ababa: Addis Ababa University.

Bernard, Colas. 2008. *Comparative Study of the Real and Transactional Costs Involved in the Process of Access to Justice across Jurisdiction, UNEP/CBD/WG-ABS/7/INF/4*. Convention on Biological Diversity: Montreal.

Bhat, Mahadev G. 1996. Trade-related intellectual property rights to biological resources: Socioeconomic implications for developing countries. *Ecological Economics* 19 (3): 205–217.

———. 1999. On biodiversity access, intellectual property rights, and conservation. *Ecological Economics* 29 (3): 391–403.

Bhattarai, Madhusudan, and Michael D. Hamming. 1998. *Environmental Policy Analysis and Instruments for Biodiversity Conservation: A Review of Recent Economic Literature. Vol. 9/1998, Department of Applied Economics & Statistics Working Paper*. Clemson, SC: Clemson University Press.

Boisvert, Valerie, and Armelle Caron. 2002. The convention on biological diversity: An institutionalist perspective of the debates. *Journal of Economic Issues* 36 (1): 151–166.

Boisvert, Valerie, and Franck-Dominique Vivien. 2005. The convention on biological diversity: A conventionalist approach. *Ecological Economics* 53 (4): 461–472.

Botanic Gardens Conservation International. 2001. *An International Review of the Ex Situ Plant Collections of the Botanic Gardens of the World: Reviewing the Plant Genetic Resource Collections of Botanic Gardens Worldwide, as a Contribution to Decision V/26 on Access to Genetic Resources of the Conference of the Parties to the Convention on Biological Diversity* (accessed 04/25/2007). Available from: http://www.biodiv.org/doc/ref/bot-gard-overview.pdf.

Borooah, Vani K. 2003. *Market Failure. An Economic Analysis of its Causes and Consequences.* Ulster, Ireland: School of Economics and Politics University of Ulster.

Braga, C.A.P. 1996. Trade-related intellectual property issues: The Uruguay-round agreement and its economic implications. In *The Uruguay Round and Developing Countries,* edited by W. Martin and L.A. Winter. Cambridge: Cambridge University Press.

Brockington, Dan, and Kai Schmidt-Soltau. 2004. The social and environmental impacts of wilderness and development. *Oryx* 38 (2): 140–142.

Brown, K., D. Pearce, C. Perrings, and T. Swanson. 1993. *Economics and Conservation of Biological Diversity. Vol. 2, Working Paper.* Washington, DC: World Bank.

Brunnengraeber, Achim, Kristina Dietz, Bernd Hirschl, and Heike Walk. 2006. *Interdisciplinarity in Governance Research. Vol. 08/2006, GARNET Working Paper.* Berlin: Freie Universität Berlin.

Brush, Stephen B. 2000. The issues of in situ conservation of crop genetic resources. In *Genes in the Field: On-Farm Conservation of Crop Diversity,* edited by S.B. Brush. Boca Raton: IDRC/IPGRI/Lewis Publishers.

Bruyninckx, H. 2004. Sustainable development: The institutionalization of a contested policy concept. In *Palgrave Advances in International Environmental Politics,* edited by M.M. Betsill, K. Hochstetler, and D. Stevis. New York: Palgrave Macmillan.

Bundesamt für Naturschutz. 2007. *ABS-Informationsplattform—Deutschland* (accessed 04/20/2007). Available from: http://www.abs.biodiv-chm.de/.

Bundesverband der pharmazeutischen Industrie. 2005. *Pharmadaten 2005* (accessed 04/15/2007). Available from: http://www.bpi.de/download/pharmadaten_2005.pdf.

Busch, Fabian, and Florian Kern. 2005. *Governing Biodiversity—The Realisation of Access and Benefit Sharing under the Convention on Biological Diversity.* Roskilde: University of Roskilde, Department of Environment, Technology and Social Studies.

Butler, M.S. 2004. The role of natural product chemistry in drug discovery. *Journal of Natural Products* 67 (12): 2141–2153.

Cabrera Medaglia, J. 2002. Bioprospecting: policy, regulatory and market incentives. Paper presented at *Megadiverse Countries Meeting on Environmental Legislation on Access to Genetic Resources, Protection of Traditional Knowledge and Intellectual Property Rights.* Cusco, Peru, November 27–29.

———. 2004. Costa Rica: Legal framework and public policy. In *Accessing Biodiversity and Sharing the Benefits: Lessons from Implementing the Convention on Biological Diversity,* edited by S. Carrizosa, S.B. Brush, B.D. Wright, and P.E. McGuire. Gland and Cambridge: IUCN.

Castro-Salazar, R., and G. Arias-Murillo. 1998. *Costa Rica: Toward the Sustainability of its Forest Resources (Technical Report).* San Jose, Costa Rica: Fondo Nacional de Financiamiento Forestal.

Chape, S., S. Blyth, L. Fish, P. Fox, and M. Spalding. 2003. *2003 United Nations List of Protected Areas.* Gland and Cambridge: IUCN, UNEP-WCM.

Coalition Against Biopiracy. 2007. *Captain Hook Awards for Biopiracy* (accessed 04/20/2007). Available from: http://www.captainhookawards.org/winners/2004_pirates.

Coase, Ronald H. 1960. The problem of social cost. *Journal of Law and Economics* 3:1–44.

Columbia University. 1999. *Access to Genetic Resources. An Evaluation of the Development and Implementation of Recent Regulation and Access Agreements.* New York: Columbia University, School of International and Public Affairs.

Convention on Biological Diversity. 1998. *Decision Adopted by the Conference of the Parties to the Convention on Biological Diversity at its Fourth Meeting COP IV.* Bratislava.

———. 2002. *Decisions Adopted by the Conference of the Parties to the Convention on Biological Diversity at its Sixth Meeting COP VI.* The Hague.

———. 2004. *Decisions Adopted by the Conference of the Parties to the Convention on Biological Diversity at its Seventh Meeting COP VII.* Kuala Lumpur.

———. 2006. *Decisions Adopted by the Conference of the Parties to the Convention on Biological Diversity at its Eighth Meeting VIII.* Curitiba.

———. 2007a. *Database on ABS Measures* (accessed 04/15/2007). Available from: http://www.biodiv.org/programmes/socio-eco/benefit/measures.aspx.

———. 2007b. *Report of the Meeting of the Group of Technical Experts on an Internationally Recognized Certificate of Origin/Source/Legal Provenance.* Montreal: UNEP/CBD/WG-ABS/5/2.

———. 2009. *Parties to the Convention on Biological Diversity* (accessed 03/06/2009). Available from: http://www.biodiv.org/world/parties.asp.

Cookson, Clive. 2006. *Ethiopia Signs Deal on Vernonia* (accessed 12/04/2007). Available from: http://www.grain.org/bio-ipr/?id=487.

Cooter, Robert. 1982. The cost of Coase. *Journal of Legal Studies* 11:1–33.

Cornes, R., and T. Sandler. 1984. Easy riders, joint production, and public goods. *The Economic Journal* 94:580–598.

Correa, Carlos. 2003. *Establishing a Disclosure of Origin Obligation in the TRIPS Agreement.* Geneva: QUNO.

Costanza, Robert, Ralph d'Arge, Rudolf de Groot, Stephen Farber, Monica Grasso, Bruce Hannon, Karin Limburg, Shahid Naeem, Robert V. O'Neill, Jose Paruelo, Robert G. Raskin, Paul Sutton, and Marjan van den Belt. 1997. The value of the world's ecosystem services and natural capital. *Nature* 387 (6630): 253–260.

Costello, Christopher, and Michael Ward. 2006. Search, bioprospecting and biodiversity conservation. *Journal of Environmental Economics and Management* 52 (3): 615–626.

Creswell, John W. 1994. *Research Design: Qualitative and Quantitative Approaches.* Thousand Oaks, CA: Sage Publications.

Cunningham, David, Wendy Elliott, Carmen Richerzhagen, and Brendan Tobin. 2006. *Micro-Organisms Sustainable Use and Access Management Integrated Conveyance System (MOSAICS) ADaM—Access and Distribution Management. The Development of Standard Documents and Procedures for Access, Transfer and Tracking of Microbial Resources.* Yokohama: United Nations University.

Darby, M.R., and E. Karni. 1973. Free competition and the optimal amount of fraud. *Journal of Law and Economics* 16 (1): 67–88.

Datamonitor. 2006. *The Future of Personal Care Occasions* (accessed 04/27/2007). Available from: http://www.the-infoshop.com/study/dc27565_personal_care.html.

Dávalos, L.M., R.R. Sears, G. Raygorodetsky, B.L. Simmons, H. Cross, T. Grant, T. Barnes, L. Putzel, and A.L. Porzecanski. 2003. Regulating access to genetic resources under the Convention on Biological Diversity: An analysis of selected case studies. *Biodiversity and Conservation* 12:1511–1524.

Davis, L.E., and D.C. North. 1971. *Institutional Change and American Economic Growth.* Cambridge: Cambridge University Press.

Dawyndt, P., T. Dedeurwaerdere, and J. Swings. 2006. Contributions of bioinformatics and intellectual property rights in sharing biological information. *International Social Science Journal* 58 (188): 249–258.

Day-Rubenstein, Kelly, and George B. Frisvold. 2001. Genetic prospecting and biodiversity development agreements. *Land Use Policy* 18 (3): 205–219.

Day-Rubenstein, Kelly, Paul Heisey, Robbin Shoemaker, John Sullivan, and George Frisvold. 2005. Crop genetic resources: An economic appraisal. *Economic Information Bulletin* 05/2005 (2): 1–45.

Dedeurwaerdere, T. 2006. The institutional economics of sharing biological information. *International Social Science Journal* 58 (188): 351–368.

Dedeurwaerdere, Tom, Selim Louaf, Carmen Richerzhagen, and Brendan Tobin. 2005. Roundtable on practicality, feasibility and cost of certificates of origin. Workshop summary of the 2nd Paris Roundtable on ABS Governance. Paris: IDDRI-UNU/IAS-CPDR.

Demel Teketay. 1999. History, botany and ecological requirements of coffee. *WALIA, Journal of the Ethiopian Wildlife and Natural History Society* 20:28–50.

——. 2002. Personal Communication. Ethiopia Agricultural Research Organisation, Director, Forest Research. Addis Ababa.

Demsetz, Harold. 1967. Towards a theory of property rights. *American Economic Review* 57 (2): 347–359.

Denzin, Norman K., and Yvonna S. Lincoln, eds. 2000. *Handbook of Qualitative Research*. 2nd ed. Thousand Oaks, CA: Sage Publications.

Devlin, Rose Ann, and R. Quentin Grafton. 1999. *Economic Rights and Environmental Wrongs: Property Rights for the Common Good*. Cheltenham, PA: Edward Elgar Publishing Ltd.

Dhillon, B.S., R.P. Dua, Pratibha Brahmi, and I.S. Bisht. 2004. On-farm conservation of plant genetic resources for food and agriculture. *Current Science* 87 (5): 557–559.

Diller, Wendy, and Herman Saftlas. 2005. *Healthcare: Pharmaceuticals*. New York: Standard and Poor's Industry Surveys.

Dixon, John A., and Paul B. Sherman. 1990. *Economics of Protected Areas—A New Look at Benefits and Costs*. Washington, DC: Island Press.

Droege, Susanne, and Birgit Soete. 2001. Trade-related intellectual property rights, north–south trade, and biological diversity. *Environmental and Resource Economics* 19 (2): 149–163.

Dross, Miriam, and Franziska Wolff. 2005. *New Elements of the International Regime on Access and Benefit-Sharing of Genetic Resources—the Role of Certificates of Origin*. Vol. 127, *BfN Skripten*. Bonn: Bundesamt für Naturschutz.

Dutfield, G. 1999. *Sharing the Benefits of Biodiversity: Access Regimes and Intellectual Property Rights*. Vol. 6, *Science, Technology and Development Discussion Paper*. Cambridge, MA: Center for International Development and Belfer Center for Science and International Affairs, Harvard University.

Dybas, Cheryl Lyn. 2006. Biodiversity: The interplay of science, valuation, and policy—report from the AIBS 2006 Annual Meeting. *BioScience* 56 (10): 792–798.

Earth Negotiations Bulletin. 2006. *Summary of the Eighth Conference of the Parties to the Convention on Biological Diversity*: 20–31 March 2006. 9 (363). Winnipeg, Canada: International Institute for Sustainable Development.

Egziabher Tewolde Berhan Gebre. 1990. The importance of Ethiopian forests in the conservation of Arabica coffee gene-pool—Proceedings of the 12th Plenary Meeting of AETFAT. Hans-Dieter Ihlenfeldt, ed *Mitteilungen des Instituts für Allgemeine Botanik Hamburg* 23a:65–72.

——. 2002. The African Model Law for the protection of the rights of local communities, farmers and breeders, and for the regulation of access to biological resource in relation to international law and institutions. In *Ethio-Forum 2002 Conference*. Addis Ababa.

Ekpere, J.A. 2000. *The OAU's Model Law. The Protection of the Rights of Local Communities, Farmers and Breeders, and for the Regulation of Access to Biological Resources. An Explanatory Booklet*. Lagos, Nigeria: Organization of African Unity, Scientific, Technical and Research Commission.

EU Commission. 2001a. *Commission Recommendation No 2001/680/EC of 7 September 2001 on Guidance for the Implementation of Regulation (EC) No 761/2001 of the European Parliament and of the Council Allowing Voluntary Participation by Organizations in a Community Eco-Management and Audit Scheme (EMAS), OJ L 247/1*. Brussels: EU Commission.

———. 2001b. *Compendium on Co-Operation Strategies, Partnership Agreement between the Members of the Group of African, Caribbean and Pacific States and the European Community and its Member States, Belgium*. Brussels: EU Commission.

———. 2003. *Communication from the Commission to the European Parliament and the Council, The Implementation by the EC of the "Bonn Guidelines" on Access to Genetic Resources and Benefit-Sharing under the Convention on Biological Diversity, COM(2003) 821 Final, Brussels, 23.12.2003*. Brussels: EU Commission.

EU Parliament and Council. 2006. *European Parliament and Council, Decision No 1982/2006/EC of the European Parliament and of the Council of 18 December 2006 Concerning the Seventh Framework Programme of the European Community for Research, Technological Development and Demonstration Activities (2007–2013)*. Luxembourg: EU Parliament and Council.

European Community. 2002. *Second Report of the European Community to the Convention on Biological Diversity, Thematic Report on Access and Benefit-Sharing*. Brussels: European Community.

———. 2007. *EC Access and Benefits Sharing Portal* (accessed 04/14/2007). Available from: http://www.abs.eea.eu.int/.

Evenson, Robert E., 1999. Intellectual property rights, access to plant germplasm, and crop production scenarios in 2020. *Crop Science* 39 (6): 1630–1635

Ferraro, Paul J., and Agnes Kiss. 2002. ECOLOGY: Direct payments to conserve biodiversity. *Science* 298 (5599): 1718–1719.

Ferraro, Paul J., and R. David Simpson. 2001. Cost-effective conservation: A review of what works to preserve biodiversity. *Resources for the Future* 2001 (143): 17–20.

Feyissa, Regassa. 2006. *Farmers' Rights in Ethiopia. A Case Study. Background Study 5, FNI Report 7/2006*. Lysaker, Norway: Fridtjof Nansens Institute, GTZ.

Finston Kling, Susan. 2004. Relevance of genetic resources to the pharmaceutical industry. Paper presented at the *International Expert Workshop on Access to Genetic Resources and Benefit Sharing*, 24–27 October 2004. Cuernavaca, Mexico.

Firn, R.D. 2003. Bioprospecting—why is it so unrewarding? *Biodiversity and Conservation* 12:207–216.

Food and Agriculture Organization of the United Nations. 1996. *Global Plan of Action for the Conservation and Sustainable Utilization of Plant Genetic Resources for Food and Agriculture*. Food and Agriculture Organization of the United Nations: Leipzig.

———. 1997. *State of the World's Plant Genetic Resources for Food and Agriculture*. Food and Agriculture Organization of the United Nations: Rome.

———. 1998. *The State of the World's Plant Genetic Resources for Food and Agriculture. Vol. 17—23 June, 1996, Background Documentation Prepared for the International Technical Conference on Plant Genetic Resources*. Food and Agriculture Organization of the United Nations: Leipzig.

———. 2002. *World Agriculture: Towards 2015/2030. Summary Report*. Food and Agriculture Organization of the United Nations: Rome.

———. 2003. *State of the World's Forest 2003*. Food and Agriculture Organization of the United Nations: Rome.

Fowler, Cary, and Pat Mooney. 1990. *Shattering: Food, Politics, and the Loss of Genetic Diversity*. Tucson: University of Arizona Press.

Fritsch, Michael, Thomas Wein, and Hans-Jürgen Ewers. 2003. *Marktversagen und Wirtschaftspolitik*. 5th ed. München: Franz Vahlen.

Fuentes, Rodrigo U. 2009. *Biodiversity Issues and Challenges in ASEAN: APFED Policy Dialogue, 25 January 2009, Elizabeth Hall.* Tokyo: United Nations University.

Gámez, Rodrigo. 2003. *The Link between Biodiversity and Sustainable Development: Lessons from INBio's Bioprospecting Program in Costa Rica.* Santo Domingo de Heredia, Costa Rica: Instituto Nacional de Biodiversidad.

Gámez, Rodrigo, Alfio Piva, Ana Sittenfeld, Eugenia Leon, Jimenez Jorge, and Gerardo Mirabelli. 1993. Costa Rica's Conservation Program and National Biodiversity Institute (INBio). In *Biodiversity Prospecting: Using Genetic Resources for Sustainable Development*, edited by W.V. Reid, S. A Laird, R. Gámez, A. Sittenfeld, D.H. Janzen, M.A. Gollin, and C. Juma. Washington, DC: WRI, INBio, Rainforest Alliance, ACTS.

Garrity, G.M., L.M. Thompson, D.W. Ussery, N. Paskin, D. Baker, P. Desmeth, D.E. Schindel, and P.S. Ong. 2009. *Studies on Monitoring and Tracking Genetic Resources, UNEP/CBD/WG-ABS/7/INF/2.* Convention on Biological Diversity: Paris.

Gebre, Markos Selassie, and Deribe Gurmu. 2001. Problem of forestry associated with institutional arrangements. *Biological Society of Ethiopia: Imperative Problems Associated with Forestry in Ethiopia.* Proceedings of a Workshop. Addis Ababa: Addis Ababa University.

Gehl Sampath, Padmashree. 2005. *Regulating Bioprospecting: Institutions for Drug Research, Access and Benefit-Sharing.* Tokyo: United Nations University Press.

Global Environmental Facility. 2006. *GEF Biodiversity Strategy in Action.* Available from: http://www.gefweb.org/projects/Focal_Areas/bio/documents/GEF_Biodiv_Strategy.pdf (accessed 01/02/2007).

Gollin, Michael A. 2001. *Biopiracy: The Legal Perspective* (accessed 01/02/2007). Available from: http://www.actionbioscience.org/biodiversity/gollin.html.

———. 2005. Feasibility of national disclosure requirements. Paper presented at *ICTSD/CIEL/IDDRI/IUCN/QUNO Dialogue on Disclosure Requirements: Incorporating the CBD Principles in the TRIPS Agreement on the Road to Hong Kong, WTO Public Symposium, 21 April 2005.* Geneva.

Grafton, Quentin, Wiktor Adamowicz, Diane Dupont, Harry Nelson, Robert J. Hill, and Steven Renzetti. 2004. *The Economics of the Environment and Natural Resources.* Malden, MA, Oxford, and Victoria, Australia: Blackwell Publishing.

Grifo, F., D. Newman, A. Fairfield, B. Bhattacharya, and J. Grupenhoff. 1997. The origins of prescription drugs. In *Biodiversity and Human Health*, edited by F. Grifo and J. Rosenthal. Washington, DC: Island Press.

Hardin, Garrett. 1968. Tragedy of the commons. *Science* 162 (3859): 1243–1248.

Hardon, J.J., B. Vosman, and Th.J.L. van Hintum. 1994. Identifying genetic resources and their origin: The capabilities and limitations of modern biochemical and legal systems. In *Commission on Plant Genetic Resources, First Extraordinary Session, 7–11 November 1994.* Rome: FAO.

Harrison, Paul, and Fred Pearce. 2001. *AAAS Atlas of Population and Environment.* Berkeley: University of California Press.

Hart, Oliver, and John Moore. 1990. Property rights and the nature of the firm. *Journal of Political Economy* 98 (6): 1119–1158.

Hawkes, J.J. 1997. Back to Vavilov: Why were plants domesticated in some areas and not in others? In *Harlan Symposium—The Origins of Agriculture and Crop Domestication*, edited by A.B. Damania, J. Valkoun, G. Willcox, and C.O. Qualset. Aleppo, Syria: ICARDA.

Heal, Geoffrey M. 2000. *Nature and the Marketplace: Capturing the Value of Ecosystem Services.* Washington, DC: Island Press.

Hein, Lars, and Franz Gatzweiler. 2006. The economic value of coffee (Coffea arabica) genetic resources. *Ecological Economics* 60 (1): 176–185.

Henne, Gudrun. 1998. *Genetische Vielfalt als Ressource. Die Regelung ihrer Nutzung.* Baden-Baden: Nomos.

Henne, Gudrun, Klaus Liebig, Andreas Drews, and Thomas Plän. 2003. *Access and Benefit-Sharing (ABS): An Instrument for Poverty Alleviation.* Bonn: German Development Institute (GDI).

Hess, C., and E. Ostrom. 2006. A framework for analysing the microbiological commons. *International Social Science Journal* 58 (188): 335–349.

Hill, A. 1999. Trends in the international market for genetic and biochemical resources: Opportunities for Colombia. Report Presented to the *BIOTRADE Colombia Initiative Workshop Villa de Leyva, Colombia 1999, World Foundation for Environment and Development (WFED).* Washington, DC.

Hilpert, H.G. 1998. TRIPS und das Interesse der Entwicklungsländer am Schutz von Immaterialgüterrechten in ökonomischer Sicht. *GRUR Int* 1998 (2): 91–99.

Hoare, Alison L. 2006. *Disclosure Requirements in Patent Applications: The State of the Art of National and Regional Measures, Energy, Environment and Development Programme, IPDEV, Work Programme 8: Interim Report February 2006, Produced for the European Commission under its Sixth Framework Programme as Part of the Project: "Impacts of the IPR Rules on Sustainable Development" (IPDEV).* Chatham House: London.

Holm-Mueller, Karin, Carmen Richerzhagen, and Sabine Taeuber. 2005. *Users of Genetic Resources in Germany Awareness, Participation and Positions regarding the Convention on Biological Diversity. Vol. 126, BfN-Skripten.* Bonn: Bundesamt fuer Naturschutz.

Horaeau, Lucy, and Edgar J. Da Silva. 1999. Medicinal plants: A re-emerging health aid. *Electronic Journal of Biotechnology* 2 (2): 3–4.

Illing, Gerhard. 1992. Private information as transaction costs: The Coase Theorem revisited. *Journal of Institutional and Theoretical Economics* 148:558–576.

Institute of Biodiversity Conservation and Research. 2007. *IBCR Homepage* (accessed 07/14/2007). Available from: http://www.telecom.net.et/~ibcr/.

International Centre for Trade and Sustainable Development. 2006. Model agreement adopted for access and benefit-sharing of genetic resources (ITPGRFA). *Bridges Trade BioRes* 6 (12), 4–6.

———. 2007. ABS experts flesh out certificate of origin. *Bridges Trade BioRes* 7 (2), 8–9.

International Chamber of Commerce. 2004. *Access and Benefit-Sharing for Genetic Resources, Prepared by the ICC Commission on Biosociety and Commission on Intellectual Property. Vol. 212/12, Discussion Paper.* International Chamber of Commerce: Paris.

International Plant Genetic Resource Institute. 2005. *Geneflow '05. A Publication about Agricultural Biodiversity.* Rome: IPGRI.

Jahn, G., M. Schramm, and A. Spiller. 2004. Differentiation of certification standards: The trade-off between generality and effectiveness in certification systems. Presented at the *14th Annual World Food and Agribusiness Forum, Symposium and Case Conference.* Montreux, Switzerland.

James, Clive. 1996. Agricultural research and development: The need for public–private sector partnership. *Issues in Agriculture* 1996 (9), 1–48.

Janssen, J. 1999. Property rights on genetic resources: Economic issues—a generalised framework for the analysis of the problems of endangered species and biodiversity losses. *Global Environmental Change* 9:313–321.

Kanowski, P., D. Sinclair, and B. Freeman. 1999. *International Approaches to Forest Management Certification and Labelling of Forest Products: A Review.* Canberra: Agriculture, Fisheries and Forestry.

Kaufmann, D., A. Kraay, and M. Mastruzzi. 2006. *Governance Matters V: Governance Indicators for 1996–2005. Vol. 4012, World Bank Policy Research Working Paper.* Washington, DC: World Bank.

Kumilachew, Yeshitela. 2001. Loss of forest biodiversity associated with changes in land use: The case of Chewaka-Utto tea plantation. Proceedings of *Biological*

Society of Ethiopia: Imperative Problems Associated with Forestry in Ethiopia. Addis Ababa: Addis Ababa University.

La Vina, A.G.M., M.J.A. Caleda, and M.L.L. Baylon. 1997. *Regulating Access to Biological and Genetic Resources in the Philippines: A Manual on the Implementation of Executive Order No. 247.* Quezon City, Philippines: Foundation for Philippine Environment and World Resources Institute.

Landell-Mills, Natascha, and Ina T. Porras. 2002. *Silver Bullet or Fools' Gold? A Global Review of Markets for Forest Environmental Services and their Impact on the Poor.* London: International Institute for Environment and Development.

Latorre, Fernando. 2005. *Review of the Experience of Implementation by UK Stakeholders of Access and Benefit-Sharing Arrangements under the Convention on Biological Diversity.* London: Defra (Department for Environment Food and Rural Affairs).

Lele, Uma, William H. Lesser, and Gesa Horstkotte-Wesseler. 2000. *Intellectual Property Rights in Agriculture: The World Bank's Role in Assisting Borrower and Member Countries.* Washington, DC: World Bank Publications.

Lemma Teigist. 2006. *Ad Hoc Expert Meeting in Preparation for the Mid-Term Review of the Programme of Action for the Least Developed Countries for the Decade 2001–2010 Case Study on Ethiopia, UNCTAD/LDC/MISC/2006/5.* Addis Ababa: UNCTAD.

Lerch, Achim. 1998. Property rights and biodiversity. *European Journal of Law and Economics* 6 (3): 285–304.

Leykun Abunie. 2000. The challenges of conserving Ethiopian wildlife: Overview. *WALIA, Journal of the Ethiopian Wildlife and Natural History Society* 21:56–62.

Liebig, Klaus, Daniel Alker, Karim ould Chih, Dagmar Horn, Holger Illi, and Julia Wolf. 2002. *Governing Biodiversity. Access to Genetic Resources and Approaches to Obtaining Benefits from Their Use: The Case of the Philippines, German Development Institute (GDI) Reports and Working Papers 5/2002.* Bonn: German Development Institute.

Maskus, Keith Eugene. 2000. *Intellectual Property Rights in the Global Economy.* Washington, DC: Institute for International Economics.

McCouch, Susan. 2004. Diversifying selection in plant breeding. *Public Library of Science Biology* 2 (10): 1507–1512.

McGown, Jay. 2006. *Out of Africa: Mysteries of Access and Benefit Sharing.* Washington, DC: Edmonds Institute in Cooperation with African Centre for Biosafety.

Melesse Damtie. 2001. Land use and forest legislation for conservation, development and utilization of forests. Proceedings of *Biological Society of Ethiopia: Imperative Problems Associated with Forestry in Ethiopia.* Addis Ababa: Addis Ababa University.

Mengistu Hulluka. 2001. Opening address. Proceedings of a workshop. In *Biological Society of Ethiopia: Imperative Problems Associated with Forestry in Ethiopia.* Addis Ababa: Addis Ababa University.

Millennium Ecosystem Assessment. 2005a. *Ecosystems and Human Well-Being—Biodiversity Synthesis.* Washington, DC: Island Press.

———. 2005b. *Ecosystems and Human Well-Being—Scenarios, Volume 1, Findings of the Scenarios Working Group of the Millennium Ecosystem Assessment.* Washington, DC: Island Press.

———. 2005c. *Ecosystems and Human Well-Being—Scenarios, Volume 2, Findings of the Scenarios Working Group of the Millennium Ecosystem Assessment.* Washington, DC: Island Press.

———. 2005d. *New Products and Industries from Biodiversity, Ecosystems and Human Well-Being—Current State and Trends.* Washington, DC: Island Press.

Ministry of Natural Resources and Energy and Mines. 1994. *Convenio de cooperación entre el Ministerio de Recursos Naturales, Energía y Minas y la Asociación Instituto Nacional de Biodiversidad*. San Jose: Ministry of Natural Resources and Energy and Mines.

Miranda, Miriam, Carel Dieperink, and Pieter Glasbergen. 2002. Financial instruments for participatory forestry management. An analysis of the Costa Rican Environmental Service Payments. *Environmental Management* 38 (4): 562–571.

Mittermeier, Russell A., Patricio Robles Gil, Michael Hoffman, John Pilgrim, Thomas Brooks, Cristina Goettsch Mittermeier, John Lamoreux, and Gustavo A.B. da Fonseca. 2005. *Hotspots Revisited: Earth's Biologically Richest and Most Threatened Terrestrial Ecoregions*. Chicago: University of Chicago Press.

Moore, Gerald, and Witold Tymowski. 2005. *Explanatory Guide to the International Treaty on Plant Genetic Resources for Food and Agriculture. Vol. 57, Environmental Policy and Law Paper*. Gland and Cambridge: IUCN.

Moran, Kathy. 2000. Bioprospecting: Lessons from benefit-sharing experiences. *International Journal of Biotechnology* 2 (1/2/3): 132–144.

Morton, Julia F. 1987. Guava. In *Fruits of Warm Climates*, edited by J.F. Morton. Miami: Flair Books.

Mulholland, Denise M., and Elizabeth A. Wilman. 2003. Bioprospecting and biodiversity contracts. *Environment and Development Economics* 8 (3): 417–435.

Mulongoy, Kalemani Jo, and Stuart Chape. 2004. *Protected Areas and Biodiversity: An Overview of Key Issues. Vol. 21, UNEP-WCMC Biodiversity Series*. Montreal, Canada: UNEP.

Mutke, Jens, and Wilhelm Barthlott. 2005. Patterns of vascular plant diversity at continental to global scales. In *Plant Diversity and Complexity Patterns—Local, Regional and Global Dimensions*, edited by I. Friis and H. Balslev. Copenhagen: The Royal Danish Academy of Sciences and Letters.

Myers, Norman. 1995. Tropical deforestation: Population, poverty and biodiversity. In *The Ecology and Economics of Biodiversity Decline: The Forces Driving Global Change*, edited by T. Swanson. Cambridge: Cambridge University Press.

Myers, Norman, A. Russell, C.G. Mittermeier, G. Mittermeier, B. da Fonseca, and J. Kent. 2000. Biodiversity hotspots for conservation priorities. *Nature* 403:853–858.

National Institute of Biodiversity. 2004. *INBio Annual Report*. Available from: http://www.inbio.ac.cr/pdf/Memoria2004.pdf (accessed 01/02/2007).

National Science Board. 2006. *Science and Engineering Indicators 2006*. Arlington, VA: National Science Foundation.

Nelson, P. 1970. Information and consumer behavior. *Journal of Political Economy* 78:311–329.

Newman, D.J., G.M. Cragg, and K.M. Snader. 2003. Natural products as sources of new drugs over the period 1981–2002. *Journal of Natural Products* 66 (7): 1022–1037.

Nicholls, Henry. 2004. The conservation business. *Public Library of Science Biology* 2 (9): e310.

North, Douglass C. 1990. *Institutions, Institutional Change and Economic Performance (Political Economy of Institutions and Decisions)*. Cambridge: Cambridge University Press.

Norton, B. 1988. Commodity, amenity, and morality: The limits of quantification of valuing biodiversity. In *Biodiversity*, edited by E.O. Wilson. Washington, DC: National Academy Press.

Norton-Griffiths, Michael, and Clive Southey. 1995. The opportunity costs of biodiversity conservation in Kenya. *Ecological Economics* 12:125–139.

Nutraingredients. 2004. *First Devil's Claw Harvest—Progress on Sustainability* (accessed 04/14/2007). Available from: http://www.nutraingredients.com/news/ng.asp?id=50441-first-devil-s.

Oligopoly Watch. 2007. *Industry Brief: Pharmaceuticals, Sunday, May 25, 2003* (accessed 04/15/2007). Available from: http://www.oligopolywatch. com/2003/05/25.html.

Onaga, Lisa. 2001. Cashing in on nature's pharmacy. *EMBO Reports* 2 (4): 263–265.

Organisation for Economic Co-Operation and Development. 1999. *Handbook of Incentive Measures for Biodiversity Design and Implementation.* Jan Horst Keppler and Helen Mountford, ed. Paris: OECD Publishing.

———. 2001a. *OECD Science, Technology and Industry Scoreboard towards a Knowledge-Based Economy 2001 Edition.* Paris: OECD Publishing.

———. 2001b. *Underpinning the Future of Life Sciences and Biotechnology.* Edited by B.R. Centres. Paris: OECD Publishing.

———. 2002. *Handbook of Biodiversity Valuation. A Guide for Policy Makers.* Paris: OECD Publishing.

———. 2003a. *Economic Issues in Access and Benefit Sharing of Genetic Resources: A Framework for Analysis.* Edited by Working Party on Global and Structural Policies and Working Group on Economic Aspects of Biodiversity. Paris: OECD Publishing.

———. 2003b. *Harnessing Markets for Biodiversity. Towards Conservation and Sustainable Use.* Paris: OECD Publishing.

———. 2005. *A Framework for Biotechnology Statistics.* Paris: OECD Publishing.

———. 2006a. Agenda issues paper. In *Meeting of the OECD Development Assistance Committee and the Environment Policy Committee at Ministerial Level.* Paris: OECD Publishing.

———. 2006b. *OECD Biotechnology Statistics—2006.* Paris: OECD Publishing.

Ostrom, Elinor, Joanna Burger, Christopher B. Field, Richard B. Norgaard, and David Policansky. 1999. Revisiting the commons: Local lessons, global challenges. *Science* 284 (5412): 278–282.

Padulosi, S., T. Hodgkin, J.T. Williams, and N. Haq. 2002. Underutilized crops: Trends, challenges and opportunities in the 21st century. In *Managing Plant Genetic Resources—Based on Papers Presented at a Conference on "Science and Technology for Managing Plant Genetic Diversity in the 21st Century" Held in Malaysia in June 2000,* edited by J.M.M. Engels. Wallingford, UK: CABI.

Pagiola, Stefano, Joshua T. Bishop, and Natasha Landell-Mills. 2002. *Selling Forest Environmental Services: Market-Based Mechanisms for Conservation and Development.* London: Earthprint.

Parolin, Pia. 2002. Diversität von Bäumen in amazonischen Wäldern 3. Interdisziplinäre Fachtagung zur Regenwald-Thematik 19–20. Oktober. *Phyllodrom-Journal* 2:25–33.

Parry, Bronwyn. 2004. *Trading the Genome. Investigating the Commodification of Bio-Information.* New York: Columbia University Press.

Paulsch, Axel, Thomas Kamp, Gernot Bäurle, and Thomas Plän, eds. 2004. *Technology Transfer via the Clearing-House Mechanism (CHM). Vol. 160, BfN-Skripten.* Bonn: Bundesamt für Naturschutz.

Pearce, David William, and Dominic Moran. 1994. *The Economic Value of Biodiversity.* London: Earthscan.

Perman, Roger, Michael Common, James McGilvray, and Yue Ma. 2003. *Natural Resource and Environmental Economics.* Harlow: Pearson Addison Wesley.

Perrings, Charles, and Madhav Gadgil. 2003. Conserving biodiversity: Reconciling local and global public benefits. In *Providing Global Public Goods,* edited by I. Kaul, P. Conceicao, K. Goulven Le, and R.U. Mendoza. Oxford: Oxford University Press.

Petit, Michel, Cary Fowler, Wanda Collins, Carlos Correa, and Carl-Gustav Thornstroem. 2001. *Why Governments Can't Make Policy. The Case of Plant*

Genetic Resources in the International Arena. Lima, Peru: International Potato Center.

Pimentel, David. 1992. Environmental and economic costs of pesticide use. *BioScience* 42 (10): 750–760.

Pimentel, David, S. McNair, J. Janecka, J. Wightman, C. Simmonds, C. O'Connell, E. Wong, L. Russel, J. Zern, T. Aquino, and T. Tsomondo. 2001. Economic and environmental threats of alien plant, animal, and microbe invasions. *Agriculture, Ecosystems & Environment* 84 (1): 1–20.

Population Reference Bureau. 2005. *Population and Health Data* (accessed 12/29/2006). Available from: http://www.prb.org/datafind/datafinder7.htm.

Possingham, Hugh P., and Kerrie A. Wilson. 2005. Biodiversity: Turning up the heat on hotspots. *Nature* 436:919–920.

Pounds, J.A., P.L. Fogden, and J.H. Campbell. 1999. Biological response to climate change on a tropical mountain. *Nature* 398:611–615.

ProBenefit. 2007. *Process-Oriented Development of a Model for Equitable Benefit-Sharing for the Use of Biological Resources in the Amazon Lowlands of Ecuador* (accessed 04/14/2007). Available from: http://www.pro-benefit.de/.

Protected Areas and Wildlife Bureau. 1998. *The First Philippine National Report to the Convention on Biological Diversity.* Manila: Protected Areas and Wildlife Bureau—Department of Environment and Natural Resources.

Rausser, G.C., and A.A. Small. 2000. Valuing research leads: Bioprospecting and the conservation of genetic resources. *Journal of Political Economy* (1): 173–206.

Reid, W.V., S. A Laird, R. Gámez, A. Sittenfeld, D.H. Janzen, M.A. Gollin, and C. Juma. 1993. A new lease on life. In *Biodiversity Prospecting: Using Genetic Resources for Sustainable Development,* edited by W.V. Reid, S. A Laird, R. Gámez, A. Sittenfeld, D.H. Janzen, M.A. Gollin, and C. Juma. Washington, DC: World Resource Institute.

Reinhardt, Frank, Markus Herle, Finn Bastiansen, and Bruno Streit. 2003. *Economic Impact of the Spread of Alien Species in Germany. Vol. 80/03, Texte.* Berlin: Federal Environmental Agency (UBA).

Reusing, M. 1998. *Monitoring of Natural High Forests in Ethiopia.* Addis Ababa: Ministry of Agriculture and GTZ.

Richerzhagen, Carmen. 2005. *Certificates of Origin: Economic Impacts and Implications.* Yokohama, Japan: United Nations University, Institute of Advanced Studies (UNU-IAS).

———. 2007. Certificates of origin: economic impacts and implications. In *European Regional Meeting on an Internationally Recognized Certificate of Origin/Source/Legal Provenance. Report of an International Workshop Hosted by the German Federal Agency for Nature Conservation. 24–29 October 2006,* 46–48, edited by U. Feit and F. Wolff. Isle of Vilm, Germany: Bundesamt für Naturschutz (BfN).

Richerzhagen, C., and K. Holm-Mueller. 2005. The effectiveness of access and benefit sharing in Costa Rica: Implications for national and international regimes. *Ecological Economics* 53 (4): 445–460.

Richerzhagen, Carmen, Karin Holm-Mueller, and Sabine Taeuber. 2006. Users of genetic resources in Germany—awareness, participation and positions regarding the Convention on Biological Diversity. In *Access and Benefit Sharing of Genetic Resources—BfN-Skripten,* edited by U. Feit. Bonn: Bundesamt für Naturschutz.

Richerzhagen, Carmen, and Detlef Virchow. 2007. Sustainable utilisation of crop genetic diversity through property rights mechanisms: The case of coffee genetic resources in Ethiopia. *International Journal of Biotechnology* 9 (1): 60–86.

Richter, Rudolf, and Eirik Furubotn. 1996. *Neue Institutionenökonomik.* Tübingen: Mohr.

Rosendal, G. Kristin. 2006. Balancing access and benefit sharing and legal protection of innovations from bioprospecting: Impacts on conservation of biodiversity. *Journal of Environment Development* 15 (4): 428–447.

Rosenthal, Joshua P. 1998. *The International Cooperative Biodiversity Groups (ICBG) Program, A Benefit-Sharing Case Study for the Conference of the Parties to Convention on Biological Diversity, Convention on Biological Diversity*, Montreal.

Ruiz, M., C. Fernandez, and T. Young. 2003. Preliminary report. In *Regional Workshop on the Synergies between the Convention on Biological Diversity and CITES Regarding Access to Genetic Resources and Distribution of Benefits: The Role of the Certificates of Origin*. Lima, Peru: IUCN.

Samper, Christian. 2006. *Biodiversity: What it Is, Why it Matters, and How its Conservation Must Be Built into Development Strategy* (accessed 04/12/2007). Available from: http://www.scidev.net/dossiers/index.cfm?fuseaction=dossierfulltext&Dossier=11.

Sandler, Todd. 2001. *On Financing Global and International Public Goods. Vol. 2638, Policy Research Working Paper*. Washington, DC: World Bank.

Sandler, Todd. 2006. Regional public goods and international organizations. *Review of International Organizations* 1 (1): 5–25.

Sarnoff, Joshua D., and Carlos M. Correa. 2006. *Analysis of Options for Implementing Disclosure of Origin Requirements in Intellectual Property Applications, United Nations Conference on Trade and Development*. New York and Geneva: United Nations.

Schippman, U., D.J. Leaman, and C.B. Cunningham. 2002. Impact of cultivation and gathering of medicinal plants in biodiversity: global trends and issues. In *Biodiversity and the Ecosystem Approach in Agriculture, Forestry and Fisheries—Satellite Event on the Occasion of the Ninth Regular Session of the Commission on Genetic Resources for Food and Agriculture*. Rome: FAO.

Secretariat of the Convention on Biodiversity. 2000. *Sustaining Life on Earth. How the Convention on Biological Diversity Promotes Nature and Human Well-Being*. Montreal: UNEP.

———. 2001. *Global Biodiversity Outlook 1*. Montreal: UNEP.

———. 2005. *Handbook of the Convention on Biological Diversity Including its Cartagena Protocol on Biosafety*. 3rd ed. Montreal: UNEP.

Sedjo, Roger A. 1992. Property rights, genetic resources, and biotechnological change. *Journal of Law and Economics* 35 (1): 199–213.

———. 2000. Biodiversity: Forests, property rights and economic value. In *Conserving Nature's Diversity*, edited by C. van Kooten, E.H. Bulte, and A.E.R. Sinclair. Aldershot: Ashgate Publishing Limited.

Shand, Hope. 1997. *Human Nature: Agricultural Biodiversity and Farm-Based Food Security*. Ottawa: RAFI (Rural Advancement Foundation International).

Sheikh, Pervaze A. 2004. *Debt-for-Nature Initiatives and the Tropical Forest Conservation Act: Status and Implementation. Vol. RL31286, CRS Report for Congress*. Washington, D.C.: CRS (Congressional Research Service).

Siebenhuener, Bernd. 2007. Administrator of global biodiversity: The Secretariat of the Convention on Biological Diversity. *Biodiversity and Conservation* 16 (1): 259–274.

Silverman, David. 1997. *Interpreting Qualitative Data. Methods for Analysing Talk, Text and Interaction*. London: Sage Publications.

Simpson, R. David. 1999. The price of biodiversity. *Issues in Science and Technology* 15 (3): 65–70.

Simpson, R. David, and Amy B. Craft. 1996. *The Social Value of Using Biodiversity in New Pharmaceutical Product Research. Vol. No. dp-96-33, Discussion Paper*. Washington, DC: Resources for the Future.

Simpson, R. David, R.A. Sedjo, and J.W. Reid. 1996. Valuing biodiversity for use in pharmaceutical research. *Journal of Political Economy* 104:163–185.

Sittenfeld, Ana, Jorge Cabrera, and Marielos Mora. 2003. Bioprospecting of biotechnological resources in island countries: Lessons from the Costa Rican Experience. *International Journal of Island Affairs* 12 (1): 1–10.

Sittenfeld, A., and R. Gámez. 1993. Biodiversity prospecting by INBio. In *Biodiversity Prospecting: Using Genetic Resources for Sustainable Development*, edited by W.V. Reid, S. A Laird, C.A. Meyer, R. Gámez, A. Sittenfeld, D.H. Janzen, M.A. Gollin, and C. Juma. Washington, DC: World Resources Institute.

Sittenfeld, A., and A. Lovejoy. 1999. Managing bioprospecting and biotechnology for conservation and sustainable use of biological diversity. In *Managing Agricultural Biotechnology, Addressing Research Program Needs and Policy Implications*, edited by J. Cohen. The Hague: CABI Publishing.

Spence, A. Michael. 1974. *Market Signaling: Informational Transfer in Hiring and Related Screening Processes*. Cambridge, MA: Harvard University Press.

Spiller, A. 1996. *Ökologieorientierte Produktpolitik*. Marburg: Metropolis.

Steele, P., G. Oviedo, and D. McCauley. 2006. *Poverty, Health, Governance and Ecosystems: Experiences from Asia*. Manila, Philippines, and Gland, Switzerland: Asian Development Bank, IUCN.

Straus, J. 2001. Biodiversity and intellectual property. In *Rethinking International Intellectual Property, Biodiversity and Developing Countries. Extraterritorial Enforcement, the Grace Period, and Other Issues*, edited by K.M. Hill, T. Takenaka, and K. Takeuchi. Seattle: University of Washington.

Swanson, Timothy M. 1995. Why does biodiversity decline? The analysis of forces for global change. In *Economics and Ecology of Biodiversity Decline: The Forces Driving Global Change*, edited by T.M. Swanson. Cambridge: Cambridge University Press.

———. 1996. The reliance of northern economies on southern biodiversity: Biodiversity as information. *Ecological Economics* 17 (1): 1–8.

———. 1997. *Global Action for Biodiversity—An International Framework for Implementing the Convention on Biological Diversity*. London: Earthscan Publications.

Swanson, Timothy M., and Timo Goeschl. 2000. Property rights issues involving plant genetic resources: Implications of ownership for economic efficiency. *Ecological Economics* 32 (1): 75–92.

Tadesse Woldemariam and Demel Teketay. 2001. The forest coffee ecosystems: Ongoing crisis, problems and opportunities for coffee gene conservation and sustainable utilization. In *Imperative Problems Associated with Forestry in Ethiopia. Proceedings of a Workshop*, edited by Biological Society of Ethiopia. Addis Ababa: Addis Ababa University.

Tadesse Woldemariam, Manfred Denich, Demel Teketay, and Paul L.G. Vlek. 2001. Human impacts on Coffea arabica genetic pools in Ethiopia and the need for its in situ conservation. In *Managing Plant Genetic Diversity*, edited by R. Rao, A. Brown, and M. Jackson. New York: CAB International and IPGRI.

ten Kate, K., and Sarah A Laird. 1999. *The Commercial Use of Biodiversity—Access to Genetic Resources and Benefit-Sharing*. London: Earthscan.

Thomas, Chris D., Alison Cameron, Rhys E. Green, Michel Bakkenes, Linda J. Beaumont, Yvonne C. Collingham, Barend F.N. Erasmus, Marinez Ferreira de Siqueira, Alan Grainger, Lee Hannah, Lesley Hughes, Brian Huntley, Albert S. van Jaarsveld, Guy F. Midgley, Lera Miles, Miguel A. Ortega-Huerta, A. Townsend Peterson, Oliver L. Phillips, and Stephen E. Williams. 2004. Extinction risk from climate change. *Nature* 427 (6970): 145–148.

Tietzel, Manfred, and Marion Weber. 1991. Von Betrügern, Blendern und Opportunisten—eine ökonomische Analyse. *Zeitschrift für Wirtschaftspolitik* 40 (2): 109–137.

Tobin, Brendan. 1994. Alternative mechanisms for protection of indigenous rights. Paper presented at *Symposium of Indigenous Peoples of Latin America: "Indigenous Peoples, Biodiversity and Intellectual Property."* Santa Cruz, Bolivia.

Traffic, The Wildlife Trade Monitoring Network. 2002. *What is Wildlife Trade Worth Financially?* TRAFFIC, The Wildlife Trade Monitoring Network (accessed 04/15/2007). Available from: http://www.traffic.org/wildlife/wild4.htm.

United Nations. 2002. Plan of implementation of the World Summit on Sustainable Development. In *Report of the World Summit on Sustainable Development—A/CONF.199/20**. Johannesburg: United Nations.

United Nations Conference on Trade and Environment. 2006. *Tracking the Trend towards Market Concentration: The Case of Agricultural Input Industry. Study Prepared by the UNCTAD Secretariat, UNCTAD/DITC/COM/2005/16.* Geneva: United Nations.

United Nations Development Programme. 2004. *Human Development Report 2004.* New York: UNDP.

———. 2005. *Human Development Report 2005.* New York: UNDP.

United Nations Environment Programme. 2002. *Global Environmental Outlook.* London: Earthscan Publications.

———. 2003. Chairman's report, conclusions and recommendations from presentations and discussions. In *Norway/UN Conference on Technology Transfer and Capacity Building Submitted as an Information Document to SBSTTA-9 UNEP/CBD/SBSTTA/9/INF/1.* Trondheim, Norway: Norwegian Direcotrate for Nature Management (DN).

UNEP/GRID-Arendal. 2004. *Global Development and Biodiversity* (accessed 04/14/2007). Available from: http://maps.grida.no/go/graphic/global_development_and_biodiversity.

United States Patent and Trademark Office. 2007. *List of Top 10 Universities Receiving Most Patents in 2005* (accessed 04/29/2007). Available from: http://www.uspto.gov/web/offices/com/speeches/06-24.htm.

Varian, Hal R. 1992. *Microeconomic Analysis.* 3rd ed. New York and London: W.W. Norton & Company.

Vogel, Joseph Henry. 2000. *The Biodiversity Cartel: Transforming Traditional Knowledge into Trade Secrets.* Quito: Facultad Latinoamericana de Ciencias Sociales (FLACSO).

Williams, J.T., and N. Haq. 2002. *Global Research on Underutilized Crops. An Assessment of Current Activities and Proposals for Enhanced Cooperation.* Southampton: ICUC (International Centre for Underutilised Crops).

Williamson, Oliver E. 1983. Credible commitments: Using hostages to support exchange. *American Economic Review* 73 (4): 519–540.

———. 1985. *The Economic Institutions of Capitalism: Firms, Markets, Relational Contracting.* New York: Free Press.

———. 1991. Comparative economic organization: The analysis of discrete structural alternatives. *Administrative Science Quarterly* 36 (2): 269–296.

Wilson, E.O. 1992. *The Diversity of Life.* London: Penguin.

Wolcott, Harry. 1994. *Transforming Qualitative Data, Description, Analysis, and Interpretation.* Thousand Oaks, CA: Sage.

Wolff, Franziska. 2004. Industrial transformation and agriculture: Agrobiodiversity loss as sustainability problem. In *Governance for Industrial Transformation. Proceedings of the 2003 Berlin Conference on the Human Dimensions of*

Global Environmental Change, edited by K. Jacob, M. Binder, and A. Wieczorek. Berlin: Environmental Policy Research Centre.

World Bank. 2006a. *Costa Rica at a Glance* (accessed 08/13/2006). Available from: http://devdata.worldbank.org/AAG/cri_aag.pdf.

———. 2006b. *Ethiopia at a Glance* (accessed 08/12/2006). Available from: http://devdata.worldbank.org/AAG/eth_aag.pdf.

———. 2006c. *Philippines at a Glance* (accessed 08/13/2006). Available from: http://devdata.worldbank.org/AAG/phl_aag.pdf.

World Commission on Environment and Development. 1987. *Our Common Future*. Oxford: Oxford University Press.

The World Conservation Union. 1994. *Guidelines for Protected Area Management*. Gland, Switzerland, and Cambridge, UK: CNPPA (Commission on National Parks and Protected Areas) with the assistance of the WCMC (World Conservation Monitoring Centre).

———. 2006a. Biodiversity in European development cooperation. Supporting the sustainable development of partner countries. In *Conference on Biodiversity in European Development Cooperation*. Paris: The World Conversation Union (IUCN).

———. 2006b. *Red Lists of Threatened Species. Facts about Threatened Species*. Available from: http://www.iucn.org/themes/ssc/redlist2006/threatened_species_facts.htm (accessed 01/02/2007).

World Intellectual Property Rights Organization. 2001. Intergovernmental committee on intellectual property and genetic resources, traditional knowledge and folklore. Second session. In *WIPO/GRTKF/IC/2/16*. Geneva: World Intellectual Property Rights Organization.

World Parks Congress. 2003. *Recommendations (R 1-32)* (accessed 04/28/2007). Available from: http://www.iucn.org/themes/wcpa/wpc2003/english/outputs/recommendations.htm.

World Resources Institute. 2003. *Biodiversity and Protected Areas—Philippines* (accessed 04/28/2007). Available from: http://earthtrends.wri.org/pdf_library/country_profiles/bio_cou_608.pdf.

World Trade Organization. 2007. *TRIPS: Reviews, Article 27.3(b) and Related Issues. Background and the Current Situation* (accessed 04/15/2007). Available from: http://www.wto.org/english/tratop_e/trips_e/art27_3b_background_e.htm.

Wynberg, Rachel, and Sarah A Laird. 2005. The commercial use of biodiversity: An update on current trends in demand for access to genetic resources and benefit-sharing, and industry perspectives on ABS policy and implementation. In *Ad Hoc Open-Ended Working Group on Access and Benefit-Sharing—Fourth Meeting*. Granada, Spain: Convention on Biological Diversity, UNEP/CBD/WG-ABS/6/INF/4/Rev.1.

Yellowstone Center for Resources. 2002. *Annual Report 2001, YCR–AR–2001*. Mammoth Hot Springs, WY: National Park Service.

Yifru, Worku Damena. 2003. Access to genetic resources in Ethiopia. In *African Perspectives on Genetic Resources. A Handbook on Laws, Policies, and Institutions Governing Access and Benefit Sharing*, edited by K. Nnadozie, R. Lettington, C. Bruch, S. Bass, and S. King. Washington, DC: Environmental Law Institute.

Yonas, Yemshaw. 2001. Status and prospects of forest policy in Ethiopia. In *Imperative Problems Associated with Forestry in Ethiopia. Proceedings of a Workshop*, edited by Biological Society of Ethiopia. Addis Ababa: Addis Ababa University.

Zerbe, Noah. 2003. *Biodiversity Conservation and Protection of Indigenous Knowledge: Analyzing the Emergence of a Legal Framework for Access to Biodiversity, Benefit Sharing, and Intellectual Property in Africa. Vol. Paper, Université catholique de Louvain Working*. Université catholique de Louvain, Louvain-La Neuve, Belgique: (CPDR) Center for Philosophy of Law.

LEGAL DOCUMENTS

African Model Legislation on the Protection of the Rights of Local Communities, Farmers, Breeders and the Regulation of Access to Biological Resource, 2000.

Agreement on Trade-Related Aspects of Intellectual Property Rights, 1994.

Andean Community Decision 486: Common Intellectual Property Regime, 2000.

ASEAN Framework Agreement on Access to Biological and Genetic Resources, 2000.

Bioprospecting Guidelines: Guidelines for Bioprospecting Activities in the Philippines, Joint DENR-DA-PCSD-NCIP Administrative Order No. 1, Series of 2004, 2004.

Bonn Guidelines. Report of the Ad Hoc Open-Ended Working Group on Access and Benefit Sharing, 2001.

Budapest Treaty on the International Recognition of the Deposit of Microorganisms for the Purposes of Patent Procedure, 1977.

Convention on Biological Biodiversity, 1992.

Convention on the Conservation of Migratory Species of Wild Animals, 1979.

Convention on International Trade in Endangered Species of Wild Fauna and Flora, 1973.

Constitution of Ethiopia, 1994.

Constitution of the Philippines, 1987.

Cotonou Agreement, 2000.

Decision No 1513/2002/EC of the European Parliament and of the Council of 27 June 2002 Concerning the Sixth Framework Programme of the European Community for Research, Technological Development and Demonstration Activities, Contributing to the Creation of the European Research Area and to Innovation (2002 to 2006), 2002.

Department Administrative Order 96-20 Implementing Rules and Regulations on the Bioprospecting of Biological and Genetic Resources (Philippines), 1996.

Directive 98/44/EC of the European Parliament and of the Council of 6 July 1998 on the Legal Protection of Biotechnological Inventions, 1998.

European Patent Convention (Convention on the Grant of European Patents), 1973.

Executive Order 247: Prescribing Guidelines and Establishing a Regulatory Framework for the Prospecting of Biological and Genetic Resources, their By-Products and Derivates, for Scientific and Commercial Purposes, and for other Purposes (Philippines), 1995.

Forest Conservation, Development and Utilization Proclamation (Ethiopia), 1994.

Intellectual Property Code of the Philippines (Republic Act No. 8293), 1997.

International Convention for the Protection of New Varieties of Plants, 1978.

International Convention for the Protection of New Varieties of Plants, 1991.

International Treaty on Plant Genetic Resources for Food and Agriculture, 2001.

International Undertaking, Resolution No. 8/83, Twenty-Second Session of the FAO Conference, 1983.

Law of Biodiversity No. 7788 (Costa Rica), 1998.

Law of Wildlife Conservation No.7317 (Costa Rica), 1992.

Local Government Code—An Act Providing for a Local Government Code (Philippines), 1991.

National Integrated Protected Areas System Law, 1992.

National Policy on Biodiversity Conservation (Ethiopia), 1998.

Paris Convention for the Protection of Industrial Property, 1833.

Patent Cooperation Treaty, 1970.

Patent, Drawings and Utility Model Law No. 6867 as Amended by Law No. 7979 of January 2000 (Costa Rica), 1983.

Philippine Plant Variety Protection Law, 2002.

Proclamation No. 120/1998 to Provide for the Establishment of the Institute of Biodiversity Conservation and Research (Ethiopia), 1998.

Proclamation No. 482/2006 to Provide for Access to Genetic Resources and Community Knowledge, and Community Rights (Ethiopia), 2006.

Protection of Plant Variety and Farmers' Rights Act (India), 2001.

Ramsar Convention on Wetlands, 1971.

Regulation (EC) No 761/2001 of the European Parliament and of the Council of 19 March 2001 Allowing Voluntary Participation by Organisations in a Community Eco-Management and Audit Scheme (EMAS), 2001.

Rules on Access to Biodiversity, Presidential Decree No. 31-514, 2003.

Treaty of Rome, 1957.

Wildlife Resources Conservation and Protection Act (Republic Act No. 9147) (Philippines), 2001.

World Heritage Convention, 1972.

Index

For Product Safety Concerns and Information please contact our EU
representative GPSR@taylorandfrancis.com
Taylor & Francis Verlag GmbH, Kaufingerstraße 24, 80331 München, Germany

www.ingramcontent.com/pod-product-compliance
Ingram Content Group UK Ltd.
Pitfield, Milton Keynes, MK11 3LW, UK
UKHW021007180425
457613UK00019B/842